How to Book a Flight for Last Year:

Volume VII of
The Travels of
Senator & Wendy V

ISBN: 978-0-99150-937-9

Other Titles by Wendy V

Travelogues:
How to Read a Compass in the Dark (2006)

How to Change a Flat on a Unicycle (2007)

How to Start a Fire Under the Sea (2009)

How to Eat a Pizza From a Can (2011)

How to Hitch a Ride With No Thumbs (2013)

How to Draw a Map of the Forest (2015)

Poetry:
Eventually, Finally (2007)

for Senator—

...the other half of the Tenth Duo...

"The whole object of travel is not to set foot on foreign land; it is at last to set foot on one's own country as a foreign land."

~G.K. Chesterton

Table of Contents

Author's Note

Yes, by now you know that Senator is, in fact, my Essential Other, David.

Introduction

I'm sitting on a hard floor in a semi-dark bar in Milwaukee, just outside the women's bathroom. It's not really like it sounds. In fact, in many ways it's preferable to my classroom. Six feet in front of me, a world-renown saxophonist is belting out a squealing solo that captivates a moderately numbered yet loyal and appreciative audience. Performing in a duo with him is a percussionist from Norway. Along with the usual assortment of drums, cymbals, sticks, mallets, and brushes, a few gongs and another toy or two find their way into the mix. To my left, close enough to touch my foot, is Senator. His headphones are firmly in place, and his eyes are affixed to a computer screen as he monitors a waving pattern of streaming colors and dancing lights. The lights are mostly green. That's good.

And I, I am listening... and thinking... and planning... and questioning... and praying... and traveling. I am not traveling because I am a few hours away from home; I am traveling in that I am wandering. My mind is flashing through memories of places as varied as Honolulu and Berlin. I am trying to understand both of them within the context of someone who resides about 4,000 miles from each. I am wondering why I don't care if I ever see one of them again, while the thought of potentially never seeing the other one again saddens me. I am also wondering how many calories the drummer is currently burning per minute... and how much higher the saxophonist can play before the pitch supersedes that which can be heard by the human ear... and whether we should go to Florida or New Hampshire next...

~Wendy V
September 2015

Chapter 1
Hutter Holiday:
Early July 2015

I suppose it was a number of events that led to me finally taking the necessary steps to leave the continent, but let us hold off on that for now. Suffice it to say, in early July we once again found ourselves accepting a gracious invitation from our friends Bill and Marge to join them in Door County, Wisconsin. Another school year, followed by its madly compacted summer session, had ended, and we had even found enough of a break from recording music to celebrate Independence Day with my parents and aunt and uncle, followed by the simple joy of fireworks in a small river town. Two days later we were on the road, northbound.

It was a fast drive up the familiar highways. In fact, it was our fastest time yet along that route, which we later concluded was a result of Wisconsin raising their speed limit by five miles per hour. Thanks, Cheeseheads! Can we have five more? It seems like most years we drive up in the rain, but this year it was almost guaranteed that we would do so. March and early April had been moderate and fairly dry. Then came the second half of spring. Rain was regular, and humidity took every opportunity it had. By June we were experiencing almost daily deluges. As the month closed, the greater Chicago area logged a total of 17" of precipitation, breaking records and sending sunscreen stock plummeting.

We arrived at our friends' familiar rented farmhouse, and Bill enhanced the alliteration: "Farkel!" We had barely said our hellos when he introduced us to his latest, greatest investment. For the reasonable sum of $5, he was now the proud owner of Pocket Farkel. As soon as we had finished unloading our gear upstairs, we rejoined Bill and Marge for a game.

The six-dice game, as it turned out, was not just any Farkel; it was a special Door County tourist edition. The cubes were Lake Michigan-blue, and each die contained a side with a lighthouse, rather than a single dot. An amazing value indeed. We chose our places around the large kitchen table and dove in. Soon realizing that no one had a clear idea how to actually play the game, we agreed to be adventurous and consult the directions. Bill, to whom we often affectionately refer as "Chief", led us in a rousing dramatic reading of the rules of the game. Like most situations where instructions are inserted into fun, they needlessly complicated the event. The three of us contributed stupid questions and comments, stretching the affair into fifteen minutes of ridiculousness. I doubt the college intern who was hired to write the step-by-step guidelines ever considered himself a comedy writer, but we sure had a grand time with it.

Somehow we managed to glean that you needed 500 points to get on the board, singles were hundreds, fives were fifties, triplets were multiplied by 100, and four or more of the same number made your score surge, leaving the competition in the dust, especially if they 'Farkeled'.*
"Hey!" I had had an epiphany. "This is basically the same as a game my grandparents taught me, called 'Greed'. Except we needed 650 to get on the board, I think. And I seem to remember that if we topped 10,000, we could lose our points..." It was all coming back to me, including the bittersweet memory of summer nights long ago, spent around a similar oil-clothed table, surrounded by smiling family members.

Bill interrupted my thoughts. "Did your grandpa give you any other words of wisdom about the game?" he inquired.

"Yeah--" I recalled. "If the scorekeeper doesn't win, there's something wrong!" I laughed, remembering Papa's low-key, mischievous sense of humor. Farkel continued for many rounds, a sound $5 investment.

It had begun to rain harder, and the dark gray sky showed no hint of allowing the sun to peek through until at least the next day, so we collectively decided it would be a great time to go to Cana Island. Into the car we piled, with jackets and the trusty recording device into which we often documented random conversations and stories. Bill piloted us through the drops, which soon relented to a strong mist. By the time we arrived, we were anxious to get out.

---

* our own word, invented to describe a situation where an unfortunate soul loses all of his/her points, often due to his/her own insatiable appetite for rolling blue dice against the odds

3

As I may have explained in a previous book, Cana Island regularly floods across its causeway, cutting the lighthouse off from the mainland. At such times, only the adventurous who are willing to wade the ¼ mile or so can reach it. On this day, the water wasn't over the strip of land yet, but it was getting close. With the wind raging and the storm front rolling, we wandered along the gravel. Gulls cried frantically as we zipped up coats and flipped hoods over our heads. My eyes started to water, but I could still make out what looked like a loon in the distance on the water's surface.

When the wind finally became too strong to comfortably stand in the open, we walked back to the mainland and ducked into some trees that backed the beach. The breeze was now manageable, but it soon began to rain harder. When we had had enough of the outdoor aspect of our excursion, we piled into the car. Bill cranked the heat (a novelty in July), and we chatted into the recorder for an episode of his podcast, *On the Lam*.

The weather probably did more to build our appetite than the actual physical exertion, but either way, we were hungry. After several years of going to Door County, we were overdue to try Wilson's, the iconic early 1900s diner and malt shop extraordinaire. Like responsible kids, we ordered the veggie wraps. Truth be told, it was just an excuse for the cheese curds that came as a side. Plus, it vaguely justified ordering dessert. My cherry malt came with more calories than someone my size should consume in a weekend, along with more in a stainless steel cup. I was told that the cup held what wouldn't fit in my glass, so I was expecting a few tablespoons of surplus. In actuality,

4

the mixing cup held even more than my shake glass. By the time we left, I am not proud to admit that I was disgustingly full. Lesson: next time go straight for the dessert... especially if you order a malt(ed)*.

We had no real plans, or ambition for that matter, for the rest of the evening, so we lumbered next door to check out the tiny library. Senator noticed that they were about to close, so we only stayed a few minutes. On our way out, he also noticed a cart of books for sale. Among the titles, he spotted a nonfiction book. *In the Garden of Beasts*, a $2 hardcover, may have topped Bill's Pocket Farkel game for value. Senator scooped up the copy, and I couldn't wait to read it, as it took place in the center of 1930s Berlin. It would provide a fitting backdrop for a World War II history tour we would be taking in just a few weeks. I won't spoil it for you, but you'll never hear the name Tiergarten again without shuttering.†

As long as we were parked nearby, we walked one more door over and found ourselves at the community center. I remembered reading that they hosted weekly concerts in a nearby park, but that they moved indoors when it rained... which it was certainly still doing. It was dry and free, so we selected seats in the last row. My Sweet Patootie, a three-piece Canadian folk group, filled the next hour and a half of our night. Among their songs was the

---

* 'Malt' vs. 'malted' depends on your age. If you are old enough to remember actual ice cream parlors and soda jerks (not just nostalgic recreations), use 'malted'.

† Yes, yes. I realize many of you are quick to point out that you have never heard of Tiergarten anyway. First of all, it's my book; don't interrupt. Second, go remedy that fact by picking up your own copy of Erik Larson's *In the Garden of Beasts*.

5

film-noir-inspired "Bad Service"-- an ode to greasy spoon dives and the less-than-warm staff who operate them.

It was a pleasant concert, and one that involved no lugging of computers or setting up microphones or checking levels on our part. The hardest thing we had to do was digest and prepare for a final round of Farkel back at the house. *Man, did I eat too much.*

*   *   *

Like so many trips I have taken, the first rainy day was followed by a bright, sunny morning. The cool, dry breeze seemed to suggest we had passed some sort of initiation and had now earned a proper day outside. Senator was not quite ready to venture out, so I walked the country road alone. The fields swayed lightly, and I made a mental note that our favorite purveyor of pure maple syrup had their 'OPEN' sign in front of their farmhouse. I walked and prayed, just conversing with God in his magnificent outdoors. I felt so good I even prayed out loud... and then sang for a while. I was suddenly struck by the thought that I had become the 'crazy lady' to the locals. By all outward appearances, I certainly fit the role. I was probably even dressed sloppily. There's a lesson for me in there somewhere. I'll try to remember it when I see our own local 'crazy lady'.

I made my way back to the house and joined my three Door County comrades for some fruit and serious planning. For about a year, Marge and I had been cooking up a scheme to go visit Chateau Hutter. We had, once again, each stumbled upon information about it independently, deciding to present the challenge to each other and our respective partners. You see, there was just enough information to pique our curiosity, and just enough holes in the information to make us determined to satisfy our curiosity. In the late 1940s, John Hutter decided to come up from Chicago and purchase land to built a grand chalet-style resort. He harbored visions of lapping up tourism dollars, particularly from wealthy urbanites. For various reasons, it never fully materialized. There was a resort, but the grounds and facilities never lived up to his hype. Eventually the place became a mess. Originally the other resorts and camps in the area were worried that he would detract from their business, however, he ended up being their best marketing ploy. His guests arrived at Chateau Hutter, took one look at the joint, and made a bee line for the next closest accommodations. In just a few hours, we too would observe the property for the first time.

Our day started with a brief stop at a local library for a few communication essentials. Senator needed a viable internet connection to check in on a few pending jobs, and Bill and Marge needed to catch up on a few minutes of work as well. Relishing the wonderful chill-- by mid-summer Senator and I are more than ready for autumn-- we found a spot in an outdoor garden. I perused a magazine, partly under the assumption that if I started reading my new book, no one would get me to leave until it was time to pack up for home.

Our next necessary pit stop was at Koepsel's, a fine establishment that has been pickling and preserving farm goodness for decades, much to the delight of locals and tourists alike. Among fruits, jams, sweets, beverages, and a host of other items, we selected our pickled garlic (Marge, Senator, and occasionally Bill), and our garlic pickles

(Wendy, Senator, and occasionally Bill). We made room for the additions to our picnic and climbed back into the car. Since Chateau Hutter was located on the bay side of the peninsula, we drove to a county park in that general region.

By the time we reached the park, the wind had picked up severely. There was no threat of a storm, but there was also no threat of a calm afternoon. Within moments we were pulling the drawstrings on our sweatshirt hoods, rendering us a gang of low-budget space creatures. It was every guy and gal for himself/herself as we scrambled to place the weight of glass jars on items deemed most likely to take flight. Fortunately, a plastic fork can conveniently poke through a hunk of cheese and a pickle, successfully spearing all items toward the mouth. No one even considered trying to wrestle a napkin out of the bag. It would have been halfway across the bay before you blinked.

Despite the wind, we had fun, but not as much fun as a nearby dog. As his owners bundled themselves into their windbreakers, he splashed around the presumably very chilly water in pure joy. He couldn't wait for them to throw his favorite chewed up ball. I didn't notice, but he may have even caught a few morsels of our lunch, as he was downwind.

Our picnic was abbreviated, but it was only a prelude to larger, more critical mission. We were on our way to the strange, secretive, secluded Chateau Hutter. As I have stated, information regarding the resort was somewhat inconclusive. I had found some general directions, which narrowed it down to an area between two towns, along a fairly major road. Marge had dug up some better facts; she had an actual address. Between the four of us, we were confident we could find it.

Within probably twenty minutes after leaving our county park, we were on the correct road. Not long after that, we started to see some rural red fire signs along the side of the road, denoting the addresses of homes hidden back in the forest. It was getting exciting. Like kids learning to count by hundreds for the first time, we rattled off a litany of address prefixes until we were within the realm of Chateau Hutter's block. And then... more numbers. Now the addresses were numerically too far from Chateau Hutter. We could not possibly have missed it, as we saw each property distinctly. Marge looked at her notes again, and we were baffled.

Then Senator suggested we try a gravel road/path we had passed a short way back. It was the best action we had at the moment, so we tried it. Quickly after turning, we realized we were driving to someone's beach home. *Well, that could be fun too...* All along, we had been prepared for the possibility that 1.)we might not be able to locate the place, 2.)it might not even exist anymore, or 3.)we might be run off by some codger with a shotgun if we did find it. Now that we felt that we were so close, though, it was painful to give up. Senator piped up. "Let me just check the internet." Somehow he, too, found an address for Chateau Hutter, but his was a few hundred numbers off from the one Marge had. Ah, renewed vision!

With a vow to make this our last attempt, we set off a little further down the main road. Just two miles later, we were there-- wherever 'there' was. Bill pulled the car off the road, into a tall grassy meadow. Across the street was a

9

hand-painted, beat-up sign with the name of the place. On our side of the street, we surveyed several acres of the abandoned property. On the south end we could see a two-story shaker style building that may have been a main office and gathering room. In the distance the land sloped down toward Green Bay. All we could make out was a very long roof, perhaps of adjoining rooms or cottages. Butterflies, birds, and bees sure liked the place, but it did not appear to have been appreciated by a human for quite some time.

It was early afternoon and pleasantly sunny, but the place had a definite mood. We all sat silent for a moment. "Do you think there's ticks in those weeds?" Senator asked. Before I could answer, he got out of the car to investigate. Well, somebody had to. I watched a little apprehensively as his legs, torso, and eventually head disappeared from view. He had waded and walked his way over to the two-story building. We waited and formed our theories as to what activities may have taken place on the land before us. It actually seemed like it could have had a lot of potential. Maybe it still did. Maybe I should give up teaching, invest in the property, christen it Chateau Frenchie*, and give it a new life.

Bill got out of the car, just far enough to stand up. "Oh, I see Daver†. He's actually down by the long building now."

Just then I heard Senator. "Hey, this is open. You can go right in!" Bill ventured out, and Marge soon followed. I

_____

* Did I ever mention that I somehow acquired the nickname Frenchie? Once I remember how it came about, I'll let you know.

† yet another name for my Essential Other

didn't care to trudge through the tall weeds, so I stayed in the car as lookout. If trouble rolled up, I could also lay on the horn. Plus, someone had to stay back and tell the story. After a short time, Bill and Marge returned. Happily, I don't believe any ticks had joined them. Senator stayed at the bottom of the small but sharp decline. He had discovered that it actually was a sort of road, and it curved around once at the bottom. He was sure that we could drive down there successfully and just follow it around back out to the main road. This kind of optimism both unnerves me and attracts me. Bill wasn't as sure, but with Senator's slow guidance, he did make it safely down the steep hill. If the road didn't go where we hoped it would, it would be a heck of a push to get the car back up.

At the bottom, the view of the bay was lovely. I thought about Chateau Frenchie again. We were all back in the car and Bill was cautiously following the sort-of road, which led into some sparse woods, still along the water. Then we spotted the pièce de resistance de Chateau Hutter.

There, practically hanging over the water's edge, was a very narrow two-story building, about the size of a small townhouse. There were no doors or windows, so naturally we reasoned that we could not get into trouble for 'breaking' in. It looked like maybe it was fishing shack, or possibly just a place to observe the water closely. I approached first, followed by the others, who milled around the outside and stepped into the main room. On the other side of the room was a second doorway that led outside. What my friends did not immediately notice was that around the corner from that door, there was a staircase that led down to a dark basement. I ventured down a bit,

11

finding only dirt, a broken lawn chair, and a couple of crushed beer cans. A few seconds later I made my way back up the stairs before anyone had noticed I was gone. When I showed Senator, he motioned for Bill to come over. As soon as Bill saw it, he exclaimed, "Oh crap! Frenchie just found the ghost spot!" True, we were all being a bit overly dramatic, but if someone wanted to stash a stiff who he had plugged during Chicago's golden mob age, this would have been 'da perfect joint.

Deciding that we had had enough spooky trespassing for one day, we returned to the house. We needed to unwind, and Farkel provided the precise means for it. After a few rounds of losing to the others, I repacked my purse for the evening's agenda, and we were off again. No one was really hungry for dinner-- apparently the picnic lunch was holding-- but we had been planning a stop at Dewey's ever since the previous year, when Senator had developed a mad craving for ice cream. (He did get his ice cream, but it was from somewhere else which, in Bill's and Marge's expert opinion, did not measure up.) So off to Dewey's we went. It was a good choice; they also sold espresso.

Just a few short blocks away from Dewey's is the marina. We walked over and Marge approached the ticket window, confirmation in hand. Our friends had invited us on a sunset cruise that would depart about a half hour later. In the meantime, Senator walked along the sea wall, pausing occasionally to record the sound of the lapping waves and creaking docks.

Finally we boarded, filing in past a forty-ish man who looked like Elvis, a fabulous blond glamour queen with plenty of glitz, and a quiet, relaxed, polite man. They were an odd trio, but they were our hosts for the following two hours. As it turned out, the quiet man was our captain. He had a tranquil smile that suggested he could get along with just about anybody. This was probably useful, as he worked nightly with the other two while simultaneously navigating about twenty passengers through Death's Door. The blond was our narrator, who needed her cheat sheet for almost every fact she spewed. She didn't even know the most famous landmarks by heart-- the ones that routinely make the covers of the Door County travel guides. It might have been forgivable if she didn't point out at least twice that she had lived there her whole life. Even so, the Peroxide Princess was pleasantly perky.

Then there was Elvis. No, seriously. He sang tired cover songs while playing the three chords he knew on his out-of-tune guitar, but he was selling himself in some effective capacity. In fact, he made sure we knew that he was ranked 17th internationally among Elvis impersonators. Impressive, but I did not even want to imagine what that contest looked like.

Our tour continued out among the islands, past bluffs and trees, in view of lighthouses and harbors. As predicted, the weather was comfortable, and the sunset was radiant, featuring pink, orange, and various shades of blue. Our captain cut the motor long enough for passengers to take photos as the sun slipped below the horizon. On the east side of the boat, we could see residents of Millionaire's Row sitting along their lakefront property, also watching the sunset. Senator pointed out that the same cruise probably blocked their view on a nightly basis. At least

13

they got to hear free entertainment. I leaned over and kissed Senator in the emerging twilight. Cliché? You bet. Magical? You bet.

Back at the house, there was more magic waiting, in the form of a cheesecake and some more Farkel. Bill, Marge, and Senator warmed up the dice, but I broke off to take a shower before I was too tired. I was in and out relatively quickly, but as I was drying off, I could hear muffled commotion downstairs. Bill was yelling for Senator to come upstairs and turn the water off. I was confused. No water was on, and the water that had been in the shower had all gone down the drain. That was when we learned that the pipes behind the wall had a leak. When I turned on the faucet, part of my water never made it to the shower head. Instead, it trickled down onto the bed in Bill and Marge's room below. Their bedding was wet, and the bed itself had to be moved across the room.

Eventually things calmed down, and we even had time to relax to an episode or two of a 1940s action serial, as was part of our Door County tradition. Our time together was already half over, but there was still another full day of experiences ahead... just as long as those experiences didn't include showers in the upstairs bathroom. The landlord would have to be called first thing in the morning. Until then, we plopped into bed for a good night's sleep, enjoying the need for a substantial blanket.

* * *

Wednesday started gradually, giving us all time to get ready for a short bike ride. It was another cool, sunny morning, which is always refreshing and motivating. Once we were set, we hopped on our bikes and started east on the county road. I prefer riding on closed trails, as opposed to roads, but a mid-week morning in a rural area doesn't see much traffic, so we were fine. We continued for almost half an hour and then stopped in the pine-shaded driveway of some very small establishment. It really looked more like a private residence. After guzzling water, we were on our way back.

Leaving the house shortly thereafter, we were again going to attempt a picnic, hopefully without the gale-force winds this time. Also as on Tuesday, we made a few stops first. Stop #1 was yet another library. Since we were headed toward the lake side of the peninsula, this was a different library. The four of us entered the lobby area, but we young punks weren't getting any further than that. The main library was closed, and a large room had been reserved for a senior luncheon. Old ladies looked at us trouble-making foreign tourists from Down South with suspicion. We smiled and quickly exited.

Stop #2 proved more successful. At the local junk shop/general store, Senator and I procured our very own Pocket Farkel game, deducting another $5 from the entertainment budget. It would later pay for itself many times over while being stuck waiting in airports and other similar drudgery. I suggest you invest in your own set. Just make sure they are the lighthouse variety. I'm not sure regular dice can deliver on the promise of "fast-paced, high-scoring excitement".

Our final pre-picnic stop was a gas station. Of course, that was not the original intent, but it ended up supplying the need. We were looking for a roadside farm market or stand that sold cheese curds, but we didn't come across any. In Wisconsin, though, you are never too far from quality dairy, so we turned into the next place we saw. Sure enough, the non-distinct gas station had a cheese case. Senator selected a bag of smoked mozzarella string cheese, and we were on our way. Enticed and impatient, we decided to open the bag and pass the goods around. At this point, I will interject that we are reasonably strong and competent adults, yet not one of us could open the bag. It was a thick, stretchy plastic that I suppose was designed to protect the cheese-- Wisconsinites take this very seriously-- but it succeeded in protecting it from our mouths. In the end it took a sharp blade and plenty of hungry determination. We devoured it (the cheese, not the bag) within a few miles.

I have been to Cave Point County Park about five or six times, but I am always excited as I drive the winding road through the trees. Anticipation mounts as I approach the water, and finally Lake Michigan comes into view. It's not just the lake; it's the wild waves that smash into the bluffs, sometimes sending sprays upward toward the banks. It is one of my favorite places in the Midwest.

We first made our way to a bluff overlook. It was a relatively calm day, and we took advantage of the condition to record another episode of *On the Lam* while nibbling some snacks. When it was time to stretch our legs again, we walked the rocky path down to the shoreline. It was a familiar site, until we spotted the cairns.

Dozens and dozens of carefully constructed rock piles stood proudly all over the beach. They ranged in size from about 6" tall to well over 6' tall. Naturally, we were inspired to make our own, and naturally, I couldn't do this

16

simply. Instead, I engineered an arch between two smaller piles, carefully balanced (after a few experimental tumbles). I was immediately taken back to my childhood, when I loved anything that could serve my imagination as a miniature house or world or rock castle, as the case may be. Senator was convinced my creation would somehow result in self-injury, but I managed. If I had a few rock people to play with in my seaside kingdom, I could have been entertained for days. At least I wasn't like the girl further down the beach, who for reasons unknown thought it would be a good idea to rock a tipsy pile of stones taller than her.

After we disbanded the cairn construction project, we returned to the house. Pulling into the driveway, we noticed that the plumber was there. Hooray-- no more drippy ceilings! We scattered around the house and either read or napped, or did both.* At some point, the plumber finished and slipped out unnoticed. When we realized this, we checked the exposed pipes through an upstairs bedroom closet. Senator, on the other side, turned the water on slowly. Dry... dry... questionable... moist... drip... drop... stream... Nothing had really been fixed. At best, it went from an F to a D+. Oh well, at least it wasn't our home plumbing problems, for a change.

There was one more event on the vacation's agenda. For years we had been joking about booking a Door County Haunted Trolley tour. We figured it would be cheesy (no pun intended) fun, and that, if nothing else, we would see some other parts of the county. Then we suggested that maybe we could just get in our car and follow the tour,

_____

*   makes for some very interesting dreams...

bypassing the ticket price. We imagined the trolley riders pelting us with eggs as we stalked them for free stories. It had been a running joke long enough that we decided to just pay for the tickets and do it. There was probably a 50% chance we would get kicked off the trolley if we got too goofy, but that might make it even more fun.

About forty-five minutes before the scheduled departure, we stepped into what looked like a remodeled Victorian train station. We grabbed a cup of coffee for the excursion and waited for someone to announce that we could board. Time passed and no one mentioned anything, so I decided to go out and investigate. Apparently everyone else knew something we didn't, because the trolley was full, save for four seats right across from each other. I quickly motioned to Senator, Bill, and Marge to come join me.

After a few moments, Bob appeared. Our host/ driver may not have had the best scary name for a haunted trolley tour, but his persona was impeccable from the beginning. He swooped up the steps, introduced himself, and affixed his undertaker's collar to his long, black cloak. It was immediately apparent that Trolley Bob possessed in-depth knowledge of local and Great Lakes region history. He also must have had a background in theatre, as his delivery showcased his engaging raconteur skills. Just as importantly, he had a great sense of humor about the characters in his stories, his audience, and himself.

As heavy classical organ music played over the trolley's speakers, we drove by a few residences with strange stories attached to them. Then we walked through an average-sized 19th-century home that had been decorated as if in a period of mourning. While the interior was somewhat fascinating, the guide inside was trying just a bit too hard, with her badly narrated attempt to sound spooky, complete with upturned flashlight shining on her face. From there we moved on to the harbor, which was a perfect backdrop for tragic tales of shipwrecks. At the next stop, the graveyard, we were definitely haunted... by mosquitoes. Our final tour highlight was a visit to the Eagle Bluff lighthouse and more stories of unfortunate locals, as the evening dampness set in. So how do you follow so much intriguing local lore? With a group sing-along, of course! Bob drove us back to the station as the group belted out everything from "Monster Mash" to "Ghostbusters", often to the amusement of people on the sidewalks as we approached red lights. I am happy to report that we did not, in fact, at any point get kicked off the tour, mainly because our host was as crazy as we were.

We followed up our tour with a trip to the local pub-grub haunt. Coincidentally, we were seated by the window, right in view of one of the homes we had visited on the tour. As we waited for our server to arrive, we decided to record another podcast episode, so out came the portable device. When our waiter approached the table, he was apprehensive. He later admitted that he was "freaked out" by our recording device, wondering what we were up to. We explained and tried to laugh with him, but in general, he seemed very flat, clearly not getting any of our humor. I guess he didn't care about getting our humor, as long as he got our tip. Fair enough.

As we ate, we viewed some photos Marge had taken on her phone camera. She was trying to determine if she saw something in one of the windows of a home we had visited. It didn't look like anything clear to me, but we probably could have scared our waiter with it. That would just be mean, though.

When we returned to the house for our final night, it looked a little scarier in the dark than when we had left earlier in the evening. We laughed about it, considering the ridiculousness of it. In an odd way, it was nice to know that we could still have that little kid feeling of being innocently apprehensive, in stark juxtaposition to real-world horror. Although, maybe there *was* something strange in the air, as I finally won a Farkel game. It only took ten rounds.

Our night concluded with one more strange apparition. *White Pongo*, yet another black-and-white serial, featured an albino gorilla. Surprisingly, he (or maybe she) was a sympathetic character. Maybe this was by default, since none of the human characters were particularly gripping. I don't remember the plot, but I do remember trying to figure out how they came up with the idea for a white gorilla. Our best theory was that it was originally going to be one of the run-of-the-mill African jungle settings, with a random ape thrown in for good measure. Then one day in the costume department, bleach was accidentally spilled on the gorilla suit. Surely there was dismay at first, but then... aha! *White Pongo* was born.

*   *   *

Our few days in Door County had come to an end. I was surprised at how much we had actually fit in. I packed our things while Senator trekked downstairs to the non-leaky shower. No one was taking any chances with that. We then joined our friends for the traditional fruit, coffee,

20

and bird/squirrel watching of our last morning with them. Soon we ran out of excuses for chatting, and we had to hit the road. We said our good-byes and backed out of the driveway for another year.

About an hour into our trip, we made one more stop. Every year we pass a large cheese shop, but we never bother to stop. Since our supply had been depleted, we opted to get just enough for the ride home. As we turned into the parking lot of Renard's, it looked like a hot rod convention had also decided to pause there while in transit. We walked in and made our selection easily. Upon exiting, there, among pristine and well-cared for classic autos, was Reverb, Senator's 300,000-mile* Toyota Echo. That image said it all. I've always said we don't fit in anywhere, and I wouldn't have it any other way. We nodded at the sight and thudded our smoked mozzarella cheese sticks together in a toast of the occasion.

---

* not a typo, although, sadly Reverb would only be with us for another five months before it became necessary to trade him in

Chapter 2
Deutschland:
Late July 2015

For as long as I can remember, I have dreamed of, fantasized about, plotted for, and lamented the heretofore lack of my presence in Europe. I was the type of child who would get absolutely lost in the setting of the fairy tales I heard. Ultimately, I was not really interested in whether the prince and princess lived happily ever after; I just wanted to explore their castle. Likewise, the dragon could burn down half of the town for all I cared, as long as he left the ornate churches and hamlet chapels intact. In my daydreams I pictured myself residing comfortably in a thatched-roof cottage with stone walls, nestled neatly in a secluded Old World forest. A career would hardly be necessary, provided there was a suitable stream nearby and plenty of morsels to forage, whatever that meant. I would have my love by my side, and we would only part when he needed to ride our gentle and faithful horse somewhere for some reason.

Time passed and, well, at least I got the boy. The

horse and even the cottage I could live without. Still, far too many years had gone by without a trip across the pond. In high school I had turned down the opportunity to go to France because 1.)it was a quite a stretch for my part-time waitress budget, which was focused on purchasing a car, and more importantly, 2.)there was no way I was going to journey to a country known for romance with a bunch of students and a chaperon. No, my agenda included activities which only required one other person.

In college I could have signed up for a trip to Rome. It was very tempting, but two problems arose there, as well. I was still a waitress; do the math. There was also the fact that said 'vacation' came with the unwelcome catch of requiring a lengthy theological term paper. Since I have always had a hard time enjoying myself when something was hanging over my head, that was out.

As I got a little older there was the constant balance of being responsible with money and splurging on my travel addiction. I am a saver, but the time had come to take the plunge. Several factors pushed my decision over the hump. First of all, in 2013 Senator and I had completed our mission of visiting all fifty states. It was a logical time to start planning a visit to a foreign country. Then sadly, in 2014, four people I knew within my general age group struggled with very serious health problems. I was always being told that life is fragile and short, so I finally decided to listen. On a more pleasant note, the final reason that made Europe absolutely irresistible took the form of a Christmas present.

During a phone conversation with my Grandma in the late summer of 2014, we happened to discuss the memoir she wrote of her European vacation with my Papa (Grandpa) Carlo in 1972. She had recently pulled it out and reread it, after not looking at it for several years. That, of course, made me want to reread it, as I had not done so since I was a teenager. I remembered getting sucked into her vivid imagery and lighthearted narration. Naturally, I asked if I could borrow it, and naturally, she gave me permission. She gave very specific direction that I return the copy, however, since it was the only one she had left. That would not be a problem, because I had already secretly decided that it needed to be typed and saved on the computer as a historical heirloom. When I told Senator this idea, he took it a step further. "Why not publish it as an actual book?" he suggested.

"You mean like I've done for years with my own travel writing?" I had not thought of that. Talk about missing the obvious! It was settled. On a night in early September we visited Grandma, borrowing her typewriter-typed manuscript to take home. Senator also managed to take a photo of the enlarged, hand-annotated map Papa had used to document their travels. I used that for the cover. Three months later Grandma received a book for Christmas, and she was instantly surprised to see that she was the author. Since the whole process involved me reading the content four or five times, by the time I was done there was no turning back.

The task of planning a big trip was somewhat daunting to me. I had a thousand questions, yet I knew if I started asking people, I would get ten thousand answers, mostly contradicting each other. I had to start somewhere, so I gave myself a booking deadline of October. Then I assigned myself three key decisions.* 1.)Should we go it alone or go with a tour group? 2.)Should we do an overall tour of Europe, or just focus on one country or region? 3.)What, realistically, would this cost?

The first question had plagued me for quite some time. I had always pictured running away with Senator to do our own thing, exploring, driving, eating, sleeping, and touring wherever we chose to do so. We knew people who had gone on group tours, but I wondered if they were too bound by the official agenda. Maybe we would miss out on too much local flavor or impromptu adventures. We also knew many musicians who regularly ran around Europe alone or with only a few band members. They would swear by 'the real experience', but they also had foreign friends in whose homes they stayed-- friends who could show them around and steer them clear of trouble if need be.

Of course I wanted plenty of privacy, and the ultimate goal was to gain superb experiences that we would look back on fondly for the rest of our lives. As I started to picture the memories I wanted to make, the realist in me decided that I distinctly did not want these memories to include Senator getting stressed out because he was in charge of driving a strange car on strange roads in a strange land. I also did not want the burden of complete navigation responsibilities. I would already have enough planning and

* I gladly welcomed any input from Senator, but he was more content to give me free reign to lose myself in internet research and comparison chart-making downstairs in our office, while he lost himself in live concert cds upstairs on the couch. Perhaps he was just remembering the frustrating catch-22 that constituted the planning process for Hawaii.

risk-taking on my head. When I envisioned thousands of dollars (or euro) being spent for a trip where we returned frustrated, exhausted, and barely speaking to each other, the choice became clear. We would book a group tour, as long as the itinerary covered specific spots we wanted to see and the schedule included plenty of free time. I started with about fifteen companies who all had good reputations. By the time I ruled out the ones that catered primarily to college students looking to hook up, snobs who cared more about the wine selection at the hotel than the selected sites, or tourists looking to perform manual labor and pay a pretty penny for it,* I was down to two choices. Either one probably would have been good, but for various reasons, I chose Cosmos. Now all I had to do was narrow down hundreds of itineraries.

Question #2: Do we try to see lots of countries, or just focus on one? On one hand, it made sense to 'do it all' in one giant excursion. After all, once we took the plane ride, we would already be there, whether for a day or a month. Plus, who knew when or if we would ever get back? On the other hand, it could be difficult logistically and financially to be gone from home that long. There was also the fact that we wanted to get a clear picture of different countries/regions, without rushing through them and jumbling them up in our minds. In the end, we decided to focus on one country, chosen from the priorities of France,

---

* I am just old enough to remember when the term 'working vacation' was an oxymoron. In recent years, however, plenty of people shell out cash to work other people's farms, ranches, businesses and such. What a racket! Perhaps I will outsource my teaching to some happy holidayer.

Germany, Italy, and the United Kingdom. I chose the best itinerary for each country and presented Senator with the 'final four'. After a coffee-fueled discussion of the merits of each, we settled on Germany, Cosmos Tour 6040. Wow-- what a process. At least the departure date was an easy choice, as it was determined by my school schedule.

As for the third question, regarding the cost, the answer was simple: too much. It was affordable, but only because of a few years of hardcore saving. I justified it by noting that it was less expensive than other similar tours, and far less expensive than going back to college, which could never hope to produce as much of an education as travel. If those reasons were not enough to ease my conscience, I reasoned that it was still cheaper than having kids.

All of the other details were settled little by little, and eventually I met my deadline. On the last Friday in October, I entered my credit card information to secure my deposit. We were then off to spend the remainder of the weekend as photographers for my brother's wedding. November then flew by, and Christmas decorations went up. Far too quickly, they were coming down again.

To ease myself out of the post-holiday doldrums, I dove into learning everything I could about Germany, German culture, and at least a traveler's basic knowledge of German. While I had always thought it a harsh language, I was surprised to find that I was immediately enthralled with the sounds, the structure, and the relationship between words.* I wish I had time to pursue it further. In

---

* I realize that I just lost 99% of my audience there. That's okay. They can run out and get a sandwich while the remaining few of us

fact, in one of my fantasy worlds, I devote an hour per day each to French, German, and Italian. Perhaps in retirement.

The spring semester progressed as smoothly as could be expected of an alternative high school classroom. Likewise, after a quiet winter, Senator's recording business grew to a sometimes frantic pace. At some point I practically forgot about my countdown to Germany, even as I continued to study it. I'm guessing that point was June, when we were balancing summer school teaching with a record amount of recording gigs* and a four-day festival in Milwaukee. Then July brought a few days in Door County. Finally, we were home. I had reserved one solid week of sanity. We would have just enough time to catch up on home and garden work, pack, and make the necessary last-minute arrangements. Oh, yes-- we would make it a point to stock up on sleep, too.

Then our track record for pre-vacation 'challenges' kicked in. So far, in over a decade of travels, we had dealt with home emergencies, family emergencies, and the general natural disasters that seemed to target our planned destinations. Though it certainly could have been far worse, we were in for anything but a calm week. I hoped that maybe we could at least sleep on the nine-hour flight, but until then...

Saturday, two days after we got back from Door County, Senator woke up with a wicked migraine headache. It had been quite a while since he had had one,

_____

passionately extrapolate the wondrous beauty of language.

* most of which required ridiculously long commutes, thanks to the expected construction projects and the unexpected seventeen inches of rain

so it caught him off-guard. It would have been tolerable, but it was compounded by the fact that he could not turn down a last-minute recording job for a twelve-piece ensemble at a Chicago museum. By the grace of God he managed it all, but he was grateful when he was back home in bed.

Sunday was smooth, but then there was Monday. As Senator was downstairs working and I was upstairs reading, I could see that it was clouding over quickly. A few moments later I could hear the distinct tapping of hail on the roof. I went downstairs to tell him so he could shut his gear down in case of a power outage. By the time I reached the stairs, the noise was tremendous. We were yelling over the loud clatter as we pounced on the easy chair to look out the back window. There was more hail flying sideways than dropping downward, due to the impact it made while hitting objects. Normally in our part of the country, hail storms last five or ten minutes. Moments later it is usually all melted by the summer heat. This storm lasted more than half an hour, and the yard was still full of lemon and kiwi-sized clumps of ice more than an hour after it stopped. It was fascinating, as Senator's dented car attested.

Nature continued to impress us the next day, when we were amazed to find a neatly organized trail of ants protruding out of one corner of our library fireplace. They had no apparent purpose. Nothing in the way of sweets or carpentry supplies lay along their path, so I could not figure out what they wanted. Maybe they were just curious about our books and stereo. Actually, it was more likely that the torrential rains had driven them up from their subterranean kingdoms. Whatever the case, we were leaving the house in two days. Liquid poison it was; there was no time for mercy. *Feast away... and don't forget to take your leftovers back to your queen.*

We continued to check the puddles of antnip throughout the remainder of Tuesday and into Wednesday. That amusement would have to take a backseat to another project on Vacation Eve, however. Wednesday morning Senator received communication regarding a project he had been waiting to finish. He had done all he could, but he had been waiting on a client's further direction before he could wrap it up. Though the client had been warned well in advance that Senator would be leaving town, he still opted to wait until the last minute. Thankfully Senator had anticipated this, and blocked out the day-- just in case.

Down to the studio he marched, determined to finish. To his professional credit he did so, and then he proceeded to send the material through the magical internet to the receiving party. I should mention that he has done this hundreds of times. This time, however, nothing was going to be easy. First, the company who would be producing the final cd had a very inefficient, non-secured system that resulted in dragging the transmission process out from less than an hour to over four hours. We were still doing alright time-wise, until we lost power halfway through. Now even Senator had had enough.

Knowing that the clock was ticking, the project had to be finished before leaving town, and he would be in the market for a new girlfriend if he did not get on a plane with me the next day, he took action. Pulling out his version of a little black book, he flipped pages desperately looking for inspiration. "Jason and Pam!" He had the thought to call our good friends and ask if there was any way we could go out to their house and send files via their system. Thankfully Jason was home, and not at all surprisingly, he was eager to accommodate. We will forever be grateful. In moments we were on the way to their home, about forty-five minutes from ours. In the end, our minor crisis ended up in an impromptu pizza dinner with our friends. We got to see our sweet niece, and Pam and I had a wonderful chat over a cup of tea.* All we could do was sit and enjoy the company while the computers did their thing. Maybe it was God's way of starting our vacation early.

We said good-bye and headed home, arriving early enough to catch a few episodes of *Hogan's Heroes* before dozing off on the couch. I turned over on my side, which is always a sure sign that I won't even make it to Schultz's next, "I know nuss-ing!" Senator was only slightly more awake than I was. *Oh, yeah, watching this reminds me: we're going to Germany tomorrow...*

*   *   *

Thursday was surreal. It did not feel like the morning of the vacation we had been anticipating for nine months. We had made sure to get everything done before going to bed the night before, yet we did not have to leave the house until midday. Because we did not want to start any new projects before leaving for two weeks, we actually had some time for forced relaxation. What a contrast to the

---

* Pam and I have been very close friends since we were three years old. I have actually known her longer than I have known my own siblings. As such, she is my sister. Maybe someday her many wonderful traits will finally rub off on me.

previous few days. Senator sat with his eyes closed, and I read a book, both of us glancing at the clock occasionally. Finally, we locked up and left, still not entirely convinced we were about to depart the continent.

Our drive into the city was easy, thanks to the time of day. Senator decided that the best going-to-Germany thing he could play on the car's stereo was the local radio station's call-in trader show. "What, are you trying to get your last fill of our little town?" I teased as we listened to the half-dazed callers hock their lawn furniture, used car parts, old appliances, and other miscellaneous junk, followed by their usually-indecipherable phone number. Then at about the twenty-five minute mark, both the host and I lost patience. Senator flipped over to the traffic and weather report.

Speaking of weather, one of the draws of Germany in the summer is that, in almost all regions, it is markedly cooler than Illinois. That is, except in 2015. True to our record, I had booked our trip during an unprecedented European heat wave. Instead of the deliciously pleasant average highs of 73°F, we would be landing in a sweltering upper 90s. Maybe we would be sampling some of their famous *eis** on a regular basis.

Here's a travel tip, should you find yourself driving to O'Hare International Airport, approaching from the south. Some of the nearby exit roads are I-Pass only, meaning that poor saps with actual cash-- in my case hoards of coins-- cannot exit. As such, we had to bypass our exit and backtrack from the next one. It was not a big deal, though. Plus, as a bonus it allowed plenty of scenic

---

* ice cream, only not ice cream, because it is fresher and yummier

33

viewing of fast food chains, construction projects, and ugly housing.

We soon reached our parking garage. Here's another travel tip, should you find yourself driving toward O'Hare International Airport and needing to park a car. Do not use the airport's parking lot. Instead, opt for one of the nearby private garages. They are safe, clean, reputable, courteous, punctual with shuttle service, and yes, cheaper. Score another one for the private sector.

At the airport we took our ghost-driven monorail to the appropriate terminal and checked in. Lines were relatively short and security was efficient. We did not even have to scheme to circumvent the 'human microwave' screening machine. I think the zillion-dollar thing was broken.

With our customary over-cautiousness with timing, we had a good two hours on our hands before our flight would leave. Into Chili's it was. It was probably a good idea to eat something anyway, since it was unclear whether our request for vegetarian meals on the plane ever got past the confused phone attendant.* Being there also reminded us of our first meals shared together. There is nothing special about Chili's, except that it happened to be next to where we both worked. On Mondays, we always ended up having the same lunch hour. Often we would go there just to get out of the store and talk. Senator always propped his

---

* Had the airline's website not advertised this option, it never would have occurred to me to attempt to request it. I would have just packed my granola bars and hoped for the best. When I saw it though, I figured it was worth a try. Based on my brief conversation, it appears that I am the only one of the thousands of people who fly daily who has ever actually done this.

watch up on the table so we could keep an eye on our time. Those were some fast hours. Now we were sitting at a different Chili's, watching our time for a very different reason... amazing.

"Hello," Senator greeted our server. "Could I please get a cup of coffee to start? And then I think we're ready to order."

"You can order," she explained, "but you don't want our coffee. Go across the concourse and get yourself a cup." She indicated a small stand across the way. "Ours has been sitting all day. No one wants it. They're all drinking beer."

"Okay, thanks for the tip!" We appreciated her frankness. As we waited for our food to arrive, I checked my bag for the essentials for the tenth time that day. When it came time to pay, I realized that it was the last time I would use American dollars for awhile. It is strange what goes through your head (or at least mine) before a trip.

We got our recommended coffee and found a seat in the terminal. Naturally, we learned that our flight would be leaving about an hour late, though somehow we were only supposed to arrive at our destination eight minutes late. I can only attribute this strange math to the fact that we would be traveling through some Atlantic hole in the space-time continuum. Either that or the airlines just don't go as fast as they are capable of going, unless they are behind schedule. Good thing we had Pocket Farkel with us. We shook our dice onto the vinyl seat between us, to the amusement of foreigners around us.

Eventually they gave the boarding call, in a few different languages. I strained my ears to interpret the German, but I could only make out a few basic words.

Either we were about to board, or the announcer had just eaten a large airplane. Well, we were on. There was no going back. Years of hoping and months of planning were being realized. As proof, I had the receipt for the $12.99 internet usage fee from the plane. I think it worked for about two minutes. Time to attempt the near-impossible: sleeping on a plane.

*　　　　*　　　　*

Our overnight flight arrived about fifteen minutes late. I was disappointed, because it meant that we would most likely just miss our hotel shuttle, and have to wait an additional two hours for the next one. Maybe we could find a chair and sleep. I had only slept about an hour and a half, and Senator did not get much more. We made the long trek toward customs. The severe-looking guard did not flinch or say a word as he scrutinized our passports. Finally he said, "Okay." Nothing more.

We then passed through to collect our luggage. Amazingly, Frankfurt was an airport that employed common sense in this area. Overhead a giant sign listed incoming flights and where each flight's passengers could find their luggage. O'Hare should try this, as opposed to offering absolutely no information to those disembarking. There you have to literally guess and ask around, which is often a hopeless pursuit. Good luck, suckers.

As I waited for our bags to parade around, Senator made a pit stop. I thought I spotted my suitcase, so I reached in for it and slung it off the carousel with an extra *umph*. When I examined it up close, it was not mine, so back into the rotation I heaved it. As it made contact with the rotating plates, it almost pulled me with it. That could have led to a scene worthy of *I Love Lucy*. I could just see Senator coming back from the bathroom to find me yelling as I circled around amid the luggage.

Having avoided such an adventure, we made our way to the *treffpunkt*.* Listed on the kiosk was just about every travel company except Cosmos. I had a sinking feeling that I had made a very bad, very expensive mistake. We paced for a minute or two, deciding what to do next.

Just then we turned around to see a smiling woman about my age, who was quickly walking toward us carrying a clipboard. In an eastern European accent she asked if I was Wendy. "Yes! We are!" Even if she meant a different Wendy, here was someone who looked like she could help us. We were hers. Dubravka introduced herself as 'Dory' and went on to apologize for running a little late. I guess she did not realize that it was divine intervention. She then led us to a shuttle and introduced us to our driver, Ismet, and two other couples who would be on our tour. As we drove, we tried to listen to the basic information Dory gave, but we were too enthralled with the fact that we were really in Germany. Somehow the airport did not count, but once we were on the road, it felt real.

Soon we were dropped off at our hotel. It was in a quieter part of Frankfurt, but still situated among walkable streets. Our room would not be ready for a few hours, so we dropped our bags and headed back out the front door. I had my arsenal of maps for each city, so I opened my makeshift book to page one. This proved useful, as we would be on our own to sink or swim until the group officially met at dinner.

----

*meeting point, often in an airport

We could see the tram station from the corner, but in the opposite direction was a tree-lined street, so the hot weather sent us that way. A few blocks away we stumbled upon a little deli. I read the menu, excited that I understood everything on it, but suddenly shy about using my German for the first time. It was one thing to talk to myself and the cd in my car while driving; it was quite another to place an order with the native behind the counter. I did not want to propel the stereotype of the arrogant, loud, self-important American, but I also did not want to butcher the language. Senator began to speak, first fact-checking with me, and then pointing out his choice to the employee. Then I muttered my best impression of a German ordering a tomato-mozzarella-lettuce sandwich. It worked well enough. I then dug through my wallet, careful to grab the correct euro coinage.

The sandwiches, which would become our staple meal while roaming many towns, were fresh, delicious, and enjoyed at a table under a tree.[*] The *kaffee*[†] was even better. In fact, if you are any sort of kaffeephile, you must try German. It is robust, rich, well-developed, and consistently excellent, whether in a restaurant or at a gas station. I don't know what they do to it, and maybe I don't want to know, but I have missed it ever since we have been back in the United States.

---

[*] One of the most common questions we heard when people found out that we went to Germany was, "What did you eat?" As it turns out, Deutschland is not just a land of sausage and sauerbraten. There are many fresh vegetable dishes and pastas, or you can just live on the hundreds of varieties of delicious breads paired with wonderful central-European cheeses.

[†] coffee

After lunch we walked back to the tram station. From my research, I felt I had a pretty good handle on the public transportation system, which generally was superior to that in the United States. Of course, the first ticket machine we came to looked nothing like any of the examples I had seen in books or online. I was puzzled. Senator pieced together which streetcar led to our destination, but I was having trouble choosing the correct ticket. Eventually we navigated our way into purchasing day passes, which I remember were reasonable.

Our streetcar arrived, and we entered. It was clean and roomy, so I was satisfied. As we zipped along toward the older part of town, I looked for anyone who might want to see our ticket. Unlike Chicago trains, there was no one checking tickets. Unlike New York subways, we had not needed to go through a pay turnstile. As we would later learn, German public transportation is, for the most part, on the honor system. Apparently it works.

We got off at our stop and surveyed the busy district. In front of us was the massive brown stone Hauptbanhof, where all of the city's main train lines met. Behind us were streets lined with dozens of centuries-old buildings, painted in muted colorful tones or wearing the signature wooden criss-cross geometric designs. People were all over the street, especially at the café tables in front of the many restaurants. *Bier** seemed to be the popular lunch choice, with eis as a close second.

We walked and strayed along, drinking plenty of water to combat the record (for them) heat wave. At one point I ducked into a bookstore to peruse the familiar titles

---

* beer

of great literature. For reasons still unclear, I was compelled to buy a copy of Dostoevsky's work, translated into German. We also strolled through a park. In short, everywhere we would walk over the next twelve days would have a common feel: safe, very clean, and neatly kept, except for the many cigarette butts that littered the streets. I guess they do not consider cigarette debris garbage.

It was late enough to check-in, so we took the street car back to our hotel. We received our key card, but it still required personal assistance from a porter to enter our room. There was a knob to turn, while simultaneously shoving your hip against the door and inserting the card. Neither of us could get it to work. Of course, the hotel employee got it instantly. Hopefully these were not standard German locks.

We had just enough time for a shower and a nap before dinner. I set the alarm clock up and checked our luggage. It looked like everything had survived the trip. We snoozed to the sound of German and French news programs on the television.

At a buffet dinner we again met Dory and the forty or so other people with whom we would be traveling for the duration of our trip. They were all English-speakers, from the United States, Australia, the U.K., and a few Asian countries. They all seemed nice, but we smiled politely and kept to ourselves. I was still a little unsure about the group thing.

Dory gave us another briefing about what we could expect in the way of travel arrangements, itinerary, etc.. She got all of our attention when she mentioned that most restrooms/bathrooms/loos/WCs in Germany were not free. She recommended that we always keep change on hand. *Very useful information indeed*, I thought, as I sipped my third cup of coffee that day.

We finished dinner and went back to our room. It was about 8:30pm, and I assumed we would not be tired for a while since it was only 1:30pm at home. I was initially wrong, and we fell asleep quickly, but it did not last long. By 1:00am I was wide awake. I silently scrolled through German, French, and Arabic television stations for half an hour trying to kill time while Senator slept. Time was even more confused by the fact that our alarm clock was running slowly, despite having the proper power converter.

Thankfully, I stumbled upon the German version of the History Channel. Instantly I was sucked in. As an avid World War II student, it took on an entirely new significance to be watching a documentary about a failed plot to assassinate Hitler, while sitting in a hotel room in Germany. I watched until around 3:00am. Then, disgusted that Hitler had won that round, I again fell asleep for two hours.

*   *   *

I woke up Saturday morning after dreaming about fighting Nazi plots-- a surreal way to start my first full day in Germany. Senator and I got ready and followed our instructed procedure. Our suitcases were dutifully parked outside our hotel door. Not being a trusting person by nature, this made me a little nervous. Having our clothes and essentials stolen would certainly put a damper on the rest of the trip. Senator told me not to worry about it, and he was right. Up and down the hallway, everyone else was carelessly leaving their baggage as we all went down to the dining room.

Here I was introduced to the wonder that is the German breakfast buffet. I am not normally someone who eats in the morning, or even recognizes breakfast as a valid meal, but I was for the duration of that trip. Basically, think of any food you could possibly want for breakfast, and multiply it by at least four options. A variety of fresh breads, müesli, fruit, eggs, real yogurts, juices, German and Swiss cheeses, meats, fish, and more were beautifully displayed for the picking. Complimenting it all was the fabulous kaffee. I will not bore you with the reprisal of this menu each day, but to understand the context, we were not staying at top-of-the-line hotels. Yet everywhere we went, an excellent spread started our morning. The high school textbook that I had borrowed from the German teacher hinted at the breakfast ritual, but I had not expected so much.

We finished eating and filed out to our coach bus. I was glad to see that everyone was on time. Hopefully this would not change as people got more comfortable on the trip, or started drinking. The bus would be our roving home between stops for the next eleven days. In an attempt to be fair, there was an assigned seating rotation. Honestly, there were no bad seats on the bus, but the system prevented arguments from people who might insist that they were somehow being cheated. As it turned out, we were in the front seat for the first day. Next to us was our unexpected bonus of the trip, Peter.

Peter was 70-ish, friendly, personable, and full of the subtle, spunky, humorous agitation that can only come from a native Brit. Although, as we quickly learned, he was not 'British', but 'English'. *Ah, correction noted.* Peter quickly altered our strategy of keeping to ourselves. While I cannot say we would have chosen to hang out with everyone who happened to be on our tour, we began to realize the value of interacting with certain people who could tell us about their travel experiences and give us new and interesting perspectives. Not surprisingly, none of them were American. In fact, we found ourselves fitting in much more with the foreign personalities than with those of our fellow compatriots.

We continued to chat with Peter about classic films, history, and language. As he put it, "England and the United States are two countries divided by a common language." Very true. I promised to do my best to start pronouncing double 't's as 't's instead of 'd's. No more baking with *budder*. We also talked about travel. On this trip he was alone, but he informed us that he and his wife enjoyed their skiing trips. "Oh?..." we inquired further.

"Yes, that's 'ski-ing'. S-K-I, which stands for 'Spending our Kids' Inheritance'!" His ruddy complexion beamed beneath his mischievous eyes. I liked this guy.

Full and ready to roll, our bus drove through Frankfurt on our way out of the city. While we had seen some centuries-old buildings in Frankfurt the day before, other parts of Frankfurt were very modern, exhibiting innovative architecture suited to a number of business purposes. My favorite was a giant convention center in the shape of an airship or ocean liner. The massive, gleaming surface reflected our bus as we passed. Contrast that with the ugly black box of Chicago's McCormick Place, and you see why a drive around Frankfurt stands out.

We continued out of town, passing several *Ausfahrt* signs. I laughed, thinking of my Grandma's travel memoir. She wrote of seeing these same signs, each with an arrow pointing off to the right, many times along the road. Eventually curiosity got the best of her and she consulted her tour guide about the matter. "When do we get to Ausfahrt?" The guide smiled and explained that an Ausfahrt is an exit. Coincidentally, later on our trip I saw a man with a tee shirt that read, "Where in the world is Ausfahrt?!" I guess Grandma wasn't the only one wondering.

Our first stop was at the Loreley* Rock, alongside the Rhein River. Legend has it that a forlorn lover took her life there in despair. She then turned into a siren, calling out to gullible and love-starved sailors below, often luring them to destruction. Whether you believe the legend or not, it is a treacherous little stretch of river. While the river is not terribly wide here, the narrow passages, combined with steep, sometimes misty slopes and a very sharp turn, produce dangerous currents. Safety equipment having improved considerably over the years, the siren now beckons tourists to a nice photo stop, and a great rock festival every summer.

We continued on through the Rhein Valley, stopping in Oberwesel to board an hour-and-a-half cruise. This is one of the most photographic parts of Germany. On both sides of the river the land is lush and steep. Combed rows of vineyards line many of the hills. I have no idea how the

---

* I have chosen to keep the German spellings of towns and other features whenever possible.

grapes are gathered from the sharply angled ground, but somehow they manage it to produce their famous *weissweins*.* There is usually a castle in the distance of almost every view as well. Some are in ruins. Others have been given another life as private residences, expensive inns, or other ventures. Closer to the shore, rows of flat, neatly kept houses in various colors make up small villages. Always, there are geraniums. In short, yes, it actually looks like the brochure photos.

As we were admiring the view from the crowded boat deck, we also met Karol and Jules. Or, I should say, Karol decided to introduce himself to us. "Looks like a lot of people are getting off at this stop," he announced.

We nodded in agreement. "Yes, there should be a little more room now," I added, apparently giving away my Yankee accent.

"So, you two are American? What is it with all you Americans wanting guns all the time?" The question wasn't asked in an offensive way, but it threw us off-guard. *So this was how the rest of the world viewed us.*

Senator laughed and explained that, at the moment, we were not, in fact, beladen with firearms and ammo. In between the dissertation, we met Karol's wife, Jules, who was a sweet, funny, somewhat naïve counterpart to his rambling. She reminded us of one of those wonderful, carefree women from a British comedy sketch. She could easily be discussing the potential for rainy weather or serious world affairs. Either would be conducted with a smile and a glass of wine beneath her floppy sun hat.

Karol then turned the conversation toward other

---

* white wines

American domestic situations, which revealed to us just how pervasive our country has become. At home, I rarely see news produced in other countries, but our news, albeit a very skewed version of it, beams its way across the pond daily. Unfortunately, we are painted in a negative, often violent light. For example, Karol wanted to know about our police, who, according to his sources, generally spent their days wandering around shooting random black people. We did our best to give a short explanation separating fact from fiction.*

Once that matter was settled, Karol was ready to discuss the unbelievably uncivilized policies that kept Americans working far too many days each year. *Oh? Tell me more...* He and Jules could not believe that paid time off was not a mandatory condition of employment. It seemed that most European countries offered jobs with a good month or more off. I asked if he was distinguishing public sector jobs, but he claimed it was all jobs. *Hhmmm.* Perhaps I should look into this further. Overall, Karol was an amusing soul, and his wife acted as his perfect foil while he held court. She kept him from getting too serious, and he kept her from getting too lost. They were a fun pair to whom we would often gravitate during the remainder of the trip.

We soon arrived in Boppard and disembarked for our first exploration of one of the many German villages

---

* With the exception of a handful of terrible incidents which the media gladly used to grab attention and instigate division, the hard fact remains that 99.1% of United States police officers have never been accused of any wrongdoing, let alone any race-related situations.

forgotten by time.* Boppard is situated along the Rhein, giving it an automatic picturesque advantage. Add more window boxes filled with red and pink geraniums, stone streets, an open-air market with locals and tourists mingling over drinks or eis, and you have the makings of a lovely two-hour stop. We meandered the streets, skipping shopping, except for a quick stop in a store that sold many household odds and ends. There we decided to invest in a battery alarm clock, since ours had been running slowly. It was well worth the €7,00 to guarantee that we would not be late for the morning departure time. My only disappointment was that I had to repeat my request in German a few times before the kind older gentleman could understand what I was saying. Oh well. At least I didn't expect him to accommodate me in English.

With our purchase in hand, we walked another block or so to a small *platz*† in front of the train station. Senator needed to use a restroom, so I dug out a handful of coins, remembering Dory's warning. In a few moments Senator returned. Good news: the toilet was free. Bad news: it was a raised-up hole, with no seat. As it turned out, it was the only unclean bathroom we encountered during the trip, but I guess when it comes to German restrooms, you get what

---

* This was one example of why I was pleased with our travel company. Towns like Boppard were listed briefly on our itinerary, barely acknowledging them as tour features. As such, I figured they would be fifteen-minute drive-through detours. Instead, at each of these villages we were given a map and ample time to explore on our own, adding many more unexpected highlights to our vacation. Understanding the basics of marketing, I certainly did not expect to get more than advertised.

† plaza, town square

you pay for.

A nicer aspect of the platz was a statue of the author of the Hansel and Gretel story. He was cast by a bench, along with his self-sufficient juvenile characters. We inserted ourselves into the scene and took a picture. Then we walked a few blocks toward the real draw of the town.

Situated tightly between a few other buildings stood St. Severus Kirche. It was not a huge church, but its historic character and charm poured out into the street, via a noon pipe organ and vocal concert. I stood amazed as I surveyed the red and white geometric patterns on the stone or stucco. It occurred to me that it was the oldest building I had ever stepped foot in, up to that point in my life. Two rows accented with medieval style arches, iron, and candles led to tall, thin stained glass and a large suspended crucifix. We quietly took a seat for a little while. One can't help but reflect upon God's light in such a setting. When it was time to go, Senator invited me to try to move the heavy church doors. They seemed two stories tall to me, and I could barely make them budge. This would be just a taste of the architectural interests to come.

We left Boppard and drove toward Köln. The visit to Köln Cathedral was one of highlights that led me to book the trip. I had first seen the massive Gothic structure in a slide during a freshman college course. I was awestruck, partly by the ornate detail and inconceivable scale, and partly by the concept of any building that took the better part of a millennium to build. Through later years, photos of Köln Cathedral popped up from time to time in my travel, architecture, or European history books. To be fair, I was intrigued by any cathedral, but I was particularly

48

drawn to a few of them, including Köln. Now we were on the way. I only hoped the rest of the trip would not be anticlimactic after it.

As we drove toward the city, I perused the brochures advertising the extra excursions. I had already pre-booked those we were interested in, but I figured it couldn't hurt to look again. My attention was soon drawn from the paper I was reading to the distant outline of the city. The dark double spires rose far above the rest of the buildings, denoting the unmistakable landmark. In fact, the cathedral is so large that Allied forces did not bomb it in World War II, opting instead to leave it as a reference point marker for other targets.

In the foreground a bridge spanned the river. All along the bridge hung brightly colored padlocks. Dory explained that the fad had begun when couples attached the locks to the bridge to symbolize their love, which was presumably locked in place. Some of the romance was negated when the practice caught on to the degree that too much weight had been added to the bridge, rendering it being declared unsafe. Bye-bye love locks. Perhaps I should have taken it as an omen about Köln...

After several loops around the very busy intersection, our bus pulled up to the curb. There was some discussion between Ismet and Dory, after which she explained that we would have to disembark quickly, and meet back at a very precise time. The area was so busy with tourists that each bus was only allowed a small loading/unloading period. Then Dory passed out headsets with little receivers. She directed us to keep them on while we walked the block to the cathedral's plaza. That way we could hear her commentary amid the throngs of people. As she led us to the square, she mentioned that hearty folks interested in a challenge could climb the stairs of the bell tower. That sounded good to us. After all, there were only 533 of them.

Our group broke up, like billiard balls that had been launched in all directions. Not wanting to run out of time, and not caring about the fluffy pastry shop with the expensive cakes that attracted some of our tour mates, Senator and I headed straight for the south tower. This meant first making our way through the circus on the platz. I knew it would be touristy, but I had expected some level of class. Instead, we encountered a host of freaks. In one corner a mime did all of the things for which mimes are detested. Not far from him, a bachelor party was making their loud, obnoxious presence known, complete with pink bunny suits. Another section featured Hare Krishnas, while a solitary man knelt on the hard stone at the church's entrance, in some sort of self-imposed penance. The only person I saw whom I liked was a traditional European bird-lady, who was gently feeding her feathered friends. I was most likely drawn to her because she reminded me of a character in *Mary Poppins*. In short, it was the Las Vegas Strip of Germany.

Upon reaching the tower entrance, it was hot, and there was a line, but it was moving quickly. In fact, it quickly approached the counter collecting the €4,00 apiece. We agreed that it was a bit steep, but so were the spires, so I reasoned that it was going to a good cause. We paid our coins and started up the narrow, cramped, endlessly winding stone staircase.

50

In very little time it became apparent that Germany was not a land of overcautious safety regulations, contrary to the United States. As nonstop lines of people ascended and descended the stairs, all maneuvering around each other, we found it amazing that no one fell. If anyone did, I can't imagine the injuries would be minor, especially since it would be almost impossible for emergency personnel to get up there. Then there was the heat. It was already unusually hot outside. Compounded with lots of sweaty bodies, no ventilation*, and a cardio workout to rival a 1980s L.A. aerobics instructor, it was not going to end well.

After many dozens of steps upward, Senator called it quits. I was seriously thinking about it, but I felt that I had invested too much time, energy, effort, and euros to turn back. I had to be getting close to those stinkin' bells. Too out-of-breath to speak in coherent sentences, I nodded and panted that I was going to go a little further... "af-fer... I... res... minute..."

Senator began his return trip, and I pressed on, wondering what the other passers-by would do if I fainted. Probably they'd just march over me, shaking their heads at the dumb American. As I pondered the possibility, after turning the same type of spiral I had done seemingly a hundred times, the stairway opened up and a two-story room held the huge, iron bells that such a treasure demanded. I can't imagine how people would get them up

---

* Based on my limited knowledge of giant church architecture, I had assumed there would be window slits along the way. Then again, maybe that was just in castles, and maybe just in cases where damsels would surely be in distress and need to call out or signal to chivalrous knights.

there today, let alone hundreds of years ago.

I circled them once along the perimeter balcony, and then began the slow, dizzying descent. "Aren't you going further up? There's more to see," a plucky voice demanded. I looked up and saw Karol. Of course he was going to the top.

"No, I'm done," I declared. "I'm heading back down. David's waiting for me anyway." He seemed surprised that anyone would come that far and not go to the top. Maybe he thought my guns were weighing me down.

I finally made it to the bottom, squeezing my way all the way past the line of incoming people, still steadily forking over their €4,00. When I got back to the entrance, Senator was not there. Around the corner there was a display in a grotto-like setting, so I peeked in. He was not there either. My next theory was that he had gone to the bathroom, so I waited for a few minutes. When he still did not show up, I began to get nervous. There was no way he could have passed by me without me seeing him, and I couldn't imagine he would just leave without telling me.

Right now, Reader, you are asking the obvious question, "Why didn't you just call him?" Well, that's a question with a rather complicated answer, but suffice it to say we had no operating cell phones while in Germany. Yes, I know. You don't need to lecture me; that was the fact of the matter. Inconveniently, we also had no way to get a hold of our tour director. While we did have a rendezvous time and place, I was not sure Senator had paid attention to it, and if he had, I was not sure he would find it, and if he did, I was not sure he would proceed there without me.

My childhood camping and field trip training led me

to take two steps. First, I prayed-- a lot. Second, though it took extreme willpower, I stayed put. When two parties are separated, everyone knows that at least one of them must remain in place. Otherwise, they will likely keep missing each other, and the next thing you know you have another *Fievel* sequel on your hands. So stay I did. Whether he had just casually wandered for a moment or was frantically searching for his Wendy V, I was sure that Senator would return. After all, it had to occur to him that he knew where I was, but I did not know where he was.

An uncomfortable amount of time passed, and now I was sure Senator had missed that chapter in the Girl Scout survival handbook. I then saw a couple whom I recognized from our trip. Desperate, I explained my situation, asking/begging them to wait there in case Senator came back that way. I did my best to describe him, as they really did not know us yet.* My only other option would have been to flag down the *polizei*,† but that was a part of my German language cd that I was really hoping not to use.

The American couple waited in the entrance while I tore up the ramp to the platz. Quickly scanning the crowd of nut jobs, I focused my attention on one sane-looking person. Senator was sitting on the edge of a short wall,

---

* I never realized how inadequate I am at this. To me, Senator is completely distinct. When I went to describe him in a practical, non-poetic way however, it sounded completely generic: "tallish, medium build, light brown hair, not quite down to his shoulders and not nearly as long as it used to be, chameleon eyes whose color I have not been able to determine for the twelve years we have been together..." I think the lesson here is that I would be the absolute worst person to give an eyewitness account in court.

† police

donning an expression that was something between tired, mildly irritated, and bored. None of these were what I had anticipated upon our grand reunion, but as long as I saw him it didn't matter. "Don't move!" I yelled. I blurted out my nightmarish twenty-minutes of panic, and then ran back down the ramp to tell the American couple I had found him. I am still grateful to them.

Back with Senator again, I was still dumbfounded that he did not stay where I would know to find him. I was flattered by his faith in my mind reading powers, but I implored him not to be so dependent on them next time. His only reaction was, "I wasn't lost." *No kidding.*

It seemed like hours had passed, but we actually still had some time before meeting back at the bus. We decided to venture inside the main sanctuary of the magnificent cathedral. Having recovered my tranquility, I entered my first medieval cathedral. For scope, workmanship, and detail, it could not be beat. My eye wandered in all directions at once, taking in the altar, a triptych the size of an exterior wall of my house, and a pipe organ reaching to the heavens.

The problem, however, was the atmosphere. Unfortunately, the inside of Köln Cathedral reflects the outside, if to a somewhat lesser degree. While there are not street players and drunken revelers, there are mobs of photographing tourists roaming all over the sanctuary. Greeting us as we entered, before our eyes could even adjust to the darker interior, were clergy members with boxes strapped around their necks. Whereas other historical churches have a donation box in the back, possibly with a simple sign attached, these gentleman found it more profitable to stare down visitors, subtly glancing down at their portable offering-box-necklaces.

Overall it was a disturbing vibe. Worse, Senator was in a funk, almost mentally writing off the rest of the trip. It was not a pleasant mood, especially considering the financial investment. Still, I was not about to have my German adventure dampened. We filed back onto the bus, wondering if the next several days would feel like Köln. Thankfully, Peter was in good humor as we drove outside of town to our hotel.

Things improved as we checked into our room for the night. It was clean and comfortable, and we had enough time to wash the grime and stress of the afternoon off of us before heading down to dinner with our group. As an added blessing, we ended up sitting next to Peter, along with Bob and Christine, a Welsh couple. Bob had a thick Welsh accent and a wind-blown complexion to match. When he wasn't sneaking out for a smoke break, he was telling stories or lightly critiquing a number of situations. Christine was as prim and proper as Bob was casual. We had nothing in common with either of them, and we had a great time with both of them.

As we waited patiently for our 'vegetarian option', we visited with our new friends, gleaning more travel knowledge and unplanned entertainment. We learned that Peter, through his son's work connection, was once a guest at Buckingham Palace. While relaxing and conversing with the staff, he made a comment about "Charles not liking" something that was currently going on in the country. He was immediately and curtly corrected. "Do you mean The Prince of Wales?"

We finished chuckling just as our dining room host lay plates of a meat entrée in front of us. We tried to explain that we were waiting for a vegetarian dish. Dory had even confirmed it. The man was thoroughly confused and flustered. We weren't upset, but he was getting antsy, and our table mates had taken up our cause, unsolicited. After several exchanges and reassuring the host and Dory that we were fine, it all ended in the dramatic delivery of large plates of pasta, an unintelligible proclamation, and monster hugs for both of us. I think the guy may have been Italian...

After dinner we lingered for a while with Peter, Bob, and Christine. There was a lagoon just beyond the patio off the hotel's dining area, so we also took a short walk. One of consistent criticisms of Cosmos is that hotels are not usually in the city centers or concentrated tourist areas. On this night in particular, we found this to be a distinct plus. We were situated at the edge of a large, peaceful park-- the very antithesis of the cathedral platz.

*   *   *

Sunday morning was an early departure, after eating breakfast seated next to the American couple who had helped me at the cathedral. Also sharing a table with us was an active Australian couple. Everyone on the tour seemed ready for the next adventure, heightening the anticipation. We were just ready to move on from Köln.

The sky was overcast, but it brought welcome cooler temperatures. We were on our way north, up the west side of the country. Since it would be one of our longest driving stretches,* Dory wanted to provide us with a little

---

* Technically, due to the make of the tour bus and our route, we can

entertainment. We relaxed and listened in, enjoying the fact that we were cruising around in luxury, letting someone else deal with the hassle of driving and directions. During 'fun facts with Dory', we learned a few fascinating bits of trivia:

> 1. The country that consumes the most amount of beer per capita is not Germany. That award goes to... Czech Republic.
> 2. Germany does, however, boast over 300 varieties of native-produced breads. I have only tasted a sample of these, but based on that, I can confidently declare them all delicious.
> 3. In Germany, sensitivity to the events surrounding World War II still runs high. As such, it is actually illegal to perform the "Heil Hitler" salute, unless you happen to be a teacher or stand-up comic.* I have mixed feelings about this. On one hand, it is good and appropriate to admonish any aspect of the Third Reich. On the other hand, one of the key components of fascism is to suppress free speech. I suppose it all comes down to balance.

We rode awhile longer. Senator dozed off while I worked on notes for this book. After a while we made a

---

say we've taken a Mercedes Benz on the Autobahn. Pop in the Kraftwerk cd!

* Here's another bit of trivia. Question: Who was the first person to portray Adolf Hitler on the silver screen? Answer: Moe Howard. To experience the magic for yourself, view the 1940 short *You Nazty Spy*.

stop at a rest area/gas station/buffet/convenience shop. I was feeling daring, so I bypassed the turnstile outside the restroom, which had been left open while a janitor was cleaning. This saved me a cool €,70. Senator, who was either more honest or less stealthy than I, paid the full amount outside the men's bathroom. As a consolation prize for pay toilets, doing so yields a €,50 rebate coupon. He promptly invested this in a German chocolate espresso bar in the store. It was too milky/rich for my taste, but he enjoyed it, claiming that it even settled his stomach. The moral of the story has something to do with giving and receiving, or maybe just paying to pee. I'm not quite sure which.

After a while we were in Hamelin. The bus parked along a curb. To the right a wine festival was about to begin. About a quarter of our group headed that way. The rest of us followed Dory across the street and down through a pedestrian walkway that might as easily have been a time-traveling portal. When we emerged, we were in a fairy tale.

Hamelin's *Altstadt** consisted of several blocks of colorful, tall buildings with sharply-angled peaks. The streets, of course, were cobblestone, converging at the town center, near the *ratthaus*† We were fortunate enough to be there on a Sunday afternoon, just about the time local actors were about to reenact the story of the Pied Piper. After

---

* old city: Many German towns have districts that are beautifully preserved and referred to by this term. The strategy of seeking out the Altstadt in any possible town never disappointed us.

† town hall: Many Altstadts contain these elaborate stone structures. Of course, in English one can draw his/her own puns regarding the politicians within the local government building.

grabbing what was quickly becoming our favorite German sandwich (cheese, tomato, and lettuce on fresh bread), we staked out a spot to watch for the glockenspiel that would announce the play's beginning.

As I looked in all directions at the storybook setting which surrounded me, I heard a sound in the distance. Senator pointed down a side street, where we could see a small parade of people emerging. Leading them was a man in medieval costume, playing a sopranino. We realized it was, in fact, the Pied Piper, or the Pied Sopraninoist at any rate. Following him merrily were a dozen or so little children, each dressed as *rattens*.* They were holding their tiny gray paws in front of them as they danced along, bobbing their pointed felt noses. I melted. *Maybe I do really want kids-- just as long as they are German and dressed as happy rats!* Senator was smiling at me, knowing what I was thinking. "No, I don't think they are for sale in a souvenir shop, Wendy..."

When the play was over, we entered St. Nikolai Kirche, which stood at the edge of the platz. Like the church in Boppard, it was simple and sincere. It was also very cheerful and inviting. There were only a few people inside, and they were quiet. I sat for a while in the pew and thought.

We then walked around the sanctuary, viewing the altar and a modest display off to the side of the room. It contained information about the historical church, as well as a few classical cds that had been recorded there. Hosting visitors in the church that day was a lady who spoke less English than I spoke German, but together we worked out a

___
* You don't really need me to translate this one, do you?

cd purchase. It was Senator's only souvenir from Germany, but we have listened to it many times since then.

It was time to leave Hamelin, so we retreated the way we came, walking through the tunnel back to the twenty-first century. Hamelin was like a dream. It was the fulfillment of many childhood visions of folk tales and faraway stories. I could have spent several days there, but we had many more adventures ahead.

When we got back on the bus, we could see Dory and Ismet speaking in a private conversation. Then they let us in on the secret. Dory explained that we would be about an hour late to our evening destination, due to the necessity of changing our route. It seemed Hannover was locked down, as authorities had discovered an unexploded World War II bomb. Passengers joked, wondering if it was one of 'ours' (American), or one of 'yours' (British). Senator and I knew, however, that only we could be blamed for such an usual interruption to a vacation. It was our pattern, throughout the better part of twelve years of traveling together. It was also proof yet again that we had made the correct decision in going with a tour group instead of going by ourselves. I could just picture us trying to reroute ourselves, while getting yelled at by the polizei because we were too close to Allied explosives.

So we had plenty of time to relax and watch the countryside go by. We were out of the Rhein Valley, leaving the lush vineyards behind. In their place was now fertile, rolling farmland, similar to that of southern Wisconsin. It makes sense that so many German immigrants settled there in the 1800s.

Dory entertained us with an interesting addendum

to our visit to Hamelin. Historians who have studied the town records found an instance several hundred years ago where there are references to the town's children being absent. Whether disease took them, or they were relocated for safety or health reasons, or a Pied Sopraninoist seduced them away, we may never know. Or maybe a tourist who was taken by the sight of a sweet mob of rat-costumed children innocently kidnapped them all.

Then Dory announced that she was going to put on some music for the remainder of the day's ride. Senator and I perked up. Exactly what kind of *musik* was in store? Bach? Beethoven? Klaus Schulze? Kraftwerk? *Nein*. We had come thousands of miles to hear Lionel Ritchie-- who hailed from our very own home town in Illinois of all places. In between the cheesy, outdated love songs were interspersed other choices that must have qualified as 'relaxing'. I think I fell asleep during Enya.

By early evening we were in Hamburg. It was comfortably cool, gray, and rainy. In short, it was a perfect night for an industrial cruise. Before that, Ismet detoured us for a fifteen-minute stop at the Wedding Cake Kirche. Actually, the church was St. Michael the Archangel, as depicted outside the front door by a larger-that-life statue of the highest-ranking angel stabbing a spear into the cowering beast. (European church imagery tends to be less cautious and blandly sanitized than that of the United States.)

The inside really was reminiscent of a wedding cake, though. There were a few curvy tiers, each with a white background accented by ornate detail. I pointed out the majestic pipe organ to Senator. He said he could see it, but

61

his back was turned to mine. Then I realized that we were looking at two different pipe organs. Upon turning to see the organ each other was talking about, our eyes rested on the main, and third pipe organ. It was situated at the altar. Near it was an awe-inspiring crucifix, which I assume is the point. This was just another bonus that was not even on the itinerary.

We then drove on to our hotel in Hamburg. Surprisingly, the rooms were each suites, complete with a bar and two televisions. Great! We could watch twice as many channels that we could not understand. After a quick pit stop, we walked a few doors down to grab some dinner.

September was the name of a pub/restaurant with a great feel. The wood interior was warm and cozy, with the added interest of antiques throughout the dining room. We found a table and ordered a dish with a lot of vegetable vocabulary in it. As we waited, Jules and Karol walked in and sat at the next table. As always, Karol was at no loss for words, and we all had a good time discussing music, politics, and most importantly, our plans for the evening. They had opted to go on the harbor cruise as well. We ate quickly and paid the poor lone soul who seemed to be acting as server, host, bartender, and cashier. We had just enough time to make it to our rendezvous point.

Our cruise departed around 7:00pm. No, that's not right. Our cruise departed exactly at 19:00. Germans do not waste time. They also expect you to use your own common sense. The captain and tour guide were a husband and wife team. He drove the boat and she narrated. In what I would soon understand to be the classic dry and sharply clever German sense of humor, she began the 'safety talk'. "Goot ev-en-ing. Ve are going to be cruising for one and one-half hours. Before ve begin, ve must go over a few safety items. If you happen to fall overboard, stay put. Ve vill pick you up on de vay back. Or tomorrow at de latest..." Naturally, there were no visible life jackets, and no reference to them. The Litigious States of America this was not.

Our boat was small, holding about twenty passengers. That allowed us to get up close and personal with the many types of vessels that traverse one of the world's largest harbors. While the Rhein cruise highlighted the romance of the region, the Hamburg harbor on the Elbe was a marvel of logistics. Foremost in our memory were the monstrous container ships. Dwarfing cruise ships and even battleships, these transports sail the world, exchanging goods between continents as though they were neighboring towns. It was staggering to see thousands upon thousands of box cars, each 20-40 feet long, stacked as if they were children's blocks. It was kind of scary when we pulled up practically beneath one ship. If the captain hiccuped too hard, one of those box cars could easily tumble right over the side. Then it would be good-bye Senator and Wendy V, Peter, Jules, and the rest of the gang. Somehow I think Karol would manage a trick to survive.

We floated along to the edge of the open water. The Hamburg skyline was very diverse, with as many new construction projects as well-preserved buildings. I could see the top of St. Michael's, unintentional patron of wedding cakes. I sipped my weisswein, which was included in the tour, but it was not anything special. While everyone's attention was turned starboard, I flipped the contents of my glass over the port side, dumping the remainder of my drink into the drink. If anyone had seen or questioned me, I was going to pass it off as a romantic ritual.

With the same amount of passengers as we left with, we returned to shore. Our guide had been excellent. I never would have thought a cruise through an industrial area would be so fascinating. It was raining and dreary out, and we could not have asked for a better night. It was not long after reaching our room that we drifted off to the sounds of a Hamburg street and German news reports about Greece ruining the euro.

*   *   *

Monday morning we started with a sunny drive around Hamburg. The most interesting building I saw was yet another ratthaus. This one was much larger than the others we had seen, taking up two city blocks. We had just enough time to walk around it. As we reached the front side, I noticed the large German flag waving in the breeze. It struck me that we had seen very few German flags since we had been in the country. National flags seem much more prevalent in the United States.

Our daytime stop was the city of Lübeck, famous for its marzipan. By now we knew to head straight for the Altstadt. It was an easy walk from where our bus was parked. There was no time-traveling tunnel like there was in Hamelin, but we did pass beneath the stoic Romanesque city gate, Holstentor. Several blocks later we were in the shadow of St. Mary's Kirche, which to date is my favorite church anywhere.

St. Mary's was constructed surprisingly quickly,

given the fact that it was the thirteenth century, and like so many others, it demanded great engineering capability and artistry. As the legend goes, this was partly due to the assistance of none other than Satan himself. It is said that he sped up the process by flying large stones and other necessary pieces into their proper places. Why would the Evil One help build a church, of all things? Simple-- the townspeople lied to him and told him they were building an ale house. Knowing the destruction that strong brew can bring about, he was happy to lend a hand, or wing. Christians: 1; Devil: 0.

The inside of St. Mary's featured muted soft hues, interspersed with geometric patterns. From floor to ceiling craftsmanship was evident. Like other churches from the same era, lines were long and lean, leaving space between arches for Gothic windows to let in natural light. The front quarter rows of seats were gated off within closer proximity to the altar. Naturally, the acoustics were heavenly.

Depending which part of the nave we were facing, there were treasures at every turn. Much of the bas relief art incorporated the danse macabre theme, using skeletons, skulls, and angels to remind man of the brevity of life on Earth. Other nooks featured stained glass depictions of coats of arms, miniature statues of saints, or even crypts of faith. In the rear of the church was an interpretive display on the church's history.

Three features in particular could have kept me there for hours. In an area carved out not far from the altar was a World War I memorial. Painted on the wall was "1914-1918", and there were several rustic crosses, loosely bandaged around their entire length. Each one contained many nails pounded in at haphazard angles. It was striking, to say the least.

The second side area was dominated by an astronomical clock. Minutes, hours, days, months, phases of the moon, zodiac signs, and more were represented on this big clock. No, Reader, I mean BIG. Senator and I stood in front of it, and we probably could have fit another five people across the front. It was several stories tall. If the skulls and skeletons didn't remind people of passing time, the giant clock surely would.

Finally, there was a small chamber just off the back of the church. In fact, it was an out-of-commission bell tower. Situated in the room, behind a locked iron gate, were a few items. A stand that held a book, (possibly a Bible, but I can't remember) faced viewers. Alongside of it was a lit candle, holding vigil. The centerpiece lay on floor, in the form of shattered church bells. During an Allied air raid one night in 1943, the bells came crashing down. Now they lay there as a silent memorial. The war was fresh in Germany, as I would continually come to understand during our trip.

After the solemn beauty of St. Mary's, we switched gears to lighter pursuits. On our way to acquire some requisite marzipan, we happened past the Western Store. Had I only seen the name, I might have been inclined to wonder, *west in relation to where?* No explanation was necessary, however, as there was a glass storefront sporting American flags, Confederate flags, and plenty of flannel and denim. A few Australian Outback items were also thrown in for good measure. We scratched our western heads and proceeded to the sugary destination.

I really knew nothing of marzipan, save that it was some sort of confection involving almond paste. Now I understand. We entered what we thought would be a nice little bakery, but in Lübeck, marzipan is serious stuff. The almond paste was dense and high quality. It stood to reason then, that the chief purveyor of it would be a fine establishment where one approached an artisan behind a counter who personally waited on him/her. Thick cake-like pieces were carefully packaged and bagged, as though one had made a fine perfume purchase. Of course, there were sampler packs and candies for the lightweights, but we didn't mess around. We made our selection, requested two forks, (which the marzipan representative had already anticipated,) and took our treat to a bench in the formal gardens just outside Holstentor.

Afterward, we walked back to the bus, meeting a few other members of our tour group as we arrived. Soon everyone was seated, Dory was at her station, and Ismet was set to drive. The intersection near our parking spot was busy, but pedestrians, bicyclists, and drivers had all been sharing the road successfully... until we started to make our turn. A 40+ passenger tour bus has a wide turning radius, but Ismet was a very cautious and experienced driver. When there was a break in the pedestrian and bike traffic, he slowly began to make a right turn. Out my window I could see a man on a bike on the sidewalk coming toward us, but I assumed that, like everyone else, he would stop at the corner when he saw the large white bus turning. In fact, he did not. He continued to come as we continued to turn. I never took my eyes off of him.

When it became apparent that he was not stopping, I realized that he would get caught under our bus, and most likely crushed beneath our wheel. Everybody screamed for Ismet to "Stop! Stop!" as he could not see the cyclist. Actually, I later learned that I was the only one who had seen the whole thing, and the only one who had yelled.* At any rate, Ismet slammed on the brakes just in time. The cyclist bumped into the side of the bus hard enough to bend his wheel a little and knock himself off of his bike, but no real harm was done.

I was shaking from the adrenaline and the prospect of having almost witnessed a violent injury or death. Out my window I could see Dory and Ismet talking to the bicyclist, who was smiling, nodding, and assuring them that he was okay. Though the bicyclist was Australian, we were once again schooled in the different attitude toward personal responsibility in Germany. The man even turned down a box of marzipan Dory offered him. Back home, there would have been police, medics, insurance companies, and certainly lawyers involved in the whole affair. And the guy probably would have snatched up the marzipan, too.

---

* To this day I have two clear recollections of that moment, which seemed to occur in slow motion. In my mind, everyone was yelling loudly, and though I was joining in, my voice was barely audible. Senator and several other witnesses assured me that it was definitely just me, and I was *definitely* audible. The other thing I remember is worrying because my mind had gone blank as to the German word for 'stop', and Ismet did not speak English. Again, Senator confirmed that my foreign message was clearly received. "Anyone who heard your blood-curdling scream would have hit the brakes no matter what you said!"

I eventually unwound as we motored our way south toward Berlin. Dory was showing a dvd that featured highlights of Germany in all four seasons. It was peaceful... so peaceful, in fact, that I think I was the only one who stayed awake on the bus. Winter was my favorite.

We entered Berlin in late afternoon. I was filled with anticipation for visiting such an iconic city-- one that had been the setting for so many books, movies, and documentaries that had captured my interest. As we drove into the city limits, I learned several notable facts about Berlin. First of all, it is a very green city, with much of its land reserved for public parks, most famously Tiergarten. I knew from booking reservations that the Spree River ran through the city, but I did not realize how much water weaves its way throughout Berlin. There are actually more canals than Paris and Venice combined. Not surprisingly, it is a very international city, which could partly account for it being the third most visited capital in Europe, after only London and Rome. Cafés are everywhere, and on any decent night they are teeming with patrons. The population is roughly the same as Chicago, but somehow it never felt even a tenth as crowded. Perhaps this is because the public transportation system is clean, reliable, and efficient. To offer concrete evidence, we never saw a single traffic jam!

As we approached our hotel, Dory made a pitch for anyone who would like to purchase the evening's optional excursion. It was a family-style dinner at Ziko's Grill. Even though we had now made several friends among our tour mates, we were planning to skip the dinner, figuring our vegetarian dining choices might be scant, and not really caring about eating in a restaurant. Then Dory said the

69

magic words. "As a little bonus, after the dinner at Ziko's, we will be taking a driving tour of Berlin at night, including Brandenburg Gate." Sign me up! I didn't care if we had to eat crackers.

After checking into our room, we joined the majority of our tour group, who had decided to go to Ziko's. The evening can best be described as going to a wedding reception without having to sit through a boring wedding, give a gift, or see distant relatives you don't like. Ziko himself was the robust, crazy, fun uncle. He was a boisterous and jovial Serbian, taking opportunities at each table to use a trick bowl to pretend to spill soup on guests.

We sat with Bob and Christine from Wales, a couple from New Jersey, and some fun Aussies. There was some sort of mediocre pasta dish, but the fresh bread would have made a premium meal by itself. As everyone was having a grand time, and the wein und bier were flowing, it was only a matter of time before Ziko announced that we would be having a sing-along. *Oh boy.* I'm still not sure how one thing led to another, but I found myself in front of the group, joining Dory and another woman about my age in an Abba song. Mainly I just felt sorry for Dory, who at that time must have been wondering how much she should really have to endure for the sake of some tips at the end of our twelve days together. I lip-synced most of it, and I was grateful when it ended, even if it meant that the conga line was just beginning.

About twenty-five people wound our way outside, around the front of restaurant. Sure a few people on the street gave us strange looks, but most seemed amused. Besides, we had the strength of numbers on our side. Our impromptu beast then snaked its serpentine way back inside, finding our seats once again before finishing our dessert and coffee.

After thanking 'Uncle Ziko' for a wonderful evening, everyone boarded the bus for the tour around the city. As if on cue, Abba was playing over the bus speakers. We started to wonder if we would hear any German music while in Germany. At least Sweden was closer than Illinois.

It was not a far drive to Brandenburg Tor, perhaps the most famous landmark in Germany. Soon we were in view of the mammoth gate. Originally it had been erected during the 1700s to commemorate a Prussian victory, but it had taken on much greater notoriety during World War II, when the Nazis draped swastika flags down the length of its neoclassical columns. On top of the gate sat a female victory symbol, driving her four-horse chariot. She faced the platz, which was flanked by various embassies and foreign consulates.

Half a block away the Reichstag* stood. Its role in Hitler's manipulative and rapid rise to power was now squelched by a glass dome top, where average citizens and visitors could gaze down and observe literal and figurative government transparency. On the other side of the gate ran Unter den Lindens,† a street with a lovely name that witnessed some of the unloveliest moments in human history. Beyond the avenue was Tiergarten.‡ At one time the beasts were the animals in this city zoo. Not long after,

---

* Germany's seat of its legislative branch; like Capitol Hill in the United States
† 'Under the Lindens'
‡ 'Garden of the Beasts'

the beasts were of a different and far more sinister nature.

It was the first surreal history-staring-me-in-the-face interaction I had in Germany. Many more would follow throughout Berlin, and in Nürnberg and München. Brandenburg Tor itself was on the cover of the book I had just brought back from Door County. I had encountered these images in documentaries, books, and movies for years, and now they stood largely unchanged, yet the antithesis of what they once were. We meandered around the platz for a while before taking our bus back to our hotel. The next day was entirely ours to explore Berlin, and we would need at least that much time to piece together such a complex city.

*   *   *

We were up early Tuesday, ready to take on our busiest day of the trip. A morning driving tour was included, so we wanted to take advantage of that first. I had also booked a free walking tour in the afternoon, because, hey, it was free. As long as I was feeling daring, booking trips over the internet in an unfamiliar city, I went ahead and booked an evening sunset cruise as well. That one had a reasonable fee, assuming the company actually existed.

As we got ready in the cramped, oddly laid-out bathroom, all at once we lost power. I stepped into the hallway and found that all of the rooms on our end of the wing were suddenly on the Amish plan. We weren't really inconvenienced by it, but some other people were more upset. The hotel admitted that their circuits were easily overloaded, but there was already someone coming to fix it.

After breakfast we boarded the bus for our driving

tour. Since Dory and Ismet needed a day off at some point, they handed us off to another tour guide and a substitute driver. It felt like 'Mom and Dad' had left us with the babysitter. "We'll probably see them light up cigarettes and peel out of the parking lot," one tour mate joked, regarding Ismet's and Dory's break from us. Nonetheless, our new guide did a great job. Like the woman on the boat in Hamburg, he possessed that stark, dry wit, with the added touch of a radio voice.

The first thing we passed was a *kaufhaus*, which is basically a department store. Of note is that a kaufhaus often has a grocery store on its bottom floor. Of greater note is that this particular kaufhaus contained over 300 kinds of cheeses. Sounds completely reasonable to me.

We meandered our way around Berlin, reaching the Bundestag* district. The massive Romanesque brown stone gave these buildings a sense of formidable permanence. Nearby was the Chancellor's residence. Our guide informed us that locals referred to Chancellor Merkel, the most powerful woman in the world at the time, as 'Angie-mami'.† We also passed the President's residence, but as he has no real power, no one seemed to care that the flag was flying overhead, indicating that he was home.

Berlin is a city of booming construction. Though decades have passed since the war, so much was bombed out that there are still opportunities to rebuild, keeping it a

---

* federal

† Many Germans have since lost their affection for Angela Merkel, after she abruptly declared that Germany would accept 1,000,000 refugees. As in cases around the world, the threat of terrorist infiltration among refugees remains a grave concern in Germany.

young city. Some of the new buildings maintain traditional styles, but many favor modern influences. Due to careful planning by top architects attracted to the city, they are neatly cast and seamless enough to blend in easily, without appearing to be soulless gray boxes. One new cathedral actually stands next to the preserved remains of its older sister.

As we rode, our driver continued to narrate. While listening, I noticed a courtyard tucked between buildings. In it were several bouquets of fresh flowers. Just as I was wondering what the occasion was, our guide explained that it was the courtyard where Count Von Stauffenberg had been executed for his role in an attempt to assassinate Hitler. Out of gratitude and to honor his courage, locals had lain flowers there on the anniversary of the event. I then put it all together. *The guy from the documentary!* It was the story I had seen on television the first night we were in the country.

As I pondered the real-life connections between the dark Berlin of the early 20th century and the lively city before me, we made our way to Checkpoint Charlie. Historically, Checkpoint Charlie was known as the border between the free democratic sector of post-war occupied Berlin and the Soviet communist sector. There is not much there, but the spot is greatly capitalized upon as a place to do touristy things like take a picture with a costumed G.I., read an information kiosk, or get pick-pocketed. To thwart any such attempts on our merry band, our tour guide and driver stood like stern bodyguards, staring down any potential ne'er-do-wells. Honestly, I think it only would have been a problem if someone was a completely oblivious target.*

Five minutes was long enough for us at Checkpoint Charlie. Everyone was ready to move on. As our guide so eloquently put it, "...iz really more like... Snackpoint Charlie." For the first time since making our stop, he cracked a slight smile. As long as he was on a roll, he also pointed out one of the many questionable modern art sculptures in the city-- this one purchased by some politician-- which Berliners have nicknamed *Verstopfung*.†

Our final stop before returning to our disembarkation point was a section of the Berlin Wall. I say a section because it exists in a broken line of bits and pieces throughout the city. Most people are familiar with the concrete barrier that isolated the "island of democracy" within East Germany, but many are surprised to find that it is only about ten feet tall. The misperception is probably due to steep camera angles when filming its destruction in 1989. Now there is metal fencing erected around parts of the intact wall so that the remaining concrete will not be taken by souvenir scavengers, as it was when it first came down. In fact, elated citizens were so ecstatic to see the hated wall's demise that some people mistakenly took pieces of a nearby business building's wall. Oops.

Our babysitters deposited us safely and soundly back at Brandenburg Tor. This would have been exceptionally handy, since that was where our afternoon tour was meeting, however we found no feasible bathrooms. Since it was a clear day and we had plenty of

---

*I should mention that everywhere we were in Germany felt much safer than metropolitan areas at home.

† 'constipation'; I told you Germans were funny.

time, we decided to walk back to our hotel for the necessary pit stop. It was a little strange, yet freeing walking around a world capital with no guides, no sanctioned maps, and no working phone. I was still pretty relieved to see our hotel emerge in the distance, though.

Our walk had convinced us that the afternoon was, in fact, hot-- not warm. Ergo, we decided to try our luck with the Berlin rail system. It was similar enough to the New York City subways that I was able to pick up the system immediately, aided by enough German to fill in the gaps. Senator then saved us by interpreting the ticket machine. Though it was not as confusing as the one in Frankfurt, it was still tricky. Again, no one checked for our tickets. I guess there must be enough honest people to keep the trains running.

After a few stops we exited the train back at Pariser Platz. We had just enough time for a variation of our favorite meal. *Salat teller* included lettuce, tomato, very mild onion, generous slices of cheese, and some pale yellow, creamy sauce. It was far more delicious than it sounds. As we finished our lunch, it began to drizzle. I looked at the sky and my watch questioningly. It was just about time to cross the platz to our meeting point.

We stood up, started walking, and the heavens opened into a full downpour. A little rain would not be a bad thing, but a deluge could seriously dampen a two-and-a-half hour walking tour. Senator had the idea to duck into a gift shop to buy an umbrella. The store probably had a maximum capacity of about twenty people, but there were at least fifty crammed in there, all hoping to avoid being soaked. The proprietor was frazzled, and no one could

76

move. After vain attempts to maneuver into a cashier's line, Senator gave up, pressed a ten euro note into the man's hand, and we took our new *"BERLIN"* umbrella outside.

It continued to pour, and our umbrella was insufficient, but we joined several others and ducked under the overhang of the French consulate building. I was beginning to work on Plan B, disappointed that we would miss our walking tour. Just then, as quickly as it had started, the rain stopped. Gradually everyone emerged from their shelter, and the platz was lively once again. It had worked out perfectly, cooling the afternoon slightly, too. "Guess you feel kinda' bad for always badmouthing the French, huh?" I teased Senator.

"No, not really."

New Berlin Tours was a company that offered free walking tours with approved guides who only worked for tips. It was a brilliant idea. Guides would have to be good to make a living at it, and tourists knew they had nothing to lose when booking. As we lined up near the giant red umbrella with the company's logo, however, I began to think we would get exactly what we had paid for. Dozens of people were crowded around. A group that big would never work. Then there was the umbrella holder, who looked like a bored college kid, who was probably in his second year as a business major. Maybe someone had told him that he should expand his horizons. Maybe he was quitting after this tour.

I was just about to leave when another representative made an announcement. We were subdivided into groups of about twenty people each, and Boring Guy gladly handed off his duties to other guides.

77

Ah, all hope is not lost. We now found ourselves in the care of a thin, Bohemian-looking, dreadlocked, English free spirit known as Alex. Well, at least it would be interesting.

Alex introduced himself, explaining that he was born in England, the son of a German-Polish couple. It was immediately apparent that he loved Berlin and loved what he did. As he gave us the preliminaries, he mentioned that if we had questions, we could stop him anytime by raising our left hand. I thought it was an unusual way to state it, but I later realized that anything regarding a Hitler salute is so taboo in Germany, that even the choice of which hand to raise was subject to caution.

Before we left Pariser Platz, Alex directed our attention directly behind us, to the Hotel Adlon. It was an upscale establishment that had catered to big shots and dignitaries for many decades. In more recent history, it had become famous as the setting where Michael Jackson elicited gasps and criticism as he dangled his baby over the balcony railing. Recalling the story brought groans from several nationalities of English-speakers on our tour. Clearly no country was voting him Father of the Year.

We then observed the massive green statue, known as Quadriga, that sits atop the Brandenburg Tor. Originally completed in 1791, just fifteen years later it fell into French hands as a spoil of war under Napoleon. When the tide turned and Paris was captured by Prussian soldiers, Quadriga was returned to its spot atop the gate. This time an iron cross was added to the statue to signify Germany's dominance. Whether the fact that the statue directly faces the French consulate building is accidental or on purpose is left up to you to decide.

Our next stop was a somber and introspective one. Just outside of Pariser Platz was the Memorial to the Murdered Jews of Europe. Upon first glance it was several city blocks of large, rectangular concrete slabs of various dimensions. The slabs were lain out in a grid pattern, but there was no adornment and no explanation. Alex explained that the artist was given the commission to memorialize the Holocaust, which he fulfilled, but he never offered an interpretation, choosing rather to let people experience and interpret it for themselves. In this spirit, Alex gave us time to wander throughout the memorial alone before meeting us at the other side.

As we explored, there were a few things that impacted us. First of all, it was stark, cold, and dreary. This, of course, had obvious implications. Going beyond, however, we also theorized that perhaps the various sizes represented people who were cut off at different stages of life. Young and old alike were represented, all stripped of their identity and individuality until they were one mass of gray. As we walked further, the full magnitude of the artist's vision unfolded. What we did not notice until we were in the middle of it was that we had gradually descended. The ground sloped gently to the center, rising again as we exited. I believe it illustrated how sly and smooth the Nazi machine had operated, especially in terms of propaganda. Things that were gradually accepted in the early days of the regime somehow led to unfathomable depths of human depravity. Upon first glance, the memorial was striking and ugly. In some ways, that was the point.

I was reflecting on all of this when my thoughts were

interrupted by some stupid Italian girls who had decided that the memorial only existed as their personal hide-and-seek labyrinth. They laughed and chased their way around, until they had annoyed several people. Thankfully they left. Just as I was calming down from the utter disrespect shown by the girls, I looked up to see an even greater affront. A couple who sounded American were changing their baby's diaper on one of the slabs of the memorial. There was a moment when I was seriously tempted to confront them. I must be getting older or wiser though, because I backed down, determining that it probably was not a good idea to get into a fist fight... at a Holocaust memorial... while temporarily separated from our tour group... while in a foreign country. Still, I hope their baby kept them up all night.

We moved on to Hitler's bunker. *Well there's a sentence I never anticipated writing.* More accurately, we stood in the parking lot that sits directly above where the bunker used to be. At the end of the war, the Russians bombed the heck out of it. Now it is just an average parking lot, next to an apartment building. Appropriately, people occasionally walk their dogs there to let them relieve themselves. Perhaps the baby-changing couple should have stopped there instead.

From there it was a short walk to the former Luftwaffe headquarters, which had been spared from bombing due to its imposing landmark status and the many valuable documents contained within. It exemplified typical Nazi architecture-- a giant gray block, purposely designed to make the individual feel small and inferior. Its most fascinating feature was the contrast between the mural on the wall and the mural on the ground beside it. During the Soviet occupation, a mural depicting the supposed glories of communism was painted along one of the exterior walls. On the ground, in blatant and poignant irony, was a mural of the same dimensions, memorializing those who were slaughtered for protesting communism. The duo worked symbiotically to depict propaganda vs. reality.

On we walked, toward the Topographie des Terrors. As you can guess from the name, this site also related to darker aspects of Germany's history. The S.S. headquarters were once housed there, but now all that is left is a long wall with information about the Gestapo's terrifying mission. In fact, despite all of the fervent construction projects taking place all over Berlin, this site is considered too evil to build upon. That pretty much sums up the S.S..

It was time to lighten the mood, so we stopped at a café across the street. As we nibbled a piece of cheesecake and sipped espresso, Alex told us the story of the Berlin air drop. When the Soviets tried to cut off supplies to East Berlin, the Americans responded with a massive aid campaign. At one point, the United States was sending one plane per minute, loaded with necessities. Eventually, the Russians gave up. U.S.A.! U.S.A.!

Some of our walking tour overlapped with sites we had seen during the morning driving tour, but we always learned something new. Alex explained that Checkpoint Charlie got its name simply because it was the third one. The first used 'A', the second 'B', and so on. Many people who escaped East Berlin actually did so by paying diplomats to hide in their cars. Other, more creative methods included a hand sewn balloon and a homemade river submarine. Usually an attempt to go over the wall itself proved too difficult. To keep the people contained, there was an inner wall of barbed wire, elaborate booby traps, mine fields, attack dogs, machine gunners, and even a regularly raked sand pit to track any footprints. Like the mural we saw earlier, that ought to speak volumes about communist regimes.

Our final stop with Alex was the *Konzerthaus**, situated between a German church and a French Huguenot church. (At one time the French comprised about one-fifth of Berlin's population.) Both structures were beautiful Baroque buildings, complete with detailed twists and turns. At a glance, the churches looked about the same height, but actually, the Germans were careful to build their church one meter higher. More kraut humor.

As we sat on the steps we listened to the story of how the Berlin Wall was opened. Though protesters had demanded for some time that the wall be torn down, a curious convergence of events involving a rushed vote and a live international press release that was not read ahead of time made it a reality. The cork was out of the bottle. Citizens fled East Berlin to democratic West Berlin, people destroyed the wall, and the drinks flowed. My favorite detail of the story was that the East German government threatened those who left by declaring that their passports would henceforth be invalid. I can only imagine that the citizens responded with, "Is that a promise?"

After our far-better-than-expected walking tour, we walked a few blocks to catch another train to Tour #3. Our

---

*   concert hall

final excursion of the day was a three-hour sunset cruise. Again the Berlin rail system was ideal, dropping us off just across the river from our destination. It was a quieter part of town, with several *brückes** spanning canals and branches of the Spree.

We were early, so we grabbed an outdoor table at a bistro in view of the dock. There were only two other parties, one of whom was finished, yet the service was slow. We had allowed plenty of time before boarding, but I was starting to think we would be late. The staff was friendly, and we even had privileged access to clean, free toilets, but no one was in any kind of hurry. In general, I think service is at a more relaxed pace in most countries, as compared to the United States. Well, unless you are in New Orleans, that is. It is indeed "The Big Easy".

Eventually our food arrived, and it proved worth the wait. Though we didn't consume the celebrated sausages of Deutschland, we enjoyed more delicious meals there than anywhere else we had visited. Our vegetable gratin, which I had never tried before, tasted exactly how one would imagine anything 'gratin' should taste. In other words, no, it was nothing like a box of dehydrated potato slices with powdered cheese.

We were a little rushed, but we still secured our place in line in plenty of time. The boat tour, which was for some reason more reasonably priced than anything comparable at home,[†] offered an English narration via headset. By this point we had listened to so much history, and seen our way around so much of Berlin, that we

---

*   bridges
†   perhaps they save money on life jackets?

decided to skip the English and instead experience the sights and sounds of the ride as they were. We walked up to the roof deck, finding our seats and enjoying the light, dry breeze.

As the other passengers filed aboard, some general directions were given over the speaker. I could make out enough German to learn that our captain was introducing himself, there were drinks for sale, and we would be leaving soon. Then there was another part of the announcement that I could not interpret. It involved some sort of explanation and a ding. Whatever it meant, we were just there to relax and literally go with the flow.

Few people think of Berlin as a romantic city, but drifting along the canals and inlets could rival any of the other famous 'watery' cities in Europe. The night was so completely comfortable that it seemed everyone was outside. The grassy banks along the river were lined with people reading, napping, smoking, playing with children, or just sitting because they could. The restaurants, bars, and cafés could have eliminated their indoor seating with no loss of business; everyone was out on a patio or balcony.

Every so often, we approached a arched bridge, and the pleasant ding sounded over the speakers. That was when we understood what the initial instruction had meant. Apparently the translation was, "Duck now!" We were seated anyway, but anyone who was standing could have had a free haircut that started somewhere around his midsection. The bridges we passed under were so low that an outstretched arm could touch the top, even from a seated position. One passenger was standing, preoccupied with focusing his camera, when the warning sounded. His friend rescued him from near disaster by yanking him back down into his seat just in the nick of time. It yet again illustrated the expectation of personal responsibility-- a foreign concept sometimes in the United States.

We concluded our lazy tour. We had seen even more of Berlin's unique waterfront features, including a building with a war plane suspended outside and several pretty little houseboats. As we disembarked and filed up to the street, we heard a few German teenagers joking. "Welcome to England!" yelled one, laughing. I guess it was their commentary on the amount of English-speaking tourists they encountered. *Willkommen!**

We found our way back to the hotel easily. As the lit city sped past our train's windows, I felt a certain sense of accomplishment. The Midwest kids had successfully navigated their way around an incredible city. All aspects surpassed expectations, considering the day had been planned from a computer in the corner of my basement, several time zones away. Passing Tiergarten for the last time, I wondered if we would feel confined by the itinerary the next day, when we rejoined our group. At least we could trade stories with Peter.

*   *   *

I awoke Wednesday with the realization that I had finally slept all the way through the night. *Well that only took a week and a day-long march around Berlin.* Anyway, I was well-rested and ready to go. This time the electrical circuits cooperated for everyone in the hotel, and we were soon on our way out of the city.

After about two hours on the road, we stopped at a

---

*   welcome

rest area. Not to devote too much of this chapter to public restrooms, but I am admittedly fascinated by the system. In this particular facility, there were no pay machines, but there was a man standing outside the restrooms collecting the comparatively-reasonable €,10. He may have been a permanent employee of the travel plaza. He may have been a custodian, filling in while the machine was out being repaired. He may have been some guy who wandered in off of some other tour that passed through years ago and found that he could stay in Germany indefinitely by eking out a living €,10 at a time. All of these were equal possibilities to be considered as we filed through and handed him our coins. I truly expected him to be gone once he had collected from our group, but when I came out, he was still there. Upon my exit, he smiled and addressed me pleasantly. "Cheers!" I do believe it was the first time I had ever been wished well upon leaving the bathroom. If I had had a drink, I would have toasted him in return.

Within a few hours of leaving Berlin, we were in Dresden, a town that dates back to the 1200s. Driving around, we passed several smaller cottage-style homes with well-maintained romantic gardens. Germans take their flowers seriously, and citizens of Dresden take it even further. As someone who has a personal vendetta against grass, and cannot understand why anyone would have a yard when he/she could have a garden, I heartily approved.

Part-way through our drive, we picked up a tour guide. This time Dory stayed aboard and Ismet continued to drive, but our new guide took over the microphone. From the first moment she did, it was 'hang on to your notebooks, kids'. New Guide Lady must have been a professor or researcher or librarian or something along those lines. She knew a ton of information, and she was spouting it off like we were cramming for a final exam. She was also all business, unlike our previous guides, who kept a humorous rapport with the group. I love history and details, but I was as lost as everyone else. As the facts spewed in all directions, I managed to catch only a few tidbits. Among them was that Dresden is the greenest city in Europe. A full 60% of its land is devoted to parks and forests.

Then New Guide Lady led us off the bus into the Altstadt. We had been anticipating the walk, but the fast-paced facts combined with the rapidly increasing heat left us less than motivated. It was now over 90°F. This was definitely not supposed to happen in northern Europe. I made it a point to keep an eye on the senior citizens in the group. Just then I remembered that we still had the "BERLIN" umbrella with us, so I popped it open for some shade, simultaneously taking another swig of water.

Despite the heat I was enjoying being surrounded by gorgeous Rococo architecture in all directions. On one side a majestic opera house stood near an an art gallery. Across the cobblestone way, a block-long intricate mosaic told the story of heroes long gone. Among the larger structures stores, shops, and apartments were sprinkled, always in the tall, flat, colorful signature buildings. The jewel of the city, however, was easily the Zwinger Pavilion.

Had it not rivaled a late July day in Chicago temperature-wise, I might have remembered more of the stories surrounding the Zwinger Pavilion. Instead, all I recall is that some rich people were involved in scandals with other rich people, but those rich people weren't related to the other rich people who had something to do with Poland. We entered a square courtyard the size of several football fields. Completely surrounding the garden and gravel paths were elaborate buildings that looked like a sprawling Italian palace. Statues and fountains dotted the various outdoor rooms and tucked away grottoes. Arches abounded on the buildings and around the balconies.

On one side of the courtyard stood a particularly regal-looking structure. While most of the heights of the buildings were about the same, a black onion-shaped dome with gold-framed corner arches rose a full story above the rest of the roof lines. We were told it was the Polish Crown, and it looked exactly like a giant crown. As the mercury had climbed to a solid 100°F, my brain responded, initiating the dumb idea to take a picture with my Polish Prince situated so the Polish Crown appeared to sit on his head. Not surprisingly, it did not work, but we did manage a nice photo of us beside one of the fountains, with the crown in the background.

At the other end of the Altstadt was another gem: St. Mary's Kirche. During World War II, all but a section of one wall of this church was demolished. Years later it was rebuilt from the rubble and topped with a Coventry Cross that was a gift from England. Ironically, the cross was designed by the son of an R.A.F.* pilot who had flown a bombing mission over Dresden.

Inside St. Mary's there were three layers of balconies. Another Baroque masterpiece, the colors were soft and the detail was exquisite. Naturally, there was a massive pipe

---

* Royal Air Force, England's military air force

organ near the altar. We later learned that we had just missed an organ concert. I was disappointed, but it might have been too hot to enjoy it anyway. Dragging ourselves back onto the bus, we saw that the outside temperature had topped out at 104°F. *Next year we're going to Siberia.*

We had another stretch of driving, which was only interrupted once, for a stop at the largest monument in Germany. I really have no idea why we stopped there, other than it was the largest monument in Germany. Essentially, it was a giant, brown ancient-looking pyramidal-type structure that you could climb if you had no better plans on a sweltering day. There was a reflecting pool leading up to it, but it was too dirty to do any reflecting, let alone any refreshing. We opted for a five-minute walk to view it from a distance. Then we returned our smelly, sweaty selves back to the comfort of the bus.

It was then on to Leipzig, home of Johann Sebastian Bach. In the Altstadt lay St. Thomas Kirche, and in St. Thomas Kirche lay Bach. He was buried under the raised section of floor near the altar, and fresh flowers are regularly placed on his grave.* It's hard to imagine J.S. Bach as simply the local church organist and boys' choir director, but I guess everyone starts somewhere.

While Bach was the star of the platz, he was not the only music game in town. Leipzig's Altstadt possessed a high concentration of street musicians. Even better, they

---

* On behalf of my better half, I will here insert a story he told me as we stood over Bach's gravestone. One day a man happened upon Bach as he was going through his works, tearing them all up. Startled, the man asked Bach what he was doing. "I'm decomposing." (Too soon?....)

possessed a high concentration of talent. The typical blasé hippie strumming a few weak chords on an out-of-tune guitar would never stand a chance there. We first saw a man playing an accordion-- quite well. Turning a corner, we encountered a Russian trio performing in full regalia. How the intense heat did not overtake them, I will never know. Further down the street was a German man singing and playing a guitar. In another area we found a string duo playing classical music. It was a free musical buffet. I realize none of the classical heavy hitters hail from the Windy City, but let's step up our street musician quality, Chicago!

On the way back toward the center of the platz, we decided a cold treat was in order. While we could not find any German eis, we did spot the line at a Turkische frozen yogurt stand, which was run by Italians.* I ordered something involving vanilla, caramel, and coffee, eating/drinking it as we walked. I hoped the rest of the trip would be cooler.

Apparently not everyone was willing to wait for more comfortable temperatures to arrive. One little girl was taking matters into her own hands. Completely stark naked, she splashed around in the fountain, oblivious to anyone else. Don't think I wasn't tempted...

Back at the bus, our 40+ sweaty bodies rode to the hotel, grateful that German plumbing was far more reliable than German wireless internet connections. After cleaning up, we enjoyed a group buffet dinner. Everyone we talked to was calling it an early night, which sounded like a good plan to us, too. As we lounged in bed, alternating between

---

* Who knew?

German and English television, a storm rolled in, complete with thunder and lightning. Thankfully, it also included a 30°F drop in temperature. Looks like no naked romps in fountains would be on the next day's itinerary.

*   *   *

The morning was clear and comfortable, and we were on our way to Weimar. About five miles outside the town we could see the giant memorial for Buchenwald concentration camp. It had been one of the largest under the Nazi regime. Now the white rounded obelisk interrupted the horizon in the distance as a reminder. I thought about my excursion to Dachau, which would take place in two days. I wondered how I would react.

Soon we were in Weimar. As in Hamelin, there was a short walk from our bus that transformed our surroundings into the Altstadt. Naturally, there was a *marktplatz** in the center, but Weimar had a more relaxed and quiet pace than many of the other towns we had visited. Along with the breeze and shady streets, it lent itself to a long midday walk.

The most famous building in Weimar, at least for historians, is the Elephant Hotel. It was from a nondescript second-story balcony there that Hitler addressed crowds early in his rise to power. Just across the platz was the much larger and grander ratthaus, with its superior balcony. Of course the ratthaus balcony was his preference, but interestingly, the town denied him use of it. As the evil fervor grew, however, he graduated to a stage far more imposing than anything in Weimar, at the Nürnberg Nazi parade grounds.

---

*   marketplace

We continued our self-guided tour, attracted by the words "City Castle" on the map. I was sure we would have noticed a castle rising above the roof lines of the town, but maybe there was an obscured estate beyond the next street. When we reached City Castle, it was really more like a relatively moderate manor house placed on a regular city lot. We did not have high expectations for City Castle, but any disappointment we harbored was easily overshadowed by the fact that we would tour an actual castle later that very day.

Just beyond the Altstadt was a small bridge that spanned a narrow river or fat stream, depending on your perspective. We walked along it, noticing the weeping willow trees below at the water's edge. A group of young children and a few adults were taking advantage of the ideal spot to eat a picnic lunch. We were immediately struck by how well the children behaved. This must be another cultural difference between Germany and the United States, because a group of five-year-olds back home would have sent us running in the opposite direction.

We circled around and started back toward the marktplatz. One more point of interest on our Dory-distributed map piqued our curiosity. After the euphemistically titled City Castle, we didn't have high hopes for the *Wittunspalais*,* but we decided to give it a shot. Again, the title was grossly overstated. The palace had three floors, but it reminded me more of a suburban apartment building that held maybe four flats. The rooms were small, narrow, and sparsely furnished. According to the pamphlet, the home had been owned by a female

---

* widow's palace

regent. In one of the parlours there was a portrait of her, painted when she was thirty. I glanced at it from a few different angles, but I could not make her out to be a day under sixty-five, poor thing. The Widow's Palais was certainly not worth the royal sum of €12,00 apiece-- not to mention the €,25 we were forced to pay for a locker-- but at least we got to use the bathroom.

We wandered around further, criss-crossing the platz. Senator was hungry, so we stopped for a falafel wrap, which was fresh, satisfying, and reasonably priced. Apparently Germany is the place to go for great Mediterranean food, despite not having one centimeter of coastline on the Mediterranean. As we passed the time until we needed to reconvene with our group, we listened to an outdoor string quartet. Overall, it had been a pleasant, rejuvenating morning.

As we continued south, we saw the landscape change yet again. We were entering Bavaria, known locally as Bayern. Rolling hills were soon lost in dense forest. Surrounded by the green were villages of red-tile-roofed homes, churches, and medieval fortresses. Bavarians have a reputation for taking life easy, finding endless reasons to celebrate, and valuing a glass of good country bier as a basic human right. With such a lovely background, who could blame them?

Ismet guided our bus up a long winding road toward Veste Coburg. Forget City Castle and the Widow's Palais; I was about to experience my first true castle. Built in the 1200s, the stone and stucco building rose high above the nearby town. The center section displayed the attractive contrasting dark wooden trim and walkways that connected to other wings. Though there were no gardens, there was a sizable lavender patch with an incredible view.

Inside we were each outfitted with an English interpretive headset and instructed to dial in the number of the display to hear the appropriate description. We were also handed a map, and then sent on our merry ways. Senator and I went on our own, but we bumped into several other members of our group at regular intervals, primarily because we were all lost. The map, which I normally would have devoured and memorized within moments of studying, was basically useless. Instead of a floor plan, it simply listed the exhibits on each floor. I say 'exhibits' because the castle did not contain chambers furnished as they would have been. Instead, the rooms were merely vehicles for a museum collection.

To compound matters, none of the numbers we punched into our headset matched the items we were viewing. We stared at a piece of armor and heard about a rare set of dishes. Entering a hallway, we were informed about a hunting room at the other end of the wing. Eventually we ran into a helpful employee who explained that the numbers we were seeing corresponded to a different tour-- one meant for children. He helped us locate the obscure 'adult' tour numbers, and things started to match up better, but the narration was too slow.

That was when we unanimously decided to roam aimlessly. This strategy proved significantly more effective. We somehow managed to stumble upon a sleigh and harness exhibit fit for fairy tale transportation. The carved wood was exquisite, and I could imagine a royal party gliding over the the snowy Bavarian countryside in one of

94

the vehicles. We also found the rooms in which Martin Luther was given asylum, after he became decidedly unpopular with the Catholic Church.

Before we left Veste Coburg, I had one more objective. Back when I had been foolish enough to try to understand the fake map, I had noticed a chapel listed on it, so I made it a personal mission to find it. Keeping an eye on our time, I was just about to give up when I saw a heavy, wooden, coffin-like door at the end of the hallway. It looked like it would lead to somewhere that would be off limits to tourists, so I decided to see if it was unlocked. Prying it open revealed a second-story balcony that overlooked a peaceful chapel, complete with font, altar, and stained glass rose window. We had located the jewel of the fortress. From what we later heard from others, we were among the few who did find it. The lesson here is twofold: 1.)always go with your gut, especially if the map is misleading, and 2.)always barge into intriguing doors, especially if no one is around to stop you.

I had to admit that my first castle tour was not exactly as I had envisioned it, but an afternoon inside a castle is still an afternoon inside a castle. I had no complaints as we settled in for the remainder of the drive to Nürnberg. For our viewing enjoyment, Dory started a dvd of the 1950s movie *Sissy*. Whether one cared for the plot or characters of *Sissy* was irrelevant. Watching the movie's outdoor scenes of the Bavarian foothills while seeing them actually go by outside the bus windows rivaled any special effects Hollywood could offer.

As we rode and watched, we chatted with more people in the seats around us. Particularly, we were entwined in conversation with Peter. Here, Senator would like me to interject his travel tip. "If you are an American traveling to Europe, brush up on your world history before you go, because everyone knows more about history than Americans." As someone who happens to be both an American and a history teacher, I concur. As Senator also observed, he had to travel 4,500 miles to discuss *Passport to Pimlico* with someone other than me.[*]

We arrived in Nürnberg by early evening. Before we entered the Altstadt, we stopped at a large stone building that was a few stories tall. I would not have known its significance except for a sign out front that presented the flags of four countries: United States, England, France, and Russia. We were standing in front of the entrance to the Nürnberg Courthouse, where Nazis were placed on trial before the occupying powers post-World War II. While some managed to escape to places like South America, and others took their own lives rather than witness the downfall of the Third Reich, many found their way to this hall of justice to face penalties for their war crimes. Interestingly, just a few weeks before I wrote this chapter, Germany was trying yet another ex-Nazi, even though he was well into his 90s.

We drove for a short while longer into the heart of the city. Dory walked us from our bus toward the center of the Altstadt, a few blocks away. There she left us to roam on our own for several hours. Cobblestone streets and narrow alleys ran in all directions, so we picked one that gained elevation and started walking up to the city's walled boundary. Nürnberg is probably one of best remaining

---

[*] 1949 comedy about a town with questionable political boundaries

examples of a walled city.

From there we turned another corner and meandered back down toward St. Sebaldus Kirche. I don't remember the church itself being open, but we browsed a historical display in a nearby building. It was another dry, lightly breezy, ideal summer evening like we had experienced in Berlin. Again, everyone was outdoors, patronizing the many cafés. We were a little hungry, but there were few available seats, and all of them were too close to smokers.* Thus, we decided to go local. We ducked into a small grocery store and wandered the aisles, obviously the only tourists in the place. After scoping out our options and ruling out items that could not be conveniently eaten without a table, silverware, or napkins, we settled on a bag of cheese pieces and a helping of toffee cashews. In our estimation, it was an impromptu meal fit for a king (or queen).

All we needed to complete our feast was a good cup of kaffee. We strolled over a few bridges that spanned the canal running through the Altstadt. Outside of one establishment we saw a sign that said "Kaffee to go", but the woman inside told us that she was out of coffee. I guess the coffee went. I don't remember ever having successfully secured any java, but since we have a photo of Senator casually walking along a Nürnberg street holding a paper

---

*   Here, I must vent slightly, no pun intended. For all of their claims to be more environmentally-friendly and socially accommodating than the United States, I really don't understand the Europeans' love affair with cigarettes. In addition to the obvious health and economic drawbacks of smoking, I would have thought it would have been long out of vogue. Yet, it seems the vast majority still light up.

cup, we must have found some somewhere. Or maybe he was carrying around an empty cup, begging.

Our group reconvened and drove to our hotel, which was located in a different part of the city. It was too early to go to bed, so I soon found myself drawn into another World War II documentary. It was on a German television station, but raw footage I had never seen before told plenty without an English translation. Images of book burnings, countless flags in parade formations, and the mysterious burning of the Reichstag flashed across the screen.

Then the war was temporarily interrupted. "Want to go for a walk?" suggested Senator. I hadn't considered it, and I was already in pajama pants and a tee shirt, but why not? Our hotel was in a quiet area, without much around it, but there were well-lit sidewalks. As we exited the parking lot, the true motive came out. Senator was hungry and hoping to find a snack.

Our venture did not lead us to any food, but it was another excuse to enjoy a comfortable night. As we stepped back into our hotel lobby, we saw a few people from our tour in the bar lounge. They invited us to join them, but we were more interested in propping our feet up and competing for the television remote. As an added bonus, Senator was able to order a sandwich from the bar, which we brought back to the room. As we stepped out of the elevator, he was temporarily turned around. "Which way is our room?" he asked.

"This way," I answered. "Right across from the painting of the giant, naked lady."

*   *   *

Friday we were on our way to München, but our day

began with a dismal yet significant stop. Before we left Nürnberg, we pulled up in a wide, nondescript parking area. Beyond a driving barricade was what looked like an abandoned race track, and not a very attractive one. Gray bleachers faced a field, with a track separating them. Along the depth of the field was a row of concrete fortresses, each the size of a small house. We were standing on the former Nazi parade grounds. Suddenly all of the images of formations of battalions goose-stepping and rallying around fields of swastika flags came uncomfortably alive.

The property was once comprised of much more land, including two lakes and a zeppelin field. The row of concrete buildings, we learned, were public restrooms, installed for the physical comfort of guests of the Third Reich brass, and the psychological oppression of all others. If you want to understand Nazi architecture, consider designs that would make humans feel inferior, usable, and depressed. Cold, gray, concrete, and very boxy lines are the signature marks.

Looking to the top of the bleachers, this same style was carried out in the grounds' centerpiece. I was so stunned by being in such a historical and somber place that I had forgotten that Dory had mentioned we could actually walk up to the balcony from which Hitler addressed thousands of Germans. Yes, it is the one you know from every documentary. It was nothing like the humble balcony at the Elephant Hotel; this one was designed to inspire fear. As I tried to take in everything I was seeing, both visually and in my head, Senator was making his way up to the balcony. He later told me that when he got there, he could not bring himself to step on the platform. In his words, "It just felt so wrong." I'll take his word for it.

The sun was ironically bright and the morning tranquil as we left the parade grounds. Our next destination was of quite a different nature. Whereas we had left a heavy scene of Germany's darkest hour, we were about to enter a town plucked right out of a fairy tale. Ismet pulled the bus to a stop outside of a solid, continuous wall. At least it looked impenetrable, but Dory led us through an obscured opening in a nook among the vegetation. Inside we time-traveled to become inhabitants of Rothenburg ob de Tauber.

Rothenburg is known as one of the best-preserved walled cities of the Middle Ages. Seeing it on the Cosmos itinerary was one of the selling points of the trip. Ever since I had read my grandma's account of it, I had been determined to go there. My only concern was that perhaps it had all changed since 1972, joining the rest of the modern world. My fears were definitely unfounded. There was not just a district of historic, uniquely German buildings; the entire town was stuck in a pre-Renaissance world. I do not mean to say there were not modern conveniences, or that you could not use a credit card, but to walk around the town's shops, homes, churches, pubs, and walls provided a 360° fantasy that could last for an entire day.

We wandered for hours, pausing to see the glockenspiel mechanism (which, incidentally, got stuck) at the ratthaus. The timed musical chimes were fascinating enough. Across the street was an over-the-top Christmas store, which was so vast that it was divided among two buildings across the street from one another. The collection of yuletide decorations was staggering, but then again, so is

100

that of Senator's mom.* I mainly entered it just to see the sheer glitz of it.

When I had all but fallen into a Christmas seizure, I met Senator back outside, and we headed toward the Castle Gardens. We had gained enough elevation to reveal a lush 180° view of winding vineyards and the Tauber River far below. Casual gardens were tucked among the walking trail, leading us from one shady nook to another. A few times we bumped into familiar faces from our tour.

There was still plenty of time, so we walked a section of the perimeter of the city's wall. Through the tiny fortress windows I could see the outside world, which just looked like fields and prairie grass. Somehow Rothenburg had managed to remain geographically isolated, adding to the illusion. I turned back toward the inside. Maybe we could move into an abandoned section of castle ruins.

Making our way back to the road we had first walked in on, it occurred to me that I should take advantage of the toy shop. For more than a week we had been on vacation, but outside of one classical cd, we had not acquired any souvenirs. This was fine for us, but we wanted to get something for our niece and nephews. When you don't travel to tourist traps or places that typically attract kids, this is easier said than done. Thus, inside the kinder store I went. After much perusing and debating, I became the soon-to-be giver of a few trinkets, including yodeling teddy bears. I could just hear my siblings when their kids' stuffed animals rang out a deranged alpine song of delight. "Thanks a lot, Aunt Wendy and Uncle Senator!"

---

* After a hefty downsizing, I believe she now only owns five nativity sets.

For his part, Senator was standing in solidarity in the street. In other words, after a few minutes of toy shopping, he turned his attention to snowballs. These traditional Rothenburg treats are basically long strips of crunchy, rather bland dough wrapped in a ball shape as though they are yarn. The ball is then dusted with powdered sugar or sometimes coated with chocolate. Either version will require a bath when you are done eating it.

After de-snowballing, we met the others from our tour and once again boarded our coach. Several travelers bore the indelible traces of having tried snowballs as well. I wish we could have stayed longer. If I ever get back to Germany, I will make it a point to spend the night in Rothenburg. Who knows what kind of mystery and romance lurk there after dark?

Thanks to Dory, I did not have to quit Rothenburg just yet. She played a documentary dvd about the town, narrated by a man performing as a medieval night watchman. He warned that there were penalties for entering the city after curfew, and they were not simply annoying tickets. We also learned that the oldest home in Rothenburg has a foundation that dates to the 900s. It probably still had less cracks than our basement.

Most interesting was the story of the town's fate during World War II. Rothenburg was saved (mostly), because an American officer offered to spare it if the Germans would evacuate and leave it to American occupation. The deal was agreed upon. Later, the portions that were bombed were rebuilt using donations from around the world, including at least one from Chicago.

According to legend, this was not the first time the

town had evaded a threat. In 1631, as General Tilly's forces threatened the town of Rothenburg, a deal was struck to save the town. Mayor Nusch wagered their security on the fact that he could guzzle a large quantity of booze in one drink. When he successfully did so, Tilly honored the bet and backed off, forever securing the story of der Meistertrunk.* True history? Doubtful. Enduring legend? Absolutely.

We must have looked like we craved entertainment, because once the documentary finished, Dory put *Sissy* back on. We picked up where we had left off, so I will insert a spoiler alert here. Since last we left our young beauty, she had given birth to a child, fought (verbally only, unfortunately) with her royal pain of a mother-in-law for control over raising the child, contracted consumption, and been miraculously cured of consumption by a mere visit from her mother. To be continued...

We had made it to München, and after checking in to our room, we flopped on the bed with maps spread out to reassess our routes for the evening. We would be on our own, which I was aware of, but the hotel was a good three or four miles from Marianplatz, and I wanted to be sure we were not going to spend the night lost in a major German city, however fun that may have proven to be. I thought it best to merge my notes with Dory's posted directions in the hotel lobby. Reviewing her instructions for public transportation confirmed my plans, so we started out with reasonable confidence.

It was just a few blocks to the first station, and it was just about where had I expected it to be. The problem was

---

* master draught

that there were no rails or ticket booth, or even a station for that matter. Instead, there was just what appeared to be a glass bus shelter. "Maybe the first part is by bus, and then we get the subway at the next transfer?..." I suggested weakly. When it was apparent that no action was taking place at that stop anytime soon, we trekked back to the hotel. Senator suggested we ask the desk attendant how to get there.

There was a friendly, pleasant woman at the desk, but I didn't have high hopes. Though I figured she knew the general area, I had overheard her giving other guests the same directions I already knew. I wasn't sure how to explain that we had done all of that and reached the intended location, but the public transportation services didn't match up. It couldn't hurt to try, though, so we began to explain our predicament. As expected, she confirmed the same confusing directions. At one point she happened to mention the 'tram'. "Do you mean a bus?" I asked for clarification.

"No, no, it is like a streetcar? A rail car. When you see the bus stop, the tram is just a little further, around a corner." *Aha!* Now we were getting somewhere. If they were that close together, that would explain why the directions seemed accurate. Likewise, if the tram was obscured around a corner, that would explain why we did not see any rails.

We were about to begin Transportation Navigation-- Take 2, when I noticed three members of our tour, (an Australian couple and an English woman,) standing near us. They were trying to make heads or tails of the directions as well, and they were even more confused than we had been. I explained that we were now clear on our route and invited them to tag along. They were immensely grateful, above and beyond what the situation called for. Now I had really better know where I was going, or I was going to make a complete fool of myself, as well as ruin five people's evenings. Upon reflection, they trusted me entirely too much, especially considering they were all about my parents' age, and had traveled far more extensively than we had.

Thankfully, just a half-block beyond the bus station, around the stealth bend in the road, was the tram station. The train arrived as expected, but the ticket machine inside was confusing. I still had not mastered that aspect of German rail, despite all of my research. Finally I found the correct buttons, but when I attempted to purchase our five tickets, it spit all of my money back out. In the end, I was fairly sure we had only purchased one-way tickets, but not due to any nefarious motives. "Well," I announced to my overly-trusting impromptu party, "if the polizei are not there to greet us at the other end of the line, we'll consider it a success." They didn't care; they were having a grand old time, laughing and goofing off the whole way. It was clear I had been nominated and elected Responsible Adult.

Four stops later, we easily transferred to our subway. I looked back at Senator, who had naturally moved to the rear of our group, much in the way that a second parent would keep the children in between. The Australian woman noticed me glance in his direction and assured me. "Don't worry, Dear. Your sweetie's right there." I smiled and nodded in appreciation, recognizing that she had no idea that it was not *him* I was worried about.

105

Upon reaching the busy Marianplatz subway station, our new friends were still confused but carefree. Though I thought it was the easiest part of the journey to simply take the stairs up to the street level, which spilled directly into the platz, they seemed amazed at my navigation skills. *Why can't my students be this easily impressed?* I caught Senator privately. "Do you mind if we take them back with us? Maybe set a meeting time?"

"No, I was thinking the same thing," he agreed. "Otherwise they'll never make it back to the hotel." Just as we were about to split up, we offered to have them meet us to go back in a few hours. Again, they were overly grateful. Just to be safe, we set our meeting point at the tall statue in the middle of the square. "See you at 9:30."

Marianplatz was thriving. There were cafés and shops, vendors and churches. From the center of the square we could hear their evening chimes as they sounded in turn. By any measure, though, the star of Marianplatz was the ratthaus. The mammoth structure, even more impressive than other ratthauses we had seen, towered into the sky, dripping with heavy Gothic niches, overhangs, and gargoyles. Its imposing, dark appearance was balanced by bright rows of window boxes of geraniums. In the center was a glockenspiel that supposedly offered a ten-minute mechanical presentation three times per day in the summer.

In one corner of the platz was Ludwig Beck, a record store. Senator had read about the store, and we were pleased to learn it was right where we were going. There are large music stores, and then there are multilevel music stores with extensive sections of each individual genre. This was the latter. Though the prices were higher than

Senator was willing to pay, he had fun browsing the vast jazz section, which was larger than the entire music department he managed at his previous retail job. He also found several cds of recordings he had done in Chicago. It was fun to think of them traveling all the way to Europe.

There was plenty to see in Marianplatz, but the strangest sight we witnessed was at one end of the main promenade. As we walked, we saw fewer historical buildings and more modern shops. In fact, they were extremely expensive, high-end shops. Shopping these establishments, in groups, were Islamic women, covered except for their eyes. Say what you like, but it was a somewhat disconcerting scene. My main question was: if they belong to a religion that supposedly eschews materialism and forbids alcohol, why were they patronizing expensive shops in a town known worldwide as the home of Oktoberfest?

We unanimously agreed to work our way back toward the platz. As we walked, we saw a few men moving a grand piano down the street-- not an easy trick, even though it was on wheels. Turning down a side street, we found an Italian restaurant. The smell drew us in, and we ordered. Service was slow, as we had come to accept in Germany, but the food was good, and the breeze floating through the open windows and patio doors of the second-story dining area was even better.

It was a little after 9:00pm, so we walked toward the vicinity of the rendezvous point. As if on cue, a classical quartet began to perform in the open air. *So that's where the grand piano ended up.* Just before 9:30pm, our English lady and Australian couple found us. We might get busted for

107

not having the correct train tickets, but at least we had not lost anyone.

Our fivesome again boarded the subway, and again they seemed amazed that Senator and I knew where we were going. Four stops to the transfer point and four more stops to the disembarkation point gave the other passengers plenty of time to be entertained by the laughter and giddiness of the two women with us. As we walked the few blocks back to the hotel, they told us about their evening and thanked us profusely. The lesson here, I believe, is that even if you are not 100% sure where you are going, if you can bring someone else further than he/she was, you have done something useful.* With that satisfaction, we went to bed.

*   *   *

I woke up nervous Saturday. It was the day Senator and I would be split up. I had opted to go on an afternoon visit to Dachau Memorial, while he had chosen not to do so. I understood and respected his decision, as I knew it would be a potentially difficult experience. We were both capable adults, but there remained the fact that we had no functioning cell phones. As he had not participated in my studies of the itinerary and maps during the planning phase, I was also concerned that he would get lost. The previous Saturday's experience at Köln Cathedral did not help ease my mind, either. If I would have been leaving from the hotel, he could have just rested and hung out there. Instead, a morning driving tour would deposit us back at Marianplatz, and he would be on his own from there. What if something happened and he could not get to

---

* In some ways, I suppose I just described teaching.

our meeting point? What if there was an emergency, and he did not even know how to say, "I only speak English"? I started to feel guilty, picturing him alone in a foreign country.

Adding to my discomfort, Senator informed me that he had a more extensive plan than simply getting back to the hotel. Apparently the success of the previous night's use of public transportation had filled him with confidence and a sense of adventure. "I talked to Dory, and the town of Dachau is not too far from the memorial. If Ismet will let me ride the bus with your group, I can walk to a bus station from there. Then I can wander around the town, get some coffee, and I'll come back to meet you." This was not making me feel better. Nevertheless, he certainly had it all worked out, and Ismet was a willing accomplice, so the matter was settled, even if my stomach wasn't.

We waited outside with our group for a morning driving tour around München with a local guide. This woman was like a female version of our Berlin driving tour guide. She looked stern, but her information was peppered with plenty of dry wit. Like the others, she was a walking library regarding her home town. She pointed out many statues and exquisite examples of Classical, Gothic, and Baroque buildings. She also brought our attention to some river surfers. We had never seen this before, but people were riding surfboards where a bend in the river made ripples. "Probably some chicky-mickeys," she murmured. *Huh?* "It means... how do you say... rich kids... don't have to work..." she explained. *Got it.*

Our drive also took us to Palais Nymphenburg for a brief stop, where our guide entertained us with stories of the crazy royals who used to inhabit it. We got out and walked around the courtyard, noting that we were enclosed in a large square of palace buildings. Now the buildings were being used for other purposes, or were just abandoned. The swans and birds did not seem to mind, and someone was obviously maintaining the vibrant flowers. It was pretty, but not a place we needed to visit for very long.

The bus dropped us off back in Marianplatz, giving us more time to explore. We wandered into another kirche, where there was an art display going on for an event that would take place later that evening. There was a white and pastel painting behind the elaborate altar, with white cords dangling from the ceiling. I wasn't sure if it was supposed to tie in to some spiritual purpose, or if it was just an odd exhibit.

It was time for a traditional snack, so we invested in some delicious soft pretzels with cheese baked on them. That just got us going, so then we chose a sort of veggie pizza bread from another bakery. As we ate, we walked, occasionally seeing street performers of a passive variety. Some were dressed in the traditional Bavarian leiderhosen, willing to pose for a picture for a tip. Another man, older and fatter than his role called for, was dressed as angel, but with silver spray-painted skin. That couldn't be healthy. Why not just go make and sell some pretzels to earn a few some cash?

We then walked back for the highlight of the square-- the glockenspiel performance. As boasted, the München glockenspiel mechanics lasted a full ten minutes. The show began with bells, which drew a huge crowd.

Then a drama involving a wedding and a joust (not between bride and groom) unfolded. It was like a miniature play in a few short acts, and the audience was duly impressed. I was very glad we got to see it.

It was getting close to time to separate for the afternoon, and again I was uneasy. We walked to another platz, near the opera house, and sat on the steps to wait for the bus. We had rehearsed the plan several times and split up cash and other essentials. It was great that Senator would have somewhere to go, and not be stuck in a hotel or waiting for me for hours in the same place, but I would be much happier when it was all over.

At Dachau Memorial the bus emptied out at a parking lot, and we all walked a quarter mile or so to the visitor center. It was a bit of a chaotic scene as Dory passed out the visitor brochure maps and English headsets. Other groups were there getting their necessary materials as well. It was not clear where one started, or which exit led to the memorial itself, so I found myself trying to interpret the map while balancing my clunky hand-held audio guide and head set. Senator was still with me, but we would separate from that point. As visitors sprawled in all directions, I kissed Senator good-bye and picked what looked like the most likely sidewalk.

Clumps of other people were wandering, not really knowing where they were going, either. I was uncomfortable and halfway convinced I had made a mistake. I was also irritated that there was no discernible direction within so important a place. Sadly, I could not focus nor devote the reverence and attention I had intended to give during the nine months I had been imagining this moment. Frustrated, I shuffled along the wide, gravel path. It seemed like I was walking into an average forest preserve, lined on both sides with uninteresting mid-sized bushes. Along the way there were a few waist-high interpretive signs, but they were general.

Then I turned the corner, and everything changed. I saw the entrance gate, with the chilling reversed "Arbeit Macht Frei"* motto worked into the iron. My entire mindset was immediately altered. It wasn't that I didn't care about Senator or his afternoon plans, but worry had vanished. I experienced a feeling of total focus, barely aware that anyone else was present, even though dozens of others roamed the grounds. I was as ready as one could be for a visit to Dachau.

Once through the gate, the property opened up to a gravel lot, perhaps encompassing the area of six football fields. The perimeter was tree-lined, and it was clearly separated from any nearby civilization. To the right I could see work buildings that were now transformed into a small museum. Though museums always interest me, my objective was to see the site firsthand; I could always read the details and history at home. To the left were rows and rows of outlined foundations where barracks once stood. In the center stood a wall translated into several languages, all condemning the evil practiced there, and vowing that nothing of the like would ever be repeated.

One of the first things that grabbed my attention was

---

* Hitler-ordered statement meaning "Work makes you free." The words only faced inward, an insulting representation of Nazi ideals that falsely euphemized concentration death camps as "work camps".

the signature sculpture for Dachau. I recognized its twisted black form from photos and the website. Many times I had seen it, assuming it was as much a piece of modern art as anything meaningful. I should have known better. Looking closely, I could see that it was not just a mess of metal or a depiction of a dead tree. What appeared to be branches were actually very skinny entangled skeletons.

Turning left, I started down the long row between the barracks' outlines. The map made sense now, but I was no longer paying attention to the audio guide. Nothing the recorded voice could say would be as loud as my thoughts. The only sound I noticed in conjunction with them was the wind, which had whipped up steadily, almost pushing me over once or twice.

At the end of the row I arrived at the memorial bell, which tolls at 3:00pm every day. Later that afternoon I was fortunate enough to hear it, not long before leaving. Next to it were the Christian and Jewish memorials, each a few stories tall. It was very beautiful to see them together, standing in solidarity for peace.

Dachau was, of course, originally surrounded by barbed wire. A large section of it was left for visual reference. At the end of the wire, where it met the corner of the rectangular property, I could see a path leading out of the camp. I walked toward it, noticing that it led to a foot bridge. Crossing the little bridge brought me to what could have been a shady, secluded picnic grove. Partly because of the pleasant setting, and partly because I am human, I was not at all prepared for what I was about to see.

A moment after entering the wooded nook, I saw a brick building, about the size of our modest 1950s house.

113

Then I looked up at the disproportionately tall chimney. I suddenly realized I was standing outside of a concentration camp crematorium. I was even more stunned when I saw people entering the building. As long as I was there as a historian, I decided that I should go in.

There were only two rooms in the building. I don't know why I was expecting some sort of office or foyer or anything to transition from the lovely outdoor setting to the horrible purposes of the chambers within, but there was no such space. Mere steps from the door were two horizontal brick ovens. If there are words to describe the impact of witnessing that scene firsthand, this writer does not know them. It had never occurred to me that the public had such intimate access to these areas.

Even stranger was the option to take pictures. For a moment, I debated. Before you judge me on my decision to proceed, please understand my motive. On one hand, I realize it could appear disrespectful to the victims and their loved ones. On the other hand, I had to consider the greater message of the Dachau Memorial. Why is it open? Why wasn't it just torched to the ground? What are we supposed to take from it? I concluded that the greatest message is that we never forget that humans can and did, and (most importantly) could again stoop to such depths of hatred and destruction. What better proof than recent, real photographs? This isn't from the History Channel; this is from life.

I capped the camera lens and stepped into the second room. It was empty, and for a moment I was grateful. I assumed it must have been used for storage or supplies. Just as I was about to exit the room, I noticed vents in the walls, close to the floor. It dawned on me that it was not a storage room; I was standing inside a gas chamber. Seconds later I was outside and it all hit me. I couldn't see through my tears as I stood alone along the tree line. *My God, it all really happened.*

After more or less regaining my composure, I walked to the opposite end of the property. There was enough time for me to visit the museum, or at least catch the short film. As I waited to enter the theatre, I saw kiosks devoted to several different countries. Each one honored the victims from their respective homeland.

Filing into the theatre, I ran into Peter. Senator and I had spent several kilometers of German highway joking around with him, but now the mood of the whole audience was understandably somber. When the theatre went dark, we were each alone with our thoughts. I don't need to narrate the documentary for you, Reader. You can imagine the footage and the details. I will just point out that, upon the liberation at the end of the war, many people from the town of Dachau, (just a few miles from the concentration camp,) had no idea what was taking place beyond that gate. They refused to believe the rumors and reports of the horror until many were literally brought face-to-face with the evidence. They had instead fallen for the propaganda. May we never do the same.

The question I am most frequently asked when people learn that I have visited Dachau is, "Wasn't it just overwhelmingly depressing?" Surprisingly, it was not. Though I knew it was not going to be a happy or lighthearted place, I must admit, nothing truly prepared me for the slap of reality that hit me as I was standing in the

115

midst of scenes that, prior to that, had only existed in the historical fiction of a classroom or a documentary. Yes, there were very vivid reminders of unspeakable horrors. Above all, however, there was an incredibly strong sense of peace, healing, and resolve that I can only attribute to the Spirit who makes all such things possible.

I left Dachau after spending exactly the right amount of time there. Walking back to the visitor center, my mind and body relaxed, and I was again aware of the people around me. Before I could fully make the transition back to the present and figure out how to reconnect with Senator, I saw him and Dory waiting in a patio area adjacent to the visitor center. He was grinning and waiting casually to hug me. Dory was checking off group members as we arrived. She paused just long enough to say in her sweet Croatian-English voice, "See, you didn't have to worry about him!" *Yes, I understand that now.*

It had been another busy day, and one that left us mentally exhausted. I wasn't ready to delve into the details of my afternoon, but Senator told me of his flawlessly executed plan, which at some point involved a blueberry pastry and another good cup of kaffee. I leaned against him, and I think we both dozed off on the way back to the hotel. The only things left on the agenda were showers, dinner, and an early bedtime.

It was good to see everyone at our large group dinner. I don't think we would have had the wherewithal to plan anything on our own anyway. I laughed as Jules pulled a pepper grinder out of her purse. "I always travel with one," she announced matter-of-factly, though no one had asked her to explain her behavior. We had known her

116

long enough not to find this odd. On the contrary, I was inspired. *Hhmmm, the one thing I had never thought to pack...* We were also touched by her righteous indignation on our behalf when she learned that there was no vegetarian soup option. We didn't care, but we felt cared for. Together we all sat back and enjoyed a final warm up of our kaffee, as we listened to another young couple from the group hamming it up singing show tunes. It was a nice mindless balance to round out our day. Good night.

*   *   *

Sunday required our earliest wake-up time-- a bleary 5:15am. I didn't mind though; it was Neuschwanstein day. Thankfully everyone was on time, including a few who had fallen into the habit of straggling.* After breakfast we drove toward the Alps. I had wanted to go to that region my entire life. In fact, I could possibly have been talked into moving there without ever having seen it. Now that it was approaching, it was like a dream. The Alps come up faster on the horizon than the Rocky Mountains. There is not the long, gradual crawl across plains while seeing the mountains slowly grow in the distance. It gives the effect of fake backdrops from a play. Before you know it, you are quickly enveloped.

Adding to the dreamlike quality of the drive were the villages that dotted the foothills. Rustic two-story chalet style homes, accented with flower boxes, had replaced the tall, narrow, medieval-looking structures of other parts of

---

* I have to give credit here to all of my fellow passengers. Though I mentioned a few who occasionally arrived at the bus a few minutes late, we never came close to missing anything on the itinerary. Overall, we had a marvelous group.

the country. We were fully immersed in Bayern. As proof, many hamlets sported their own blue-and-white maypole, representing the colors of the region. Dory told us that in times past, the poles were used as sign posts for illiterate merchants. Now the fun-loving Bavarians sees them as prized items to be captured from neighboring villages. Once they are taken, they are held for ransom in exchange for bier.

Neuschwanstein* is what you see in your head when you think of a fairy tale castle. In fact, it was the inspiration for Walt Disney's Cindarella's castle, and is often featured in photo essay books about castles. Its steep walls, turrets, balconies, and terraces are situated perfectly in the lower Alps, with a 360° view of surrounding villages, lakes, and forests. A winding drive inclines sharply, elevating visitors to refreshing, clean air. Cindarella would be a fool to leave this for Florida.

Our bus had to remain at the bottom of the drive, so we transferred to a shuttle bus, riding in two shifts. Our drive through the trees took us to a bridge overlooking the castle from a distance. Below us was a deep gorge. It was not for the faint of heart, but the views were stunning. Just looking and breathing were a treat. Thankfully, our group also had enough time to view the scenery before a large group of Chinese tourists arrived. They immediately crowded onto the bridge, body-to-body. I wondered if their weight, combined with that of the many padlocks lovers had locked to the railings, would stress the structure too much. I recalled the story of a bridge in Köln that had to be closed because of too much weight from the locks. I

---

*   New Swan of the Rock

wouldn't say I was nervous, but I was glad we were no longer on the bridge.

Security at Neuschwanstein was strict, and they ran a tight ship. There was only a five-minute window in which we could line up. Then they ushered us in and prepared for the next group, who entered five minutes after us. Each tour lasted about thirty minutes, and they kept them rolling all day.

The castle was a little deceptive in appearance. Though it looked like it had been standing strongly since medieval times, it was actually built in the 1870s. King Ludwig II* commissioned sixty rooms, but only sixteen of them were finished when he died, possibly from suicide or murder. He had only lived there six months, but construction stopped upon his death. This left the exterior beautiful, but the interior largely empty. As such, the tour only took us through about eight rooms.

The castle rooms were not nearly as large as I had expected, but they were regal nonetheless. Many featured murals of fairy tales on the walls and even ceilings, adding to the story book quality of the place. In keeping with the name, the swan theme was vividly carried throughout. Unfortunately, photography was strictly *verboten*.†

Three rooms in particular stood out. The first was the throne room. Though I have visited dozens, if not hundreds, of historical homes, I can't say I had ever been in a throne room before. Far from being the cavernous hall depicted in movies, it was more of an intimate setting that could comfortably hold about twenty people. The walls

---

*   perhaps better known as Crazy Louis
†   forbidden

and ceiling were covered in gilt and sparkle, and the centerpiece was, indeed, a throne. It was raised up a few steps, but I had the distinct feeling that Crazy Louis would have preferred to hang out on the floor level.

Another surprising room was the king's bedchamber. By today's standards, the room was not outlandishly spacious; most new homes in the suburbs have a master suite at least as big. In Ludwig's bedroom, however, the architectural features were what set it apart. Atop the bed canopy, for example, was a collection of heavy wooden Gothic spires. The three-to-four foot spikes produced a artistic hand-carved skyline. Among the luxuries in the room was full plumbing-- certainly a rarity for its time. Tap water flowed out of a swan's mouth into the bedside basin, in keeping with the theme. We were told there was also a flushing toilet, but it was behind a closed door. I can only assume there was a swan involved somewhere in its design as well. Perhaps the seat was a giant open swan mouth.*

Finally we reached the celebrated concert hall. This was the one room that struck me as legitimately 'palatial', whatever that means. Designed for optimum acoustics, the concert hall provided a fitting backdrop for singers and musicians alike. There our tour guide made the mistake of asking if anyone in our group sang. The two spotlighters immediately volunteered their services. Despite the

---

* Just for the record, swans do not necessarily deserve their reputation for grace and gentility. When I was about five years old, I approached one. As I stretched my innocent little hand out toward the fowl, whom, thanks to cartoons, I was sure would nestle up to me or swim heart-circles in the pond for my amusement, the rotten sucker bit me-- hard!

120

inspirational setting, we were not treated to an aria or other such vocal marvel; I believe we heard a verse of another show tune. At least they enjoyed their moment, even as everyone else kept filing out of the room.

If you visit Neuschwanstein, you may not get to see as many rooms as you are picturing, but you will certainly get to see gift shops. The castle itself boasts two of them, which, conveniently and predictably, are the last stop on the tour. Just in case you did not get your fill of fairy tale themed shot glasses, fake wooden swords, "Bayern" tee shirts, or random crystal pieces for your own palace, you can catch about ten more such shops on the way back down to the parking area. We bypassed all of them, and headed for the *imbiss*.*

As we ate our staple German veggie/cheese sandwiches outside, we watched the throngs of people descending the hill. Some were taking shuttle buses. We had opted to walk, taking every advantage of breathing the alpine air that drifted down from the higher elevations. Melodic hard rock played over the patio speakers where we ate. Senator was intrigued enough to seek out the owner to find out the name of the band. He learned they were called Sohne Mannheim, and as he pointed out, they wrote in my favorite key-- minor.

Neuschwanstein truly lived up to the pictures. Even the photos from our unprofessional camera looked like stills from a fairy tale movie set in a very far away land. The setting and weather were ideal. The afternoon temperature stayed between 72°F and 75°F the whole time we were there. Still, given the choice, I would rather visit it

---

* snack shop, not to be confused with "Snackpoint Charlie"

in the dead of winter, trudging through mounds snow in a blue-white wilderness. But that's just me.

Back on the bus our group reconvened for the drive to Bad Herrenalb through der Schwartzwald.* Dory treated us to the thrilling conclusion of *Sissy*, which most of the group slept through. I'm sure Sissy triumphed vibrantly, but she hadn't been up since 5:00am. Our next triumph was the final rest stop of our tour.

Ismet parked the bus and we dispersed. If you play your euros right, you can collect your various toilet refund coupons and amass them toward a greater purchase. In a special pocket of my travel binder, I had done just this. By the time we stopped, we were able to knock about €5,00 off of some salads from the self-serve buffet. With our cafeteria tray and change in hand, we found a table with Karol, Jules, and Peter. We had just enough time to eat while doing some heavy-duty b.s.-ing, mainly led by Karol.

The strange thing about taking a tour with a group this size is that you naturally fall into smaller groups, and you do get to know some personal aspects of these complete strangers. You go on as if you will all get together for coffee once a month once the trip is over, when in reality, you understand and accept that you will probably never see each other again. Not even email and social media have changed this much.† The only difference is that

---

* Black Forest

† I do have to add one exception. One particular member of our group returned to Europe a few times to visit Dory, which Senator accidentally found out several months after our trip, when he contacted the guy about some music they were both interest in. Less than a year after that, our tour mate and our tour guide were married!

you all exchange information before forgetting each other. We knew this at the time, but Senator and I still reference our Germany buddies from time to time. Considering we went into the trip not really intending to interact with others beyond basic friendliness, I think we surprised ourselves.

Our route took us deeper into tall pine territory. It started to drizzle, adding to the mystery and tranquility of the area. This part of Germany, unlike the north or east, reminded me of the American Pacific Northwest. I could see how its dense, dark cover could provide an appropriate setting for terrifying morality tales. Who knew what lurked in the depths of the forest?

As we drove, Dory led us in a game. Each passenger wrote down two facts and one false statement about himself/herself. Then of course, we had to guess which were true and which was the lie. My fellow tour mates were mildly shocked that I had a tattoo. They also enjoyed Senator's explanation of his relationship to Liberace.*

Soon we were at our hotel, tucked in the small town of Bad Herrenalb. The outside and the bedrooms looked like a typical southern German lodge, with lots of wood trim and a balcony that ran around the back side. The lobby and lounge area, however, looked like a retro take (perhaps 1960s) on earlier art deco. The large white geometric accents and an unusual attempt at glamour seemed a little out of place, but it was all comfortable. Like everywhere else we had been, we never saw a bug, so it was an easy choice to leave our sliding door open, even with the light rain.

---

* See *How to Change a Flat on a Unicycle*

Sunday night was our last group dinner. We found our usual suspects and made a few plates from the buffet. Through the long window near our table we could see that the drizzle was now a full-fledged rain. Whereas it would not have been welcome when we were running around Berlin, it now gave the tall pines a solemn glow. It was the perfect backdrop for sipping an after-dinner kaffee while discussing social and political situations with Peter. Too bad college can't be like that.

The rain also made it an easy choice to forgo our planned walk around the neighborhood, which we were probably too lazy to do anyway. We decided to call it an early night and relax in our room instead. As we walked toward the elevators though, we saw our U.K. coalition in the adjacent pseudo-1930s lounge. Jules' enthusiastic invitation to join them for more of the crazy stories and laughs that were already in progress was too good to pass up. A few minutes later we were situated in over-sized plush chairs, Irish coffees in hand. Needless to say, it was several hours later by the time we finally stepped into the elevator. Here's to our British/English/Welsh friends-- cheers!

*   *   *

Monday morning was still overcast and cool, which provided more ideal atmosphere for our last glimpses of der Schwartzwald. I wish we would have had more time to spend in the region, but we had only one more night in Germany, and we had to get back to Frankfurt. As we watched the scenery roll by, we saw a lone horse strolling across a brook, pausing to drink, unconcerned by us or the world. When he was finished, he walked back into the hilly forest, disappearing easily among the dense cover.

Before completing our round trip, however, we had one last stop in Heidelberg. Ismet pulled our bus into its parking spot as usual, but Dory asked us all to wait outside the bus before we dispersed to our separate adventures. Then she arranged us into a semi-organized mob in front of the bus and took a group photo. As anyone who knows me is aware, I hate having my picture taken, but in a group of forty people, I was able to blend in fairly well.

In other towns, we had always started exploring with a map, prioritizing sites according to interest and time. In Heidelberg, we toned our pace down overall. From the riverfront we could see the town rising up along the hillside. At the top, we could see castle ruins, which, thanks to our vast travel experience, led us to believe they were, indeed, the "Castle Ruins" we had vaguely remembered Dory mentioning. As I believe an abandoned, dilapidated fortress is always a worthy pursuit, we started our hike upward through the narrow streets.

As we soon found out, many of the streets led to dead ends, so we side-stepped our way up the hill, changing direction as necessary. Once we reached the top, it was apparent that we had definitely taken the road less traveled. Our journey led us to cool, green seclusion, as opposed to the proper path up, which brought tourists to a paved walkway, an open space, and a gift shop. I think we surprised a few people as we emerged from the nether regions around the back way, especially since we were drenched from a brief downpour.

At the top of the ruins we found an overlook. The wind gusted upward toward us as we scoped the town below. Red roofs dotted every crooked, cobblestone street. As if the scene was a planned panoramic mural, the Neckar River ran along the backdrop, with more homes and buildings asymmetrically scattered along its embankment. From our vantage point, we could also see the large black tower of Heiligeist Kirche.* It was the obvious choice for the remainder of the time we had in Heidelberg.

We lost our breeze as we zig-zagged back down the hill through the neighborhood. I was glad we were on foot, as I could not imagine trying to navigate even our small car through the narrow, twisted streets. Walking also allowed us to see local detail. Outside of one home, an elaborate and colorful array of terra cotta pots was wired together to create a bountiful window bouquet. Below it was a well-used bicycle leaning against the wall. This was the stuff calendar pictures were made of. *Why, exactly, did we have to return home the next day?...*

Using Heiligeist Kirche as a landmark, we reached a bustling platz. Along one row sellers manned their outdoor stands, offering the usual assortment of souvenirs. Other people ducked in and out of pubs and bakeries, tempted by various yeast-induced aromas. We passed up the spirits in lieu of the Spirit.

I did not think about it at the time, but Heiligeist Kirche was the last European church we entered on our trip, as well as the last to date. Like the others, it was a stoic marvel of medieval architecture, and beautifully adorned inside. Unlike some of the larger churches, it maintained its peaceful atmosphere, in spite of its attraction to tourists. After walking around quietly, we found a seat and listened

*   Church of the Holy Spirit

to an organist playing. It was easy to slip into prayer, and difficult to imagine the chaos of a new school year that was fast approaching. Maybe I could quit teaching and just be a nun-- who happens to have a boyfriend.

Then a man came to the front and made an announcement. I could not get all of it, but I picked up enough German to understand that they were about to begin a short noon service. We glanced at the time. Since we did not have to meet our group for another hour, we decided to stay. The mass was only about fifteen minutes long, but it was enough time to experience the tranquility and begin to unwind for the transition back to reality. Though none of it was in English, I recognized parts of the Lord's Prayer/Our Father. It was good to be among believers from a different culture.

The brief service left us enough time for a snack before walking back to the bus. Following the best smell on the street led us into a small deli, where we selected pretzel sandwiches. I really think I could live on German veggie sandwiches. Apparently one of the pigeons felt the same way. The bold scavenger got as close to us as possible, without actually flying onto our laps. *Sorry, buddy. This is too good to share.*

On the way back to our meeting point, we ran into Jules. "Where's Karol?" Senator asked.

"Oh, who knows?" was her unconcerned reply, as she grinned and bobbed her head under her floppy sun hat. "We were walking together, and then we got separated. He'll find us." I was struck by the juxtaposition of her casual attitude and my practical verge of panic when Senator and I were separated in Köln. Maybe that comes from decades of marriage, or perhaps vast international travel experience. Or maybe just from having phones that actually work.

Everyone was situated and we drove on to Frankfurt. Just before our round trip was complete, Dory surprised us one more time by presenting each party with a group photograph. Unintentionally, the image of the Heidelberg hillside had been captured in the reflection of the bus windows. As Senator and I looked at the picture, we realized how much we had learned from our many unofficial travel agents. We had received a bonus education simply by listening, asking questions, and honing the correct blend of a sense of adventure and a sense of humor.

The hotel in Frankfurt was the tallest of all of our accommodations, providing great views of the city. I was glad we were not returning to our first Frankfurt hotel, where we never really figured out how to open our own door lock. Here, our room was on the twelfth floor, ideally situated to take advantage of the extreme breeze that had developed. In fact, as soon as I opened the balcony door, the wind swept through the room, creating strange whining moans in the ventilation system. It was refreshing and fun. Then I opened the door to the hall, to see if our luggage had been delivered yet. In so doing, I must have let the wind into a vacuum. With my hand still on the door handle, I was almost sucked out of the room into the corridor. We agreed that we would take advantage of the unique atmosphere and definitely sleep with the balcony door open. It felt like being on a ship.

The afternoon was morphing into evening, and I was acutely aware that we had only one more opportunity to walk in Germany.* It was our last chance to roam an Altstadt unattended, so we grabbed our travel bag and started out toward the waterfront. It was at least a mile and a half, but it looked like the rain would hold off. It was also considerably less windy than up in our room.

We walked along a main street, pausing every block to wait for the traffic lights. I had finally adapted to the German custom of waiting religiously for the iconic green man walk signal to appear, rather than the Chicago look-look-run method of crossing urban intersections. Along the first mile nothing in particular grabbed our attention. There were businesses, some apartment buildings, and an occasional convenience market, but I needed to step back in time once more.

When we reached the waterfront, there was a wide pedestrian bridge spanning the Main River. It was clear we were on the modern side of the river. As we took our last step from the bridge, the architecture, crowds, and streets all seemed different. The cars were left behind, and almost everyone was on foot. A centuries-old church stood guard over the old platz. Beyond it was a square of colorful, tall, flat buildings, each with its distinctive criss-cross pattern of wooden trim. A fountain marked the centerpiece, and a perfect spot to rest and people-watch for awhile.

We were both getting hungry, but we had trouble finding anything suitable to eat. Surprisingly, it was the first time we could not locate a good sandwich stand. Sausage abounded in every direction-- veggies, not so much. We had also not seen anything tempting on the walk

---

* That is, unless you count the hustle through the airport, which, like Mark Twain's definition of golf, is merely a "good walk spoiled".

there, so we decided to head back to the hotel and hit up the room guide for suggestions.

On the way back, we overtook Peter, who was walking alone. He did not seem to mind our company, and we were always happy to chat with him. Before we knew it, our hotel was in view. Like us, Peter had not had any luck in his quest for dinner either. "I guess I'll try that traditional German restaurant across the street-- the one Dory mentioned." The food did not sound especially appealing, but we had no other viable options. More importantly, it would offer one more chance to glean travel wisdom from across the pond.

A small walkway along the side of the restaurant led to the covered outdoor patio. As soon as we stepped into the area, we were greeted by about ten familiar faces. There was an American family from our tour, along with the Australian couple we had helped in München. They were all smiling and invited us to join them. As we browsed the menu and ordered, more and more people from our group trickled in, until there were about twenty-five of us. We had formed our own impromptu last group dinner, much to the consternation of the servers who kept trying to accommodate more of us.

Everyone ate and drank as the memories of the past week-and-a-half poured out in random snippets. The Australian couple told the others how we had assisted them, making a much bigger deal out of it than it had been. They were very sweet, treating us like a long lost niece and nephew. Others were talking and enjoying typical meat dishes, but our *pfunffkuchen mit gemüse** may have had them

---

*   thicker than a crèpe, thinner than a pancake, bursting with sautéed

beat. It was outstanding. As the daylight disappeared, we raised a final toast to each other and our safe returns to many different time zones. Just as everyone had gradually joined the party, we all trickled out, a few at a time.

Back in our hotel, we took the elevator to the twelfth floor again. Inside our room, we were happy to find the wind just as wild as it had been before. The lights of the city shone through our window, as the curtains near the balcony door swayed. For the last time, we flipped through channels in four different languages. After a good walk and a great dinner, none of them could keep us awake for very long.

*   *   *

Tuesday morning the hotel was extremely busy. Dozens of people were exiting the floors, creating a long wait for the elevators. Feeling ambitious, or maybe just impatient, we took the stairs. At least the stairway had windows, providing an ever-changing vantage point as we spiraled our way down to the breakfast room. It was vigorous and kind of fun, but I couldn't imagine evacuating a high rise in an emergency.

We found a table in the corner of the buffet area and ate our fruit and müesli. As the crowd thinned out and more people left, we recognized a few familiar faces from our group. They were people we had not met in depth, but friendly nods were exchanged nonetheless. In silence, we finished our last German kaffees, forever spoiling us against American coffee.

The elevators no longer had a wait, so we stepped in

----

veggies, and dripping with a fresh, delicious, lightly spicy thin red sauce; difficult to pronounce, easy to devour and hit number twelve. After packing a few last-minute items, we rolled our suitcases out into the hall and returned downstairs. There we met Dory for a final check-out, and she grouped us with a few other people who had flights at similar departure times. We were pleased to see that Peter happened to be in our group.

At Frankfurt International Airport we were dropped off and left on our own. After all of the walking through romantic town squares, it was a little depressing to be trekking through the sterile, gray terminals. As most airports are basically set up the same way, we approached the long row of counters and looked for United. At home, you could not miss United's check-in stations if you tried; they were everywhere. Here, Lufthansa was king, and we did not see any other counters beside their fifty. I double-checked my paperwork. "Well, we are definitely in the right concourse..." I was getting antsy, even though we were early. Doubling our tracks, we walked a good extra mile out of our way. Right on cue, we happened to run into Peter again. Unfortunately, he wasn't sure where United was either.

Just then a small counter, completely separate from the rest of the check-in area, caught my eye. It was somewhat hidden, as though it was only a service area off to the side. As we walked toward it, we could see the United logo. *Finally.* I had been getting nervous.

Without incident, we registered, checked our two bags, and proceeded to security. I was happy to see there was no human microwave to step through. A few years prior, in Hawaii, I had requested a pat down instead of the scanner. Somehow I figured that would not go as smoothly

132

in Germany. One unintentional slip of the vocabulary and I would probably be handcuffed to a large security guard in a small room, most likely without the German sense of humor I had come to expect.

We were once again sitting and waiting. I glanced at a clock, just as the announcement of delay came over the intercom. It would be another forty-five minutes. In a mutual sigh, Senator and I leaned our heads against each other. It was mid-day, but flying west would land us in mid-afternoon. From there it would be another hour to our car, and who-knows-how-long until we reached home through the weekday rush-hour traffic. I did not really want to think about it. Hopefully we would be exhausted enough to sleep during the flight.

After all of the transportation logistics had been accomplished, we eventually stepped into our home. I never really get that glad-to-be-back feeling. I'm happy to return to my own bed and bathroom, but beyond that, nothing particularly grabs me. As long as Senator is traveling with me, there is not much appeal to coming back. This time I actually felt confined, especially when we ate indoors. I already missed Europe and felt somewhat out of place. It would take some transitioning, as it always does. Yet, as any real traveler knows, there is only one remedy to getting over the conclusion of a vacation...

Chapter 3
Spikes, Chains, and Hard Rock: Late March 2016

Of course, after Germany I did transition back to real life, and, of course, there were things at home that I would have eventually missed. In fact, as fulfilling as traveling to Europe was, it was sort of nice to be on hiatus from planning. For the time being, I did not have to worry about making transportation or lodging arrangements, translating a language, or navigating unfamiliar territory. I was able to settle back into a somewhat normal routine, whatever that meant within our strange schedules.

Throughout the fall we continued to teach and to record live music. A few times we picked up some intensive multiple-day sessions, creating new challenges that were met one way or another. This pattern continued right through the new year, forgoing the usual slow period of recording from mid-December until late January. In fact, January was only second to the previous June in the busyness of the business.

It was fine that our schedule was packed. Between the lack of time and snow, the 2015-2016 winter was a bust. It was clear that no skiing would take place, so the antidote was to look forward to the spring. As I perused the calendar, I realized that Easter was very early, making my school spring break early. It occurred to me that we might be able to coordinate a visit with my grandma, who wintered in Florida. Doing the math, I realized it had been six years since we had done so. Usually she was back home in Illinois before my spring break took place, but this seemed like the perfect opportunity. Excited, I called her.

"Oh, Honey, I'm so sorry. I'm actually leaving earlier this year..." She sounded so disappointed that I felt like I should apologize to her. My impeccable timing had chosen the one year when other events required her to return to Illinois about a month earlier than usual. Oh well; either way we would get to see her at some point. Giving up the time off, however, seemed like a waste, so into plotting mode I went.

The natural choice was to return to the White Mountains. This was partly for the simple reason that I love it there, but also because my familiarity with the region meant minimal planning effort. Too many things, good and bad, were going on in my late winter to devote much time or thought to the process. Visiting New Hampshire in spring would also offer the opportunity to see a somewhat touristy area in the off-season. I reasoned that people would be scarce and bugs nonexistent. The biggest unknown factor (besides virtually everything when traveling), was how 'our' inn was faring under new ownership. The place we had enjoyed staying twice before had changed hands the previous autumn. I figured it would still be good, so I booked five nights there. If it was a flop, well, times change, circumstances change, and even the mountains are temporary to an extent.

Not surprisingly, Easter was upon us before we knew it. That Saturday afternoon, with clothes, traveling necessities, and the ingredients for Easter brunch and an Easter Eve pizza, we left for Senator's mom's house. We took her to church and then returned to her house. It was strange to see some of her furniture gone and boxes lining the sides of rooms. She was in the process of waiting for an opening in a senior community in the next town over. As she was in hold mode, I realized that it might well be our last holiday at the home in which Senator grew up.

Senator was not in a mindset to be sentimental, though. He was just hungry for the pizza I had promised to make. I could relate; my stomach had started growling somewhere between the third and fourth readings at church. As I assembled the pies* and popped them into the oven, I could hear Senator and his mom scrolling through television channels in the living room. "Anything good on?" I asked, walking in to enlist Senator's help in maneuvering the pizzas off of the small, rectangular baking sheets that had survived his mother's Great Kitchen Downsize.

"Not so far..." he responded, much more interested in choosing between pizza toppings than channels. We made up three plates and joined his mom, who was still

---

* I suppose I will have to get used to this term to describe pizza if I ever want to migrate to New England.

faithfully looking for something suitable to watch. Soon she found it, via the classic biblical epic *The Ten Commandments*. Christian, Jew, or atheist, if you grew up in the United States during the latter half of the twentieth century, Charleton Heston most likely went head-to-head with Yul Brynner at some point on your family's television each spring. As Pharaoh's daughter had just instructed her servant to pluck a mysterious basket out of the reeds, we settled in for a long stretch. It was nice that some traditions could remain the same, even if their commercials changed.

As Moses struggled with his true identity, we continued to visit and relax. Maybe all out-of-town trips should start this way. A yawn or two circulated the room. Then Senator's mom went to bed just before the plagues began. That was just as well; I suppose they could induce some nasty nightmares in conjunction with a heavy meal. Senator and I made it all the way through the Red Sea, but we dozed off in our respective cozy spots before the Israelites turned into whiny, ungrateful partiers. Satisfied with our quiet evening, we dragged ourselves upstairs to bed. No golden calf this year.

*   *   *

Easter morning our simple brunch went as planned. We even squeezed in a visit to Senator's aunt, who lived on the other side of town. After covering current events, family gossip, and a litany of other unrelated topics, we said good-bye and went back to Senator's mom's house. After the car was loaded, she presented us with a bag of essential snacks that she had decided we needed for the road. Who could argue with someone hugging you as she foisted chips and trail mix upon you?

We were off, ten minutes before the planned departure time. Traffic was a little busy through Illinois, probably due to others trying to escape, too. (The state tends to have that effect on people.) Regardless, the weather was good, and things moved along swiftly through Indiana and into Ohio.

That is, they moved along swiftly until we were a little west of Toledo. There we came to a complete stop, due to an accident a few miles ahead. No one was moving, so there was nothing to do but watch the dwindling daylight and the gradually emerging lightning show. We could see a considerable storm skirting the horizon, but we were not sure which way it would go.

I turned the car on temporarily to check the clock. Over forty minutes had passed. I felt like I knew the drivers of the cars around us better than I knew some of the people on our block. A steady spring rain had started, breaking the monotony a little bit. "At least there's no hail," I pointed out, suddenly remembering that we were in a three-month old car that had mainly seen the inside of our garage heretofore.

During the next hour, we traveled the grand sum of one and one-half miles. On the side of the road we could see a semi-truck with its trailer caved in. It must have rolled, sprawling across both lanes. Hopefully there were no serious injuries.

Finally we passed the accident site and the pace picked up, despite the pouring rain. Up ahead vehicles were quickly accelerating to 70mph. We, on the other hand, had to lay back at 50mph, due to being stuck behind a car that weaved its way haphazardly along for the next ten miles. We did not dare attempt to pass the erratic driver. How he or she managed to stay on the road is still a mystery to me. Eventually he or she exited off and became someone else's problem.

Fighting the strong wind gusts and adjusting our eyes to the celestial strobe show, we gained speed and began to watch for an exit with fuel. We were not in the danger zone yet, but we agreed that a full tank of gas was next on the agenda. A bathroom sure wouldn't hurt, either. That's when the hail began.

"I can't believe this is your second car to get hailed on in less than a year! I knew we should have taken the older one instead," I vented, fully knowing that nothing I said would hold any weight by the time the next road trip rolled around. It was by no means a catastrophe, but it definitely was not part of the grand vision. In the meantime, we just needed to find a stop.

Fifteen minutes later, we did. The hail had stopped, leaving us with the torrential rain and high winds so as not to diminish too much of the drama. Senator pumped gas while I called our hotel to make sure they would hold our reservation beyond midnight if necessary. Then we drove over to the travel plaza building for restrooms and bad coffee. Adding to the fun was my irritation at remembering how terribly inconvenient it sometimes is to be a girl when traveling.

Finally we reached our hotel. As promised, they had saved the room for us. I settled in, got things ready for the morning, and set the alarm clock. Senator had to check his email before going to bed. Just as my eyes were drooping, I heard him. "Oh, shoot. They shipped the microphone."

140

"What mic...phone?" I mumbled vaguely, not knowing what he was talking about.

"I ordered a microphone before we left, but I did not expect them to ship it Fed-Ex. The mail's stopped, but this is different. I can't have it sit on the porch for a week." He was right about that. Lately the feral cat population had increased in our neighborhood. I pictured one of them spraying the box. A hungry coyote would be useful on the porch, but certainly not a microphone. Either way, nothing was going to be solved that night, which had already become the next morning.

*   *   *

Monday morning was easier than expected. Everything came together faster than anticipated, and we checked out a little earlier than planned. As other spring breakers around the country probably stepped onto their beaches in minimal clothing, Senator and I fought the pelting sleet as we put our luggage in the car. It was brisk, but as we cranked the car heater and shared a cup of coffee, I was actually enjoying it. Maybe it meant there would still be some snow in the mountains.

As we made our way through the remainder of Ohio and into Pennsylvania, the temperature warmed enough to change the precipitation to rain. It continued on and off for most of the day, but with the light traffic, it was tranquil. I counted down the miles to the halfway point, which was roughly near Buffalo. In southwest New York, we also noticed a few dozen vineyards along the highway. Somehow, though I had driven that stretch of interstate several times before, I had never seen them. Upon further reflection, I guess most of the times it had been dark. There was, of course, also the time that we were too preoccupied with reports of a tornado spinning its way from western Pennsylvania to appreciate the local wine culture. Anyway, we were cruising, making good time as we turned east to transverse the rest of the state.

Gladly leaving the cities in our rear view mirror, we crossed into New England. It was apparent that we had done so, too. Traffic dropped off, and forested areas separated small towns-- the kind with rushing brooks meandering along the highway and among the valleys. A darker sky and drizzle permeated all of it, enhancing the shift to a greener corner of the country. There was also an abundance of home-based, nonessential shops selling curiosities and collectibles. For example, who knew one could make a living as a purveyor of a variety of life-sized animal statues, each painted black and white to look like cows? Likewise, I had to double-check with Senator that we were all stocked up, lest we needed to stop at the Colonial Lamp Shoppe. "Yeah, I think we're good..." was his unfazed reply. I was seriously tempted to stop by one event in Chester, Vermont, though. According to the sign, they were holding a fundraiser to benefit their historic hearse house, conveniently located next to the church yard.

Unfortunately, among the beauty of any rugged, rural area, there is also the smattering of junkyard-worthy, shacky compounds. These are properties that probably served as family farms at one time. Since then, they have been abandoned or at least neglected. Alone, they are not a problem, and even add visual interest and a certain historical dignity to a place. Combined with acres of garbage, old furniture, rotting mattresses, demolished

142

building supplies, and rusted out pieces of vehicles, however, they tend to lose their charm. I guess that is a factor we will have to consider if we ever run away to the great woods of the Northeast.

We needed to make one more gas stop, so we pulled into a station near the state line. As Senator went in to use the bathroom, I stepped up to the pump and followed the directions for using a credit card. The machine claimed to be authorizing my card, but it never worked beyond that, despite trying a few times. Frustrated and wet, I went inside to ask the cashier for assistance. The girl-- although she was at least ten years older than me, I didn't think of her as a real adult-- was talking loudly on her phone. She did put her friend on hold to see what I wanted, but her usefulness ended there.

"Yeah, whatcha' need?" I explained my predicament and asked if she could somehow reset the pump or get it to start. "Oh, I don't know," she laughed and shrugged. I did not get the sense she was being rude or messing with me; I just think she genuinely found the situation amusing. Since it appeared that my credit card had not been charged or left vulnerable, I gave up on the Village Idiot and went back to the car.

A moment later Senator arrived. "Let's get out of here! Get me to New Hampshire!" I barked. As he has never been a particular fan of Vermont quirkiness, he gladly obliged, noting that he had seen some odd characters outside the gas station, too.

We drove two blocks, turned a corner, crossed the Connecticut River, and we were in New Hampshire. This time the gas station was normal. Gradually the rocks became boulders, the forests included more pine and birch, and we rose in elevation. I had to admit, it kind of felt like a homecoming.

If you have ever looked at a road map of New England, (which is something I assume sane people regularly do,) you have likely noticed that there are no east-west interstates across the northern half of the region. Whereas you have a few solid north-south interstates to easily facilitate American-Canadian tourism and commerce, you are left to explore the smaller highways when traveling east or west. For our purposes, there were three viable options. I chose the one that was shortest, by a whopping twenty-five minutes, according to the internet. As it turned out, I was as effective at picking the best route as I am at picking the best line at the grocery store.

We had actually taken the same road a few years before, and I remembered that it had been a little bumpy, but spring added a whole new level of bumpiness. In the Midwest we are well aware that the freezing and thawing cycles wreak havoc on the roads. Even so, I was not prepared for the rough ride ahead. It seemed every minute brought another of the ubiquitous orange warning signs inserted near the side of the road. Frost heaves lurked everywhere, slowing us down considerably.

Because of the slow speeds, the overcast day, and the mountain and forest shadows, the darkness fell quickly. Though we were not climbing very high, it was soon enough to bring us into dense fog. *Well this was not exactly what I had in mind when I imagined arriving at our vacation destination.* Just in case we were starting to get bored, yellow "Moose Crossing" signs now joined the "FROST

144

HEAVES" warnings.

As we were approaching the apex of the topography, the temperature dropped a few degrees, which was sufficient to freeze the fog. It was also snowing lightly. The crystallized trees were definitely beautiful, but we were doing more praying than sightseeing. We rounded a sharp corner at about 5mph only to find yet another sign, this time white. "Icy Road" confirmed our assumption, but I wasn't sure there was anything else we could do to be more cautious.

Finally, just to round out the experience, and because New Hampshirites* are polite enough to share their knowledge of road conditions at every opportunity, we saw one last sign. Our icy road was apparently going to help us descend an 8% grade. *Well, if you're going to pick a bad road, you might as well be thorough.* On the bright side, the gauge that reads the car's miles-per-gallon was off the charts on the way down. Ultimately, thanks to Senator's driving skills and the fact that the moose were not stupid enough to be out on such an evening, we arrived into town safely.

The previous forty-five minutes had not been fun, but there was our cozy inn, just as we had remembered it. It was quiet, but the door was unlocked and there were plenty of welcoming lights. Inside I looked around, but I did not see anyone. Then I noticed the note and key on the desk. It basically told us to check in and make ourselves comfortable. We would not meet anyone until breakfast the next day.

We settled in and sat down, taking a few moments to

---

* probably not their preferred term, but I can't think of a better one at the moment unwind. The room was comfortable, and it was tempting just to drop off to sleep, even though it was only 8:30pm. Once we rested though, we realized we were hungry, as we had only snacked lightly throughout the day. "Want me to go get something and bring it back?" I asked, figuring Senator had had enough car time for one day. It was only two miles along the well-lit road to several carry-out places, and I was very familiar with the area.

His answer surprised me. "No way! Let's go eat.... but you drive." We just wanted something fast, so we stopped at a small place that sold pizza and grinders*. We remembered that the pizza had been nothing special, but a hot, drippy sandwich sounded pretty tasty.

In fact, it was not-- hot or tasty, but we were excited to be there and having fun planning our next four days of freedom in the mostly-deserted mountains. Senator perused a local paper while I rattled off some tentative ideas. I could not wait to get started the next morning. I only wished we had more time. "Let's remember to check the weather when we get back to the room," I suggested. "Then we can decide which itinerary to do on which day." Senator agreed, and we finished our crummy sandwiches.

We drove the few minutes to the inn and immediately turned the heat up in our room. The 'wintry mix' was chilly, and we were glad to be in for the night. As we cleaned up and scrolled through the limited cable selection, I checked the weather forecast on the computer. Our first day of outdoor activities would begin in the low 30s, with snow and high winds. *Woo-hoo! Spring break!*

        *   *   *

---

*   New England speak for sub sandwich

Tuesday morning we enjoyed our first breakfast in view of the mountains, complete with steadily falling snow. We were the only ones who had stayed at the inn, and we were savoring the slower pace of the off-season. Alan, one-half of the new owners, came over to greet us. He was very polite and pleasant, but I could tell he was not usually in the role of front man. His normal place was in the kitchen, an extension of his previous career as a chef.

As he started us with fresh fruit and warm homemade muffins, we learned that he had grown up in California, but his mother's roots were in the same New Hampshire town as the inn. Every summer she would pack up the kids and head back east. Alan's wife, Karen, on the other hand, was from Rhode Island, but had never been to the White Mountains prior to retiring there from teaching.* Currently she was out of town for a few days, which meant that Alan would have to practice managing the office and housekeeping end of things. We were the easygoing guinea pigs, so it was a suitable arrangement. He did not bother us, we did not make demands, and we could temporarily pretend we owned a large, historic home.

As promised, the weather was more like mid-February than late March. The snow continued to fall-- sideways-- thanks to the relentless wind. We had decided to start with a drive, saving the hike for the afternoon, when the temperature would shoot way up into the 30s. Remembering the incredibly fresh and clean spring water

---

* This was inconceivable to me. If I lived in Rhode Island, I would probably run to the White Mountains any time I had two days off in a row. For the time being, perhaps it is a good thing I live seventeen hours away.

we had discovered on our last trip there, we headed to a wayside stop in Franconia Notch State Park. We had come prepared to take advantage of the free mountain-sourced flow. Armed with our plastic water bottles, we exited the car and marched/slid our way to where the water should have been. Mild blizzard notwithstanding, we were determined to fill up, even if we could barely find the basin among the snow. "So, where is it?" I asked.

"They took the pipe out for the winter," Senator said flatly.

At least I didn't feel stupid for not being able to find it. "Well, that crossed my mind, but I thought since it was constantly flowing, it wouldn't freeze."

"No, we're just dumb Midwesterners."

I grimaced. "Man, the wind is really brutal."

"Dumb Midwesterners," repeated Senator.

We threw the empty water bottles into the car and started to drive north. While the mountains were my favorite part of my favorite state, I had also been fascinated by the rugged northern country. Its remoteness meant that there were few people and even fewer major roads. Moose, however, existed in healthy numbers, so it could be our best chance of seeing one. Maybe it was mating season, which I imagined would bring them out looking for dates.

The beautiful early spring snow layered branches and covered the ground with a satisfying crunch. Trees were outlined in an attractive silvery/green/gray. As we drove further north, the small towns still depicted their hardworking history, usually in the logging industry. Some kept their classic New England town squares, surrounded by historic buildings and clapboard-bound architecture.

148

Others had devolved into a series of dilapidated shacks. Streams, brooks, and full-fledged rivers tied it all together under the quiet, gray sky.

On one of my strategic maps, I had noticed an information center on the very road on which we were driving. We had been to its sister facility at the other end of the White Mountains, and it was a nice little spot to take a break, learn a bit about the region's ecology, and stock up on useful items like brochures and "Live Free or Die" apparel. Thinking this would be an interesting counterpart, I asked Senator if he would mind stopping. He easily agreed, so I watched for the sign or building, which I estimated we would approach in about ten minutes.

Sure enough, we did find a building, right where the map indicated it would be. The visitor center, however, was definitely closed. It did not just looked closed for the season; it was boarded up securely for the duration. My guess is that it had not been open at any point during the last five years. "Look at the time we're saving," I joked. Of course, that meant a while longer until we could find a bathroom, but there was always 'God's restroom' if we got desperate.

Not long after we passed the Visitor-Center-That-Has-Ceased-To-Be, we turned east to cross a narrow portion of the state. It did not take long for us to learn how fast winds and temperature can change, even without increasing elevation. The road was difficult to see as we entered a blustery wilderness. It was not a white-out, but we were not doing any casual wildlife watching. Fortunately, the snow on the road was not accumulating much, due to the wind. This was good, as only a few

149

vehicles passed us, none of which were plows.

Eventually we completed our trek on the remote stretch of highway. It was not until then that I realized that we had passed through the northernmost of the notches.* I recalled seeing "Dixville Notch" on the map, but in keeping with the Dumb Midwesterner tradition of the morning, I had dismissed it as a lovely name for a small mountain village. This was particularly inexcusable as I knew what a notch was; it just had not registered when I was planning the drive. Naturally winds would increase and tunnel through a geologic narrowing. Add some snow and you've got yourself a half-hour party.

Turning south onto Route 16 placed us in a surprisingly different climate. The winds died down, the snow slowed to an occasional flurry, and the sun poked through a few thin spots in the clouds. Along the highway the rivers and streams met in sizable lakes, where birds casually took advantage of the ample food supply below the surface. I figured this was my best chance to see a moose, so I scanned the banks for any large, brown masses gulping drinks. Alas, the creatures that supposedly required great caution to avoid were too elusive for us.

If we could not see moose, at least we could see Moose Brook State Park. The snow had stopped, leaving us with a light but consistent drizzle. The winds had remained steady, too, justifying the bulk of sweatshirts, hats, and gloves I had packed. We were determined to get some form of hiking in during each of our our four days in the mountains, so we parked the car near the visitor center and

_____

* or 'gaps', or 'passes', depending what part of the country you are from

got out.

The building's doors were locked, and there was only one other car in the lot, presumably belonging to a maintenance worker we could see in the distance. He was probably wondering who in the world went hiking on a day like this. Maybe he figured out his answer when he saw our license plate. Whatever his thoughts, we were glad he had left the outhouse unlocked for us.

We started walking up a service road that led to a trail head. Moving into the forest cut down on the wind, and the rain had stopped for the time being, even if the clouds threatened to let loose at any moment. As we made our way downward, winding among the rocks and trees, we could hear the sound of a cascading brook somewhere nearby. Following the trail led us closer to it, where we crossed a small, wooden plank bridge. We paused for a moment by the clear, rushing water. I thought back to the first time I had planned hikes in New Hampshire. I remembered telling Senator that I had carefully chosen all of our trails based on wanting to see waterfalls. In the White Mountains this is almost laughable; it would be a much more difficult task to find trails that *didn't* eventually follow or cross waterfalls. If you can't find a waterfall in northern New Hampshire, you probably have not left your room.

We only hiked for about an hour and a half, but it was enough to get our feet wet, figuratively and, in Senator's case, literally. "I think my boot just sprang a leak."

"That's it," I declared. "There's no way you're doing three more days of hiking in wet boots. I saw a Walmart back in Berlin.* At least they should have something without holes. The town's only a few miles back." Reluctant to invest in new shoes, but knowing soggy socks would not be wise, Senator agreed.

"Wow. Even the Walmart is nicer than those in Illinois," I remarked. It was true; the staff, customers, and overall atmosphere were more pleasant than the brand generally connotes, but the hiking boot selection was still lacking.

"I don't know about the fit. They're not completely comfortable..." Senator started.

I finished the thought for him. "Then forget it. Decent footwear is nonnegotiable when going up rocky, slippery mountains." I was all for saving money, but that kind of frugality could land a body in the emergency room. I then introduced Plan B. "Actually, I noticed an outfitter store about a half-mile down the road. They should have something...."

It was divine intervention. Within five minutes the helpful local sales associate had Senator in a pair of boots that were as comfortable as worn-in tennis shoes yet as functional as the local landscape demanded. "Sold!" Leaving his old boots in the garbage, Senator stepped up to the counter.

As we paid, we were reminded that New Hampshire

---

* According to New Hampshire writer and humorist Rebecca Rule, Berlin is pronounced *BER-lin*, as opposed to *ber-LIN*. She also explains that Milan, New Hampshire, is pronounced *MI-lan*, instead of *mi-LAN*. Perhaps the towns wanted to distinguish themselves from their European counterparts. They still have nothing on Illinois. Our towns include Cairo (*KA-ro*), Vienna (*VY-enna*), and Marseilles (*mar-SALES*).

does not charge sales tax. This prompted me to look down at my own worn boots, which probably only had a few more months in them. "Do you sell kids-sized boots?" I asked the woman who had helped us.

"Only in snow boots-- sorry," was the reply, as she glanced at my feet curiously. I figured they would be hard to find. As I have always said, few nine-year olds need adult-quality hiking boots. The quest continues...

It was late afternoon when we got back to our room. We had seen the vast, wild beauty of the northern part of the state, dabbled in a blizzard, hiked, and performed an informal socioeconomic Walmart comparison. We were hungry and tired, and the chilly rain that had picked up once again suggested food that was hot and nearby. Fortunately, a pub was just a few blocks away.

Off-season was quickly becoming my favorite season of the year. With only one other couple in the tavern, the only visible employee was heavily multitasking. He was simultaneously host ("Go ahead an' sit anywhere. There's booths over there if you like that."), bartender ("Can I get you something to drink?"), and server ("Here's a couple of menus. You can let me know when you're ready to order.").

We quickly scanned the menu for the standard veggie burger that most such places offered and signaled for our guy to come over to our table. He was friendly and a little apologetic that there was not more action in town that night. We assured him that we were completely content with our evening. We were about to enjoy an ideal night on vacation, consisting of scrolling through photos taken earlier in the day, chatting and reading guide books, and falling asleep to shows about people with unrealistic expectations shopping for homes in sweaty locations. The sweet potato fries weren't bad, either.

*   *   *

Wednesday morning the sun was beaming. It was still considerably cold, though, which would balance out the temperature once we got moving. In short, it was what March should be, as opposed to the sticky mud and brown-yellow bits of dead vegetation of an Illinois March. We were anxious to get started, but first we had another breakfast as the only guests of the inn.

Chatting with the owner again, we learned that he, too, enjoyed hiking the lower mountains in the area. It was nice to see we were not the only ones 'working our way up' to the more strenuous hikes gradually. On the other hand, he had recently met a man who was completing his 4,000-footers.* This, in itself, was impressive. Learning that the man was seventy-eight years old, and that he had only started when he was seventy years old, was downright inspiring.

Our destination for the entire day was Franconia Notch State Park, just a few miles north of where we were staying. The short drive would allow more time to hit the hills. To get the blood flowing and gain manageable amounts of elevation, we started off with the double feature of Artist's Bluff and Bald Mountain. Depending how that

---

* New Hampshire boasts forty-eight mountains with summits over 4,000 feet. Some hikers have made it a personal goal to tackle each of them. Doing so successfully earns them a membership in the Appalachian Mountain Club's 4,000-Footer Club. Doing so in winter earns them an even more elite distinction. (At press time, Senator and Wendy V have set no such goals.)

went, we might take another short hike later in the day.

At the back end of a parking lot for Cannon Mountain ski area, there was an almost-obscured trail head with a sign denoting our trail names. We were in the right spot, so we started into the woods. I was surprised at how fast we got warm, even in the dappled shade of the trees. It was only in the upper 30s, but within fifteen minutes we were peeling off outer layers, leaving just long-sleeve shirts.* Up we climbed, navigating around occasional slippery patches of leftover ice. In between conversation, our background soundtrack was provided by screeching blue jays. No other humans were on the trail.

The top of Artist's Bluff lived up to its name. There was a modest opening which provided a perfect view of Cannon Mountain's ski trails. We took a break and sat facing the long, white ribbons of snow. Watching the small stick-people figures of the skiers confirmed my decision to never go downhill skiing. They looked like they could fall down off the mountain at any moment.

The lower part of the Artist's Bluff trail linked up seamlessly with Bald Mountain, so we headed up that path. It was a little narrower, but it was still fairly easy to hike. The air was still clean and crisp, motivating us and pushing us forward faster than usual. As we walked, we spiraled up the mini-mountain quickly. At least, we *were* moving quickly, until our pace was broken by a very steep section of sheer granite. The long stretch required some strategy, but we both made it up. My only disappointment was that, in the picture we took, it did not look as far as it was.

The payoff was a wide view of a quiet little valley

---

* and jeans; we kept our pants on.

below. "This is perfect. I think I'm hooked on New Hampshire as a spring break destination. Forget July..." The transition between winter and spring meant comfortable hiking, very few people, and zero bugs. If one was so inclined, he/she could even sunbathe on the boulders. Considering the limited skin exposure, a bottle of sunscreen could last a few years. "Look at the money we're saving!" I pointed out.

It was only about 11:00am, so we had plenty of time to explore another part of the park. After a quick pit stop at the room, we headed back to the state park to the Lonesome Lake trail. About two months before we left, I had found a great trail map, complete with natural details and elevation rings. According to the layout, we could take a trail up one side of the small mountain to Lonesome Lake, and then join a different trail to come back down the mountain on the Cascade Brook trail. From there, it would just be a short walk along the road back to the car. Altogether, I estimated it would take about three hours.

We locked the car and checked to make sure we had water, sunglasses, a map, and a few other necessities. It was still very sunny, and the day was quickly warming into the 40s as we started the wide, flat trail from the campground. The clear air felt great inside and outside, and we both inhaled deeply. I was motivated to see the frozen lake and another rushing brook with tiered waterfalls. We knew the incline would come soon, but in the meantime, we bounded along the path at a good pace.

Occasionally we had to glance around to find the trail markers, which were painted on trees at strategic points. For a while we followed another couple, but they stepped off to the side to affix something to their shoes. Smiling and nodding a hiker's "good afternoon", we passed by them. It did not take long before we realized why they were making the adjustment.

Around the next bend the trail became decidedly steeper. We were fine with the leg work involved, but we were not prepared for how slick it was. The sun was melting the top layer of snow, but the ground was cold enough to refreeze it as a smooth path of ice. We slowed down to less than half of our previous speed, using small trees to assist us as necessary.

A few minutes later the couple passed us. A few minutes after that, another man passed us. This time we got a look at his feet. "Does that guy have chains around his shoes?" I asked Senator.

"Looks like it..."

"Wouldn't the metal just slide even more on the ice?"

"No, because those chains are attached to spikes," he explained, as we both realized the impact of this discovery. Rubber holders stretched around their hiking boots, keeping their spikes securely in place. I had read about these crampons* before, but I had always heard of them in the context of ice climbers-- those crazy people who scale sheer frozen overhangs of ice. We were just on a dirt trail that happened to contain winter leftovers. As we saw more people pass us easily, we realized they were a necessary accessory for spring mountain hiking. "Add them to the list for next trip," Senator noted.

Due to our cramponlessness, we took much longer than expected to wend our way up to the lake. I was

---

* terrible word-- I know

starting to understand why it was called Lonesome Lake. Then suddenly the wind kicked up, and the temperature started to plummet. The sun was still warm, but it quickly dropped about 15°. Shortly thereafter, we reached the lake. The frozen openness exposed us to the elements, from which we had been protected while on the forested part of the trail. It was definitely worth the effort, though. We had made it to a strikingly scenic spot under the midday sun. Besides, it would be all down hill from there.*

In addition to the ring of pines surrounding the lake, we also noticed another sight. A sign post pointed various directions, indicating the conjunction of a few trails. Everything lined up as expected, which is always a welcome confirmation. The problem was the partially torn piece of paper attached near the bottom of the sign.

"It says the bridge over Cascade Brook is out," Senator announced. I pondered that concept for a moment. He continued, "Does that affect us?"

"Well, according to the map, we do cross the river at some point further down the trail. It might mean we have to backtrack," I explained, as we both listened to the nearby rushing water that told us the powerful stream was not something we could hop across, at least at this point. "Maybe it's smaller near the bridge?" I suggested, realizing as I said it what a stupid statement it was. Obviously water would gain volume as gravity fed other little streams and

---

*As our friend Bill later pointed out, the photo of us standing, arms outstretched, on the snowy field was reminiscent of a scene from one of our favorite cold-weather movies, 1951's *The Thing From Another World*. Unlike *The Thing*, our adventure did not lead us to any buried space ships or frosty aliens, but you never know.

melting snow into it. If anything, it would be much wider there. I threw it back on him. "It's your call..."

"I think I'd like to try it," declared Senator. No surprise there.

"Yeah," I agreed. "It might be an old sign anyway. It kind of looks like someone might have tried to remove it. Maybe the bridge has been fixed. If nothing else, we'll just backtrack. It's plenty early." Maybe I was starting to think like him. We had come this far; we might as well have a little adventure. Plus, the allure of a potential shortcut and easier route back was too great to bypass.

We walked back into the forest, and within moments we were out of the wind and peeling off sweatshirts again. Hiking downhill was still a workout, but it proved a little easier due to the fact that we were now trudging through snow rather than slipping over ice. At one point we saw a man and his dog coming up the path. *Great-- a potential source of information!* "Hello!" He nodded back, somewhat out of breath. "Was the bridge really out... over Cascade Brook?"

He looked puzzled for a minute. So did his dog. Then he answered, "Oh, I don't know." *How could he not know,* I wondered. *Had he flown in?* "I came from the other way."

"Oh, okay. Thanks anyway," Senator replied. Then he turned to me. "Can we go that other way?"

"No, it's actually a trail that goes many miles into the back country-- the opposite direction of what we need. What do you think? Should we continue or turn back?" Again, I already knew his answer. Even though his legs were starting to bother him, he wanted to continue further.

159

Either we would cut off a significant amount of time, or we would add a significant amount of time. It was about 50/50 odds either way.

As it turned out, it was a bet we lost. The sun continued to shine in random specks on the trail, and we found ourselves dropping through holes into a few inches of water every so often. Had there not been snow, we would have been able to see which parts of the path were covered with water. We would have simply stepped around them. Fortunately, our boots were waterproof-- we were extremely grateful for the boot-buying detour of the day before-- but mine had two tiny cracks on top that required careful maneuvering to avoid.

"Add gloves to the list, too," muttered Senator. His hands were getting cold, especially when we tripped over an unseen root and palmed the snow. The next section of the hike was very quiet. I could not tell whether Senator was annoyed with me, concentrating on the difficult trail, or just in pain. In any case, I felt sorry that the afternoon was turning out badly, especially after such a wonderful morning hike.

The trail still paralleled the brook, which continued to trip its way downward over boulders into various swirling waterfalls. Eventually it turned toward the water. We had to be close to the moment of truth. Senator got a second wind and bounded down the level section of trail to the water's edge.

There, indeed, was no bridge. Instead, there was a full-fledged river with New Hampshire's version of rapids. Naturally, rocks of many sizes were everywhere within the cascade. Senator wasted no time in investigating the

160

situation. I watched, impressed and nervous, as he tested the possibility of crossing. He made it about halfway across, pausing in between steps to determine the best route. Every so often he glanced at me, checking my reaction. Then he returned to the shore, and I knew what was coming next.

"I think we could make it..." he began.

"Correction: *you* could make it." I truly did admire his courage, and I truly did believe he could have made it. When it came to my short legs, however, I knew my limits. This one was too risky for me. I loved the idea of trailblazing, especially since it could have saved us time in this case, but I did not love the idea of possibly ending up in a hospital after being tossed around the rocky water.

We admitted defeat and turned back. It was an even quieter hike back, partly due to the fact that we were again hiking uphill to the summit of the small mountain. The sun was still plenty high in the sky, but I had no idea what time it was. *Add a watch to the list,* too, I told myself.

When we reached the lake again, we barely acknowledged it, except to note that it meant we would soon be turning downhill. About fifteen minutes into our walk, we met a woman with a dog. The dog seemed friendly enough, and the woman, though somewhat oblivious, nodded as she passed, so we did not think anything else of it. We were focused on the mission of not tumbling down the mountain, as we gingerly stepped and scooted our way along the extremely slippery path. Gripping tree branches and trying to ignore the odd sensations caused by toes being abruptly stopped within their boots, we weakly nodded greetings to hikers who

161

jaunted past us, fully outfitted in crampons.

Then I heard an unfriendly greeting. Looking up from the trail, I saw the dog we had met earlier quickly making its way toward us, growling. I warned Senator, who was in no mood for this new addition to the drama. I knew some dogs had an aversion to male strangers in particular, so I tried to speak to the dog in a firm but cautious manner. "Hey, Dog. Relax. What happened? You were fine with us a few minutes ago..." Of course, the owner was nowhere around.

The standoff went on for an uncomfortable amount of time. The dog continued its menacing threat, and Senator unleashed an equal verbal response, emphasized by the large stick he was now wielding. I added pepper spray to the mental list. By the time the owner appeared on the scene, we were out of patience. "Hey!" I yelled, "Your dog's growling at us. Can you call him off?"

Failing to comprehend the situation in any manner, she mindlessly responded. "Oh, he likes people."

"Yeah? Does he like mace, too?" Senator shot back, "Because he's about to get some in the face!" He was so convincing that I almost forgot he was bluffing. The woman still just stood there stupidly. I suppose the fact that she had headphones on and was winter hiking in capri pants and tennis shoes should have tipped us off that we were going to get nowhere with her. Eventually the dog gave up its stance and they passed us. Given how dense the woman was, I think the dog should really have focused on protecting her from herself rather than us.

At some point we dropped beneath the mud line. It's like the tree line, except it's the boundary where the ice

162

stops and the mud begins. Pretty it was not, but suddenly we had the gift of traction. Our second wind had finally arrived, and we flew down the remainder of the trail. I had almost forgotten that the last section was virtually flat. Senator had not forgotten; he was depending upon it.

We reached the car tired and sore. I offered to drive, and Senator eagerly accepted. I didn't tell him that I was only able to offer because we had such a short drive back to our room. All told, it had taken five hours to hike six and a half miles. That brought the day's total to eight and a half miles-- eight and a half miles on rough terrain. It was purely divine intervention that we had purchased new hiking boots for Senator the previous day.

At the room we cleaned up and elevated our feet. At first it felt like we could easily fall asleep for the night right then, but as we rested, we realized we were hungry. Senator was hurting, though. "Is there a drug store somewhere nearby?" he asked. I mentioned the Rite Aid I had seen along the main road through town. "I think that needs to be my first stop."

So our vacation night life included a stop at the local pharmacy. Specifically, we visited the ointment-for-the-elderly-and/or-ill-prepared-hikers aisle. Among the gooey options were tubes promising relief for muscle and joint paint. Senator read the descriptions. Either the cream would cure everything up to and including arthritis, or it would just burn and freeze alternately.

Having secured Senator's ointment, we drove a few blocks down the street to an Italian place. Last time we were in town, we had ordered calzones there. We took them on a stake-out to observe unsuspecting moose, to no avail. This time, no one was going anywhere. We plopped in a booth and awaited our hot, sloppy, cheesy delights.

As we sat, I wondered if the rest of the vacation would be spent in the room. It seemed like Senator was wincing in pain more often than he was comfortable. Well, I had brought a book with me. At least we had been able to enjoy two days of hiking.

"How's your calzone?" I asked.

"Really good. There's a lot of food here," Senator answered, more upbeat than expected. I have to say, by the time we reached Rite Aid, he was maintaining a pretty good sense of humor about the whole affair. I think the garlic further helped. "I think I'd like to stop and get some gloves when we're done here."

"You mean you want another souvenir, in addition to your muscle cream?" I teased. Then I thought about his request. *Did that mean there was a chance he would attempt another hike on this trip?* "Maybe Wayne's would have gloves," I suggested.

Wayne's Market is the convenience store attached to one of the local gas stations, and we have deemed it a destination unto itself. In addition to the usual chips and motor oil assortment, Wayne's carries camping supplies, groceries (including local favorites), odd clothing items, and other fascinations. Perhaps their most important function within the community, however, is their role as purveyor of homemade maple fudge. I don't mean the corn syrup and filler junk you can get at any grocery store; this is the real melt-in-your-mouth deal.

After dinner we did, in fact, go to Wayne's. They did, in fact, have a rack full of reasonably-priced gloves.

164

Senator actually found a pair that he claimed were the most comfortable he had ever owned. The next aisle over from the gloves brought us to the maple fudge. We selected a hefty chunk of it and paid for our essentials. God's sense of humor was apparent as the store's speakers played The Proclaimers' song "I Would Walk 500 Miles".

As long as we were doing the town, we stopped at a coffee shop on the way back to our room. There were only two or three other people there, and it had a serene vibe to it. The night was warm enough to sit outside in a sweatshirt, and the large open patio beckoned, so we took our coffee and Wayne fudge and found some seats. We only saw two other people on the street.

Twilight slipped away as we parked at our inn. Before we went upstairs to our room, we borrowed a few hiking guides from the bookcase in the living room, for future reference. Browsing them revealed several mistakes we had made while spring hiking. *Now you tell us.*

As I read, Senator slathered his cream onto sore areas. If you are familiar with the aroma of such creams, you are already smiling. I was not-- familiar or smiling. Intense menthol does not begin to describe the asphyxiating smell that fills the room as soon as the ointment is squirted out. "Whoa!" I burst out. "I had no idea it smelled like that!" Since we were still the only ones in the inn, I opened both windows and the door to the hallway to try to get a cross breeze.

"Yeah, it's pretty intense," agreed Senator, "but I think it might be working already..." I sure hoped so. Anything so strong must have some kick to it. I handed him a book and we both continued to peruse.

"Ha-- yeah right..." I could tell Senator was reading trail difficulty ratings. Our experience has taught us that New Hampshire's scale is shifted from that of every other hiking region. On most lists, a rating of 'easy' means that a trail is practically accessible for wheelchairs, strollers, and danger-seeking four-year olds. A New Hampshire 'easy', on the other hand, means steep inclines, roots, and rocks. You had better have good boots, be in halfway decent physical shape, and allow at least 1½ times the stated guide book times before you even consider it. Who are these people-- mountain goats?

*   *   *

Given the events of the previous day, we had no unreal expectations for Thursday. Thus, we were quite surprised to wake up to Senator feeling so good. I actually felt pretty good myself, too.* This opened the day for new opportunities.

While eating breakfast, we worked on a compromise somewhere between climbing a thousand feet and vegetating. We decided to start with a morning drive on the Kancamagus Highway for scenery and potential moose spotting. Then we would attempt an easier walk to the top of Sabbaday Falls. From there, we would play it by ear. Agreed. We finished the last of our coffee, grabbed the backpack, and got into the car.

Lily Pond, you may recall from one of my previous books, is touted by the guide books as a "popular place to see moose". We had stopped there several times on our

---

* Senator and I later admitted to each other that we both figured he would be down for the day (or two). We halfway expected the rest of the trip to consist of reading and playing dice games in bed.

first trip to the White Mountains in 2012. Then we had stopped a few more times when we returned in 2014. At no point did we see moose, despite the peaceful seclusion of the spot and the plentiful, presumably delicious water plants. Why bother again, you may wonder? I reasoned that perhaps it just wasn't a summer hang-out. Maybe in early spring it would be a hot spot for activity-- kind of a moose singles joint.

"There's the turn, ahead," I pointed out to Senator. We parked in the familiar turn-off and sat in silence, scanning the horizon in all directions. I adjusted our binoculars, but all they did was magnify the fact that the pond was 100% mooseless. I guess not seeing moose there had become a tradition. If we ever come back, I'm going to throw that guide book into the pond!

A short drive along the same scenic highway brought us to Sabbaday Falls. Not only would it be a relatively short walk to a dramatic cascade, but it would be good for research purposes, too. In the summer, especially on a weekend, the place is buzzing with tourists. Going there in late March would provide another good indication of how tourist numbers compared in the off-season.

Pulling into the parking lot gave us our first clue. Only two other vehicles were there, as opposed to the usual twenty or more. One was empty; the other had a family just climbing out. Good-- we would have the place virtually to ourselves.

Upon climbing out of our own vehicle, we immediately noticed the mound of ice blocking the parking lot from the trail. It was only a few feet tall, but it was very slick and took some maneuvering to cross. From there it was less than a minute until we were on the trail. Though it was steep, for the most part we were hiking up dirt. Ice lined the sides, but the center was safe. We would just have to resist the temptation to go to the edge and look over the railing, so we did not fall into the falls.

As we continued to make our way up, the dirt parts of the trail became fewer and further between. Ice was now the dominant carpet. Gradually we slowed down to a cautious pace. It was working, but certainly not as I had envisioned on the normally-simple trail. More importantly, it occurred to me that, if it was this hard to get up the ice safely, it would be a heck of a time getting down, *safely*. I looked at Senator, who's return expression told me that he was already concurring with my thoughts. No family meeting was necessary; we carefully turned around, balancing and gripping any useful objects.

Sabbaday Falls, or more accurately, our failed attempt to reach it, determined our next item on the day's agenda. We had proven we were physically capable for more hiking, but if we could not even manage a basic walk up a wide trail, crampons were in order. Back into Lincoln we drove, stopping at the first outfitter store we passed. It looked like we were about to add a third vacation souvenir to the Wayne's Market gloves and the Rite Aid Salonpas.

Inside Lahout's, I felt outside my element. For starters, every other store in town seemed to have some variation of the same name, so I was suspicious of a monopolistic conspiracy. I was pretty sure we would be overpaying for whatever gear we bought, but I also did not want to waste time comparison shopping. In the second place, everything I saw looked like it had been designed for more intense purposes than stick-to-the-trail day hiking.

A few minutes later, a nice man offered assistance. After getting a feel for our needs, and doing an excellent job of hiding any mirth he may have felt at our ill-preparedness, he led us to a wall. From it hung a tangle of what appeared to be thick rubber bands and spikes. *Okay...* Then he explained the three different levels of crampons. *So an education is included. This is good.* On one end of the spectrum were the ones for level walking on ice, which would basically only get us across the parking lots to the trail heads. At the other end of the crampon scale were the ones for people who, for reasons unknown, scaled walls of ice. It was a Goldilocks moment. "We'll take the middle ones."

As the man helped us secure the rubber straps and chains around our hiking boots, I could see how they would provide much more traction. They fit perfectly. Now it was a Cinderella moment. With kid-sized feet, I may never own a pair of spiked high heels, but damn it, I would have a pair of spiked hiking boots.*

Armed with metal and confidence, we proceeded to the Mount Pemigewasett Trail. The difference was amazing. In less than five minutes we were used to our crampons, and in another five minutes we were purposely looking for ice to tread. *What an invention! I'm going to wear them everywhere.*

The real advantage came during the last twenty minutes before the summit. We had ascended into a slightly cooler zone, but it was just enough of a difference to

---

* I was also glad to later learn that we had paid a fair price for our crampons. I would hate to think we had paid the suckers' rate.

prevent the ice from melting. The steep mound could not be avoided there. The dense trees on the sides prevented alternate trails, while the trees along the trail were too far apart to grab onto. Without our spikes (and possibly the muscle cream), we might still be edging our way down the mountain.

We celebrated our success back at the car with an impromptu tailgate party. The fruit, cheese sticks, and water were flowing. "Woo-hoo! Spring break!" yelled Senator, as he pretended to throw our garbage into the lot. No one lying around on a beach could possibly be having this much fun.

It was only 2:00pm, but it was starting to sprinkle. Rather than attempt a hike that would end up soggy, we started a driving a tour of several small towns on the northwest part of the mountain range. Ultimately, we just wanted to explore the mountains and find a good place to sip some coffee, but I also had another motive. This was the area where I someday hoped to retire, so I figured we might as well begin the long-term process of narrowing down the towns.*

Our first destination was Bethlehem, which is the highest elevation town east of the Rocky Mountains. That distinction alone won it some points, as mountain altitudes meaner cooler, drier summers. It was a quiet little town, with neatly kept homes and a tiny main drag. There were no big stores, but such conveniences could be found within a reasonable distance.

From there we entered the outer limits of the

---

* Plus, if the state of Illinois implodes-- which is likely at any given moment-- we might be moving sooner than expeced.

booming metropolis of Littleton. With its massive population of roughly 6,000 inhabitants, you can understand why its downtown was thriving. In all seriousness, though, it is amazing that the area could support so many small businesses. It was clean, well-planned, convenient, and active. By contrast, new, independent businesses in our hometown of about the same size struggled to survive beyond their first year. After much consideration over a cup at the local java shop, we attributed the tale of two cities to a difference in values, as well as the fact that they existed in two oppositely managed states.

Leaving Littleton, we headed south on the lesser-traveled highways, past the big box retail establishments that were pushed to the far outskirts of town. After driving among more river streams, we entered the smallest village on the list. Sugar Hill was affordable and still had incredible mountain views from many of the properties. There was not much in the way of services, but Littleton was close, and Harman's Cheese Shop could keep a body stocked in enough cheese, crackers, pickles, and country goods to survive a few snow-bound days.

Our last excursion took us through Franconia. Upon first impression, it did not seem like a place where we would fit in. Though it looked attractive, it was apparent that a lot of money was floating around, and it did not feel as casual as surrounding towns.* We were still keeping open minds, but they were closing quickly as a family of oblivious bicyclists meandered around the highway. They

---

* Cue the indignant letters from warm, wonderful, hospitable Franconians.

were annoying and dangerously daring as they ignored the cars coming around curves and up and down the rolling hills. "That's it-- no Franconia," declared Senator. *Done.*

We drove back to the inn and made our way from the parking area to our room. Before we reached the house we ran into Karen, the owner who had been out of town. She was now back at the helm and in command. Immediately after introducing herself to us and asking if we needed anything, she turned to the construction workers who had been doing some renovations on the building and instructed them to stop working so they would not bother us. We assured her that we did not care if there was some noise,* but she had made up her mind firmly as to our comfort needs.

Senator checked some business correspondence and I perused a few local menus before we ventured out again. We decided to try an international café that had received consistently good reviews. As expected, the food was good, but it was also overpriced. I mean, how much should you really expect to pay for some seasoned veggies and smashed beans? Next time I'll just take my greens inside of a giant calzone.

We took a short walk after dinner, along the main street in town. It was brisk, and I think we were the only non-locals around. I was getting spoiled by these low-key nights. Already I could sense the dread of returning to work in the chaos of Chicago. *Can't we just move 100 recording clients here?...*

*   *   *

All too fast, it was Friday, our last full day in the

---

* She should hear some of the things we have recorded.

White Mountains for the foreseeable future. Though we were motivated by Thursday's hiking success and the fact that we felt great, we did not want to overdo it, just in case. The next day we would be sitting in the car for at least ten hours, which could be extremely uncomfortable if we were too sore. Additionally, we were not sure the sky would cooperate. As it debated whether to rain or not, we planned a few mild walks.

Leaving town, we again hopped on the scenic Kancamagus Highway. No, we did not waste time scouting out nonexistent moose; we had finally learned our lesson in that department. Instead, we pulled into the parking lot for the Forest Discovery Trail. The short loop, which served as an introductory sampling of the ecology of the local national forest, had been our very first trail in New Hampshire, four years before. There were more elevation changes than I had remembered, giving us a nice little warm-up. There was also a brook than ran under a wooden bridge, creating an opening to a deeper view into the woods. Both times we walked the trail there was not another soul on it, giving it an especially fairy tale-like quality.

One of the benefits of flatter trails is the ability to talk with the person with whom you are hiking, as opposed to vaguely nodding while panting. A couple can also hold hands, as opposed to grasping tree parts or extending arms creatively for balance. We continued to take advantage of these features on another level trail with which we were already familiar-- Lincoln Woods. As the former site of railroad tracks, the Lincoln Woods Trail parallels a river and runs from The Kanc into the back country. It is the main trunk of several trails that later split off and wander to remote regions. Until that point, it is suitable for casual promenades* and probably cross-country skiing if snow is present. It is not, however, suitable for a family of four who looks far too clean and nicely dressed to attempt to push a stroller through the mud to reach the trail's beginning. *I think someone missed the turn for Disney World...*

As we returned to the trail head, we scrambled the boulders that led down to the river bank. The wind was cool coming off of the water, preventing the last pockets of snow in the lower elevations from melting. In one direction, we could see the path up to the ranger station. In the other direction, the river seemed to run endlessly into wilderness. Alas, the wilderness was for another day, but I thought a brief visit to the ranger station might be enlightening.

I was correct. Inside the small log cabin were two gentlemen seated near a wooden table, both drinking coffee. The first, who was perhaps in his mid-to-late 60s, was clearly the ranger on duty. He greeted us right away and asked if we needed any information or help. Meanwhile, his sidekick, who was about eighty and looked like he had just returned from a long stint in an isolated mountain cabin, just rocked in his chair contentedly.

"No, we're just stopping in to say 'Hi' after a morning walk," I answered.

"Beautiful, isn't it?" he asked.

I was not sure if he meant the scenery or the weather,† but either way, it got me going. "We've been to all

---

* even with a broken toe, as Senator can attest from two years earlier

† In New Hampshire, a 'beautiful' day can range anywhere from 0 to 75 degrees Fahrenheit, with anything from a mostly sunny sky to a

fifty states, and this is my favorite spot in the country," I volunteered. I could see Senator nodding in agreement out of the corner of my eye, and probably simultaneously wondering how long I would go on about it. At this, the second gentleman lit up, beaming in solidarity. We were in.

The younger ranger continued to comment. "Yes, you can go all over, and see lots of natural wonders, but there's nowhere any prettier..." He went on to tell us how he had grown up in southern New England, then moved to Missouri (poor guy!), then settled in New Hampshire as soon as he retired. I told him that was my goal, too.* When he informed us that 80% of the state was still rural, with little chance of changing, I may have completely passed the point of no return. I think Senator might just be getting a little hooked, too...

As if on cue, when we left the ranger station it started to rain. Satisfied at having walked several miles, we decided to treat ourselves to an afternoon of browsing bookstores. The first place we stopped had changed significantly since we were there the last time. (Come to think of it, it is really the only thing about the town that did change.) It now smelled like stale cigarettes, and though the owner was not smoking, he was ranting about something on the phone, adding to the oddness of the place. Junk that had nothing to do with books filled the front quarter of the store. Since we had time to kill, though, we wandered to the back to glance through the titles. After ten minutes, nothing caught our eye, so we started to leave.

Bad timing. The owner concluded his phone call in

_____

light blizzard. More proof that these are my people.

* minus the Missouri incarceration

just enough time to acknowledge us. He actually was friendly, and he asked us if we had found anything, despite our obviously empty hands.

"No, not really..." we smiled, anxious to make our exit lest he try to assist further.

"Yeah, sorry," he muttered, while stepping outside to light up. "We just need a flood to get rid of it all!" he declared, gesturing the demise of the entirety of the stock with his hands. Then he laughed, so we did, too, as we awkwardly slipped past him toward the parking lot. I have been to a lot of bookstores in my lifetime, but it was the first time I ever ran into an owner who had zero interest in what he was selling. Perhaps a flood *would* be his best solution...

After leaving Crappy Books,* we headed to Maps-Books.† While chatting with Alan at breakfast, we had learned that the owner of the bookstore was also the recognized local expert on trails, hiking, mountaineering, and all things White Mountains. He had even published several respected books on the subject. We were looking forward to browsing his map selection and picking his brain on a few key questions. Among them was whether the infamous 'black fly season' was merely a nuisance or a full-blown hiking debilitation. Unfortunately, Maps-Books was closed that day, so the mysteries of the mountains would have to be unraveled at a later date.

There was a pause in the showers, so we drove to the north side of the mountains to attempt another short hike.

_____

*   not actual name

†   also not actual name, but that's what the sign in the window said, and it was considerably more noticeable than the sign with the real name of the place

By the time we arrived, however, it was raining. We continued past the historic train station and parked in a lot across from a picturesque pond. Our initial thought was to wait out the rain and then walk again. When it started pouring, we changed the plan to eating cheese while sitting in the parked car, in view of the Silver Cascade flume. Good thing we had our emergency picnic kit with us.

When it became certain that no more outdoor activities would take place during this trip, we drove back toward our home base, stopping at a third bookstore. Books-Books* was a cramped and damp portal of many wonderful and intriguing titles. Inside, seated in a sort of booth, the owner chatted away at himself, or any one of us browsers, or no one in particular. I actually found a few local books I was interested in, but they were far overpriced, presumably due to their distinction of being "signed by author". If the author was Robert Frost, well, okay. If the author, as was the case, is someone no one outside of town has ever heard of, not so much. By that math, my books could be worth a small fortune. Where's a pen?!

Three strikes and we were done with bookstores. We had been wanting coffee ever since we met the rangers at the Lincoln Woods station, so it was time to duck into a café. Fortunately, we found one that was open for another hour or so. As 3:00pm is not a prime coffee-drinking hour, we had the place to ourselves. The experience was significantly enhanced by the carrot cupcakes with loads of cream cheese frosting. *There goes any calories we burned off during the morning.*

---

*   also not actual name; same reason as Maps-Books

The rain took a short break, but we weren't falling for it. We used the remainder of the afternoon to drive south and see what those small villages looked like. 'Village' turned out to be a stretch, as they were mainly rural residential areas with more trees, brooks, and rocks. I could be content somewhere like that, provided I didn't live next to the unofficial junkyards that seemed a little too prevalent on some people's properties.

When we had exhausted that region, Senator suggested a game of Farkel. Not wanting to waste time in our room, however, he took us back to Franconia State Park, so we could play 'Farkel with a View' in the car. A paper plate served as a flat surface on which to roll dice, and I kept score alongside of the trip notes I had been writing. Mountains surrounded us, and I was enjoying our game, but something about rain streaming down windows always makes me sleepy. Senator was getting tired too, so we finished our game and drove to our final stop before calling it a night.

According to a few publications, at some point while in New Hampshire, one must make a pilgrimage to a Common Man restaurant. The local chain is noted for decent, home-style food in a rustic, cozy atmosphere. That sounded good on a chilly spring night, so we went in and got a table. As we waited for our food in the dark dining room, we were told to help ourselves to the cheese-and-cracker station downstairs. I could understand the appeal of the place given that feature alone.

It continued to rain hard, offering an appropriate backdrop against which to unwind. Our conversation dwindled somewhat as relaxation passed the boundary into tiredness. I looked at Senator across the table and wondered if there was any chance that we would actually move there someday. He seemed to think it possible. I pondered a cautious optimism about the whole affair. Only time would tell.

Our server approached, interrupting my thoughts. "Will that be all tonight?"

"Yes, thanks," *We have everything we need.*

*   *   *

Saturday morning's breakfast brought our last meal in the shadow of the mountains. We savored it, grateful for the chance to rejuvenate for a week. Behind our table sat another younger couple. They were the only other guests who had been at the inn during our entire stay. We could overhear them discussing their ambitious plans to hike one of the 4,000-footers. I thought about interjecting when I heard the girl mention that they "probably wouldn't need to worry about ice this time of year", but it did not seem my place. They, too, would soon have to add 'crampons' to their vocabulary.

We thanked our hosts and started south on Route 3, avoiding Route 118, which had given us a harrowing hour on our drive into town earlier in the week. From there it was a lazy ride around the countryside for most of the first four hours, until we reached I-90. In New York, rural highways end and the mad dash across the state begins. On the welcome sign at the state line it might as well read, "Vacation over; accelerate toward home".

The day's travels were non-eventful. We drove along and occasionally listened to another installment of a cd lecture series about the early founders of the American

Colonies and the Revolution. It rained a little on and off, but nothing slowed our pace. We were even pleased to find that the traffic was not backed up at the Buffalo toll plaza, for a change. We were not pleased, however, to see a large, white mass rolling in from the west.

You know by now, Reader, that I love snow. Even so, I did not relish the prospect of encountering a blizzard, especially when our route called for us to follow the east side of Lake Erie for hours. Throw in the Cleveland hotel hell hole*, and we were facing all the ingredients for a fairly miserable evening. Senator gripped the wheel as we entered the blowing snow, slowing down with the rest of the traffic.

I flipped through the radio stations in search of a forecast. As we could see, it was not going to pass by quickly. In fact, it was getting worse. Predictions on the amount of expected snow ranged from 6"-8", but all reports agreed that the advisory was in effect until 5:00am. There were also the high winds with which to contend, making it an easy decision to look for lodging as soon as we crossed into Pennsylvania.

It was a relief when we pulled off the highway into the lot of a decent chain hotel. We were in Northeast, Pennsylvania, which should have told us something about the town, as it was located in the exact northwest corner of the state. There was a lot of nothing around, but as visibility was so poor we would not have seen anything anyway, we

---

* Twice before we had made the mistake of ending our day's journey near Cleveland. For some reason, all of the hotels in the area were either booked solid, ridiculously overpriced, or dumpy enough to make sleeping in the car appealing.

were grateful to be there. As Senator parked under the canopy of the entryway, I battled the 70mph winds to get out of the car and into the hotel's lobby.

I brushed the snow off of my shirt while requesting a room. "All of our rooms are nonsmoking," began the woman behind the counter. "I do have availability... either two double beds, or it looks like I have one king left," she offered.

"That's great!" I answered. "I'll take the king; there's just two of us." As I began to produce my license and credit card, things started to get interesting. I had noticed a man, whom I will simply call 'Cheech', demanding a room from the other woman behind the counter. While I was securing a room from the first woman, I was not really paying attention to what was transpiring next to us, but when Cheech heard me accept the room with the king bed, the sheet hit the fan.

Possibly due to his apparent affinity for cannabis,* or possibly due to his altered perception of his relative importance to the establishment, he started causing problems. His main accusation was that the desk attendant had not informed him that a king bed was still available. She retorted by explaining that it did not show up on her computer screen. This led to louder, angrier protests from the man, citing the fact that he was "a very good customer". She, in turn, added more facts. In addition to him not having a credit card to put on file, there had been past complaints about him "always smelling like pot". I was beginning to wonder what I had gotten us into.

In between a smattering of expletives, he continued.

_____

* medical, I'm sure

"Hey... listen... everybody's got their problems. But I don't even care. Gimme my money back! I don't have to take this. Wait 'till I get a hold of the company! I'll have both of you fired!" The woman behind the counter did not back down. I think she was extra motivated by the potential to be rid of him for good, as it was apparent that this scene had taken place before. Narrowing her eyes with a determined finality, she literally threw his wad of cash back at him.

Just then, Senator walked in. I figured he was about due; I had been gone too long for a simple transaction. Cheech stormed past him, swearing and leaving a scent trail worthy of Pepe Le Pew. I had to admit, I was glad Senator had not come in a moment earlier. I feel certain he would have punched Cheech, and I feel certain Cheech would have gone down in a single blow. It might have complicated the evening to have to drive to a police station in a blizzard to bail out my Essential Other.

With lodging secured, we turned our attention to food. According to a quick internet search, we were next to a restaurant with mediocre (at best) reviews. The other option was a gas station a few blocks away, which lost out due to not being able to see it through the blowing snow, and not wanting chips and candy bars for dinner. Although, for the record, the health factor probably would have been equal. Thus, we hiked next door.

I cannot remember the name of the restaurant, but we can call it Grandma's Basement, as it immediately evoked the feel of a 1970s recreation room where one would have played with cousins after a holiday meal. The paneled, slightly musty entryway led us into a larger, carpeted 1980s dining room, complete with an abundance of muted-tone artificial floral arrangements. As the hostess/server/cashier sat us, I could see the blizzard raging even stronger than before. It was good to know we were done driving for the night. Had we gone exploring further afield, we might not have made it back to the hotel.

As promised by the online descriptions, Grandma's Basement took great pride in its hospitality and its ability to fry just about anything. Naturally, we ordered a fried veggie basket appetizer to nibble while our pizza was baking. (When in Northeast Rome...) As we waited, we chatted about the past week and enjoyed the gas fireplace glow. In the end, the appetizer was rather greasy, the pizza was rather awful, the server was rather sweet, and we were rather glad to anticipate a good night's sleep.

Inside the hotel we brushed the heavy, wet snowflakes off of our jackets. It wasn't long before we were in pajamas lazing around and watching yet another unrealistic house-hunting program. The clueless couple-of-the-week nervously deliberated over which house to buy and renovate. Their anxiety was increased by the constraints of their $800,000 budget. I did not envy them one bit as we drifted off to the howling wind outside our window.

*   *   *

Sunday morning I could see a thin stream of sunlight slicing through the slim gap in the curtain. Drawing the drapes aside, the full spectrum lit up the room blindingly. It was still breezy out, but there was no sign of the storm that had sent everyone in for an early Saturday night. Now it just looked clean, and snow reflected sun. I sat back on the bed as Senator started to emerge from a groggy pre-waking fog.

In less than an hour, (ten minutes of which was spent scraping ice and snow from its solidified shell around the car,) we were on the road. The rest of the drive was easy, until we reached Chicago. The south suburbs are always a mess, not unlike the north and west suburbs.* During our week-long trip we had encountered torrential rain, hail, frozen fog, and a blizzard. It was a little unexpected to enter our town under a calm sky, and to walk into our 65°F home. In fact, we were both starting to sweat.

---

* East of the city, it's usually not bad, but that may have something to do with the fact that it's a giant lake. Given enough years, traffic will probably be a disaster there as well.

Chapter 4
Edgy:
Late June 2016

Just as spring break had turned out differently than anticipated, our travel plans for summer changed as well. 2016 marked the third attempt by Senator and me to see my parents at their cabin in Canada. 2014 did not work out due to a scheduling conflict; we had missed our 'reservation window'. The next year brought the opportunity to go to Germany, putting off Canada for another year.* Thus, 2016 was the year.

In my classic style, I reasoned that as long as we were going to western Ontario, we might as well swing by Montana. Despite plenty of road trips and hiking, we had never been to Glacier National Park. Several relatives and numerous online reviews highly recommended it. Plus, Al Gore kept blathering on about the glaciers melting, so it seemed like a good time to go. If we made a big loop, we could take in a few sites in South Dakota on the way out

---

* I still feel badly about disappointing my parents. They were quite patient and understanding!

and see my parents on the way back. Heck, we had been to all fifty states, why not start on the Canadian provinces?

For months I planned the big road trip west. It would take about two weeks, which we loosely scheduled in late July. There would be a lot to think about, and a lot of junk to bring since we would be camping for part of the trip. I also wanted to exchange some cash, since the spring brought a good return on the American dollar.

Sometime around April, just as we were getting back into the swing of things from the last trip, one of Senator's clients approached him with a proposal for a live recording project. The event was an attractive gig, but it would take place right in the middle of our trip. While my first instinct was a dismayed *Noooooooo*, I knew how important the job was to Senator. Slowly I had been learning the blessings and challenges of self-employment, and so, at 70mph, the floor was opened for discussion as we drove to another show.

As passionately as I can get attached to travel, and as annoyed as Senator can get with my occasional frustration with his unpredictable schedule, I have to give us both points for keeping cool heads. No raised voices or disappointments ensued. Ideas and counter-offers flowed. In the end, we agreed to split the road trip into two smaller trips, neither of which would interfere with his job. The more I thought about it, the more I realized how much better it would be to pack and plan for two smaller trips as opposed to one big trip. *Actually, why hadn't I planned it that way to begin with?* I wish all such conflicts could be so easily remedied.

Satisfied with our plan, we plugged away through

April, May, and the first few weeks of June. As a result of having a very mild winter, my school year did not add any make-up days for snow cancellations, giving me an extra week of break. I was done teaching my short summer program a few days before we left, giving me an open weekend to get ready. Naturally, Senator was booked the night before we had to leave, but we would not have to get up ridiculously early.

*   *   *

On a sunny Monday morning, while the rest of our little town was off to more productive pursuits, Senator and I left for a westward adventure. It was nice not to be leaving at the crack of dawn, for a change. We even had time to take a fifteen-minute side excursion through our local state park. As expected, it was quiet, save for the birds and the light swoosh of a deer darting back into the woods.

Not as expected, however, was the very unquiet highway. As we headed toward Iowa, in the opposite direction of Chicago, we were surprised at the volume of traffic. Of course some of it was commercial vehicles and some of it was vacationers like ourselves, but I really couldn't imagine what made up the rest. It was certainly more traffic than I had ever seen in corn country. Had Sioux Falls suddenly become a holiday hot spot?

We continued westward through Iowa. Somewhere past the halfway point in the state, the heavens opened and it poured. This was not a problem. The hail, however, was. So now our six-month-old car had been hailed on twice. "Nothing we can do about it now," said Senator. I nodded in agreement. Actually, it did not seem to be hitting as hard

187

as it had during the last trip, and that left no visible damage, so maybe we would luck out again.

At I-29 we exited northward, leaving the rain and a good clipping pace behind. For the first time since leaving the house we slowed to less than the speed limit. Traffic then merged to one lane and eventually stopped. Seeing orange barriers ahead, we assumed it was construction, the ubiquitous specter of summertime road travel.

After sitting for fifteen minutes or so, we began a steady crawl. As we reached the source of the bottleneck, we realized that there was no construction. Instead, two state troopers monitored a harrowing scene. Whether other vehicles were involved we could not tell, but the blackened, charred shell of a tour bus was all that remained along the side of the road. We hoped it was a vehicle fire that took place after everyone was safely evacuated, but the blown out windows and the warped steel between them almost suggested an explosion.*

Soon we crossed into South Dakota, where the speed limit was a generous 80mph. There was not much opportunity to explore the vast, fast freedom, however, due to the fact that we had almost reached our first stop. Vermillion, South Dakota was home to the University of South Dakota, which was home to the National Music Museum. Formerly known as the Shrine to Music, I had stumbled upon the site in an old travel guide book I had purchased at a library sale. Verifying its current existence via internet reviews, it sounded like a hidden gem suitable for anyone who appreciated music or unique instruments.

* As we never heard any news about the accident, we will continue to hope that there were no fatalities.

188

Onto the itinerary it went.

We first drove by the museum so we would not waste any time looking for it in the morning. As it had not sprouted legs and self-relocated since my research, we drove up the road to our motel. I will here interject to explain that, having hundreds of hours of booking experience, I am no novice. I generally have a very good handle on reading between the lines, filtering through reviews, and choosing the appropriate accommodations for the situation. Sometimes I go with a chain hotel. Other times I reserve a cozy inn or splurge on a bed and breakfast. Since we only needed a bed and bathroom before heading on to other adventures, I opted for a modest motel. In this case, I bombed.

Don't get me wrong, Reader. Many motels are perfectly fine, and even offer a mom-and-pop charm that is increasingly rare on the American roadside. What I reserved was not that. For the first time, my Trip Advisor pals had steered me wrong. Unfortunately, to save ten bucks, I had prepaid.

I will say (and did, in my subsequent review) that we never felt unsafe. Likewise, the man behind the front desk was very friendly, if not at all fluent in English. The problem was the overall vibe of uncleanliness. Likewise, I will go on record as saying that Senator and I thoroughly enjoy a good curry, but if the smell is magnified a hundred times to the point of suffocation, it suddenly loses its appeal.

We agreed to at least look at the room, especially since everything else in town seemed to be sold out. Inside it was definitely outdated, but there were no freeloading critters, and the bed passed the bed bug test.* *Well, points for that, I guess.* I went to inspect the bathroom and found hairs in the shower. *Bluh-ack!* On the other hand, the sink and toilet looked clean.

I sighed and asked Senator for his opinion. In the end we chose to stay, with the compromise of sanitizing the shower and keeping clothes on at all other times. Ironically, there was a high-end television in the room. Still, I was not about to inquire after the complimentary breakfast that had been advertised. I could only imagine what that would have been.

We left to get some dinner, killing as much time as possible. Immediately after eating, Senator started to feel the effects of allergies coming on. Armed with over-the-counter antihistamines, we returned to the motel room, hoping to fall asleep as fast as possible. As we pulled into the parking lot, we could see three generations of the family who owned the joint smiling and playing badminton in the front drop-off area. The place still reeked as we darted toward the hallway.

*   *   *

Needless to say, we were up early. Getting to the museum when it opened, as I had hoped we would, would not be a problem. Two hours before it opened, we checked out of the motel, which was only a mile away. The last thing I noticed as we left was a sign asking guests to please rate the motel on popular travel websites. *Oh don't worry; I*

---

* According to a bed bug expert: go to the foot corners of the bed. Completely strip away all layers of bedding and give your eyes a moment to adjust. As long as you don't see any black dots around, you should be fine. If the sheets happen to be black, run!

190

will. Grabbing coffee at a local fast food restaurant gave us time to regroup and welcome the sunny morning. It would be hot later, but in the meantime we could take a walk around the attractive campus. It was a quiet Tuesday morning in a historic neighborhood. Apparently no one was awake or out, which was exactly the way we like it. Although, judging by the large branches that lined much of the curb, the locals may have just been relaxing after heavy storms the previous week.

When our circle was complete, we waited on the museum steps for a few minutes before the curator unlocked the door. Inside we found two floors of wonder. The collection more than met expectations. Thousands of instruments ranged from traditional ethnic pieces, to rare Renaissance strings, to bizarre creations and monumental firsts.*†

Some instruments were owned by famous musicians or composers, while others knew a limited and obscure existence before somehow finding their way to the southeast corner of South Dakota. We even found out more about an unusual guitar Senator had acquired several years ago. My favorite story behind an instrument involved an American banjo player who was sent to Germany under the guise of performing a concert. Actually, he was there as a decoy to allow Allied spy photography.

---

*How anyone played the first electric piano without electrocuting himself is a mystery to me after seeing the jumble of metal and wires.

† Wow-- an unprecedented double footnote, sharing a bit of trivia: did you know that the drum 'kit' developed in response to sound effects men needing several different types of drums and percussive gadgets to enhance radio shows? I bet most heavy metal fans don't.

I highly recommend the National Music Museum. While it would more aptly be called the American Instrument Museum, one can gain hours of education surrounded by inspiring and creative methods to produce sound. All in all, the experience made up for the crappy motel room. Now if we could just get Senator to stop sneezing...

It was midday when we left the museum, and the sun was high as we stair-stepped our way up to I-90. Joining one of the main thoroughfares of the nation, we were soon zipping through the wide open prairie. Senator settled in for a nap, and I took the opportunity to settle in to cruise control. It is funny how speed is relative. With such wide open spaces, and so few fellow cars on the road, it felt like we were only doing about 65mph. *Hooray for cars that get great gas mileage!*

We were making good time, mainly due to the ample speed limit and lack of idiots. People drove fast and stayed out of each others' way. I can respect that. Thus, we had enough time to take a side trip through the Badlands.

It had been twelve years since we had hiked in Badlands National Park, but the eerie, ever-changing spires were just as unearthly as I had remembered. Jutting out of the otherwise flat prairie, they must have caused more than one pioneer to utter profanities when they entered the horizon. Senator rolled down the windows to relish the dry heat, but we soon added the air conditioning to balance it out. Color-wise, afternoon is probably the least interesting time to see the Badlands, but we enjoyed the hour detour nonetheless. While we did not have time to hike, we did see a few buffalo and plenty of prairie dogs.

Thankfully, no rattlesnakes were in view, although that could have been because they were chasing prairie dogs down their holes. I will choose to believe they (rattlesnakes) have recently gone extinct, the news somehow evading the national press.

From the Badlands we drove to the Black Hills. Traffic picked up a bit, and I was glad we were not traveling during the busiest week of the year, when Sturgis becomes a mecca for motorcyclists. Besides the dramatic pine-covered granite, the most interesting sight was a license plate from Virginia that read "1 M NAKED". That one never would have made it past the Department of Motor Vehicles censors in Illinois, but we had a chuckle over it.[*]

Soon we were driving the curvy and sometimes confusing roads around Deadwood and Lead. Whereas Deadwood took the more touristy path of kitsch and casinos, Lead is still relatively quiet, with just as much fascinating history. The first thing you learn is how to correctly pronounce it. Say 'leed' as opposed to 'led'. The lead refers to veins of gold that were leads to greater deposits. Plus, there were no lead mines anywhere near the town.

We found our inn and met the friendly owner, who was excited to share knowledge of her town with us. The inn itself was a very historic building that had served as both town hall and office headquarters for the gold mine across the street. It also proved to be an immaculately clean building, which we appreciated more than the owner knew. If you're going to have a crappy motel night, better to have

---

[*]   Yes, of course I looked. And no, of course she wasn't.

it on the first night of vacation and get it over with.

After settling in, we took a stroll a few doors down to grab some dinner. Without many viable options, we took a wooden booth in a rustic western-style pub. The tall, solid-looking dining room surrounded a stone fireplace with the requisite moose head watching over us approvingly as we ate our veggie burgers. Even more enjoyable was the comfortable, dry breeze that was floating in through the open doors. No oppressive humidity. No stealthy mosquitoes. Just a peaceful summer evening in the Black Hills.

Following dinner we walked across the street and continued toward the remains of the Homestake Mine, which relieved the earth of gold for over 100 years. Like a displaced ziggurat, layers of industrial roads were still stacked, as if they had been in service that very day. Though the grounds were strictly off-limits, the landowners did provide an open viewing panel through which curious travelers could peek. Declaring Tuesday a greater success than Monday had been, we retired to our room for the night.

Allergies and the lack of quality sleep the previous night sent Senator to bed fairly early. That was just as well. It was better to knock it out sooner, before we got to the camping part of the trip. Until I could doze off, I turned on the television and scrolled through meaningless shows. Eventually I stopped at Carol Burnett reruns.

I was not paying too much attention, until somewhere between Harvey Korman trying to make Tim Conway laugh, and Tim Conway returning the favor, a red message flashed across the screen. Three loud beeps accompanied it. Generally programs are interrupted in this fashion when there is a severe storm warning. At home, that can mean a tornado, and the viewer is highly advised to seek shelter. Knowing that the Black Hills are not in tornado country, and a possible moderate storm had been predicted for the overnight hours, I did not think much of it. *So we'll probably get a bunch of rain or, with our new car's luck, hail,* I thought.

I was about to dismiss it when I read the words running across the screen. It was not weather-related, but a "civil emergency". The voice of the local chief of police overrode the show's dialogue, and my pulse quickened as I wondered if there had been a terrorist attack on a U.S. city. My mind raced to Chicago and our family and friends in the surrounding areas. I was just about to wake Senator up when the details halted me mid-turn.

Thankfully, there had been no terrorist attack. Strangely though, the chief of police announced that the people of Martin, South Dakota would be under an imposed curfew from 2:00am until 5:30am. We were not in Martin, and we certainly were not planning on going out in the pre-dawn hours, so the only course of action was to ignore the message. Before I knew it, the cartoon janitor was mopping the floor beneath the credits.

*　　　*　　　*

Wednesday I woke up with a help-your-fellow-traveler idea. We had had to purchase a pass to drive through the Badlands, and it was good for a full week. Since we would not be returning that way, I would give it to the inn's owner, and perhaps she could pass it on to someone who could use it. At least somebody could save fifteen bucks.

My idea came into play with perfect timing as we stepped outside our room to get coffee. Near the front desk, the owner was talking with a mother and daughter who were heading to the Badlands after visiting Lead. Perfect! I gently interrupted, gave them the pass, refused their offer to pay, and accepted their gratitude. *Gotta' stick it to the Man once in a while...* We all chatted for a few minutes, and then went our separate ways.

As Senator was finishing his last sips of coffee, I started walking toward our car. Upon coming around the corner, I saw the mother and daughter driving out from the inn's parking lot. I signaled for them to roll down their window. They smiled and waved, assuming I was just saying good-bye again. When I repeated and exaggerated my gesture, they took the hint, stopped, and lowered the window. I didn't say a word. I just grinned and handed them the tennis shoes and water bottle they had inadvertently left on the car roof. "Now we *really* owe you big time!" the mother said. We had a good laugh and parted ways. I hope they had a great time in the Badlands. I also hope they didn't forget their shoes there.

Our first stop of the day was only a few doors down. Now that we had viewed the site of the Homestake gold mine, we would learn the background at the Black Hills Mining Museum. At depths reaching 8,000 feet below ground, Homestake was founded after gold leads were discovered in the late 1870s. Naturally, the prosperous ground beneath the town sparked a boom. The rush was on, but no one was bothering to back fill the area. The ground was so mined out at one point that buildings in

196

town became unstable, due to lack of foundational support. The company solved this potentially deadly crisis by buying up the damaged areas and demolishing them.

Overall it was a safe mine, and wages were good, even including free hospitalization for employees as far back as the early 1900s. At least, wages were ample compared to other common careers, but the men more than earned them. When the mine first began operation, a 'single jack' operated with only two candles for his extended shift. Once 'double jacks' (two-man teams) began, one man had the burden of using the sledgehammer, while the other had the danger of placing his thumb on the bit. This allowed the very dim light to reflect off of his painted nail to mark the hammer's target. Then the brave soul pulled his thumb away just in time-- or not.

Amazing engineering and planning feats were around every corner of the tour. A walkway opened to small rooms, each modeled to illustrate various aspects of the drilling, hauling, and elevating process. A ventilation system had to be installed to prevent lack of oxygen and to cool the deepest areas, where the geothermal heat reached 130°F. Tool repair and maintenance were additional considerations. Likewise, the power of compressed air was harnessed for greater drilling efficiency. Pre-computer ingenuity was on display throughout.

A sense of humor was also imperative when living half of one's life more than a mile underground. This was apparent when it came to the bathroom facilities, or lack thereof. Imagine a miniature caboose, small enough for a man to sit atop. Perched on the rails, the potty car acted as a portable toilet that was used by everyone until it was full enough to be sent to the surface to unload. It was normally chained in place, until a mischievous coworker released it, sending the unfortunate user rolling down the track mid-business.*

As our tour concluded, the guide asked if we had any questions. I could only think of one: "Why in the world would anyone want to take on this practically-impossible job?!" I guess it was men willing to do what they had to do in order to make a decent living for themselves and their families. Between the tour and the displays within the museum, we gained an immense respect for the history and innovation of the mining industry.

It was time to head west into wild Wyoming. The land became drier, more rugged, and emptier. Elevations changed too, and eventually we could see the east side of the Rockies in the distance. To the south, we could also see a great plume of smoke. It appeared to be from a forest fire, although we did not see any flames.

"Why don't you turn on the radio to see if you can find out anything about it," suggested Senator. We did not find any news about a fire, but we did stumble upon a report that made me turn up the volume. To our surprise and endless entertainment, we learned that the situation which had called for a curfew in Martin had been none other than an old-fashioned feud. Bad blood between multiple generations of two families eventually required the involvement of local police, state troopers, tribal police, and other officials. It was like something out of an old western. We agreed that it was better to hear the report on

---

* hence the term 'yanking your chain'

the radio than to see it on television. Video footage might have been disappointing. We preferred our envisioned images of teenagers with four teeth and dirty overalls, shooting side-by-side with their pipe-smokin' grannies.

Into Montana we drove. For a while we paralleled the Rocky Mountains as we drove north, but eventually we pulled away as they drifted northwest. By no means was the land flat, however. Rolling mounds and meandering trenches surrounded endless open ranches. Mesas and gaps introduced new vistas, always with roaming cattle. If the elongated ditches happened to contain streams, they were deemed rivers. No one was complaining of population congestion.

In fact, we probably should have stopped for gas in Billings, but we were getting fairly comfortable with the fuel range feature on our new car, which claimed we still had 120 miles before we became vulture food. Looking at the map assured us that there were towns about every fifteen miles, so we pressed on. Alternating between north and west roads, we did find each of the promised towns. What we did not find were gas stations. Evidently, a handful of houses, a bar, and a dilapidated store that has been ready to cave in since the Johnson administration* constituted a town; no fuel was necessary. I guess everything is relative. When there is nothing for miles around, even a dinky village with a population of a few dozen is big enough to make it onto my trusty Rand McNally spiral map.

We did eventually find gas, but it took long enough to make us nervous. Knowing that we were down to one

---

* the second one, to be fair

bottle of water and two phones that did not function added significantly to the drama and the prayers. We had learned our lesson. When we reached Great Falls, it was time to call it quits for the night.

Before turning in, we checked the weather forecast to see what we could expect while camping in the mountains. We were shocked to learn that eleven tornadoes had passed through a few Illinois counties, including our own. Miraculously, reports confirmed that there were no injuries, but we were not sure if our home had sustained any damage. Based on what we were hearing, it did not seem like we had anything to worry about, but I emailed my brother to see if he knew anything.

*   *   *

Thursday morning the light woke me up just as my work nightmare was revving into high gear. My boss was just about to yell at and possibly fire me. Then I drifted off again, semi-conscious. *Who cares? What's at home? No mountains, possibly no house...*

Soon I was up permanently. We were both excited to see Glacier National Park. The pure air beckoned, and we were ready to trade town for timber. Maybe the atmosphere would even clear out Senator's allergies. Maybe we would get to see a grizzly bear. Maybe we would see a bright moon's glow through the tent's wall as we snuggled to stay warm in the higher elevation for the next few nights.

For the next three hours we drove toward the west entrance to the park. The mountains grew as we approached, and lush green forests carpeted the foothills. Part of our drive took us through the Blackfeet reservation, where we occasionally stopped for wandering cattle blocking the road. No one was in a hurry except us.

Amid a few motorcyclists, we reached the park entrance. It was also the gateway to the famous Going-to-the-Sun Road, which I had read about for two years. As tempting as it was to turn in and start up to the summit, we wanted to get our campsite situated first. Just another mile down the road, we entered our reserved campground.

The owner was friendly, as was the large, immovable dog that I almost tripped over as we stepped into the office. I registered, she (the owner, not the dog) directed us to our spot on the map, and all seemed in order. We got back into the car and drove up to our numbered site, which was conveniently located near drinking water and the shower house. That was the last moment that camping was fun.

Two strikes were immediately against us as soon as we stepped out of the car. As I surveyed the site, I realized that it was laid out in three tiers. Some architecture school drop-out had planned the lowest tier as the tent space. The last time I checked, water ran downhill, so this could be a major problem as it was supposed to rain for most of our second day there.

As I pondered the gravity situation, Senator slapped his first mosquito. Then he swatted another. Even though it is a well-known fact that he is a mosquito magnet, I thought he would be safe in the high, dry mountains. Not so, as he let both me and the bloodsucker know. We were not off to a banner start, but he put on long pants and sleeves and started to help me take out the tent.

Fortunately, our little tent sets up in minutes. Unfortunately, our air mattress* is too big to fit through the

_____
* I don't care how hardcore you are. After a certain age, all tent

201

door hole when inflated. This is not normally a problem, because I unroll the flat mass inside the tent, then pass the cord of the air gun out the hole to Senator, who plugs it into the car's power. When the car is parked two tiers up, however, one is faced with a dilemma. Either one can sleep on the hard ground, or one can relocate the tent to the tiny parcel of land right next to the car and the road. Reasoning that we would get no sleep on the hard ground, I moved the tent for option #2, complete with scenic view of the bathrooms.

I believe this is the moment that Senator decided he was sleeping in the car. Actually, in retrospect, this may have been the moment he began contemplating the monastic life-- no girlfriend planning crazy adventures, a small cell but no camping, and a completely mosquito-free church. Yet, he humored me by plugging in the air gun, (whose cord now reached without an inch to spare,) on my cue. "@#$% !" quoth I.

Even though I had checked the device at home before leaving, and even though it had faithfully worked since I was a teenager, the air gun was broken. It wasn't that I was opposed to sleeping in the car. After all, one of the main reasons we had chosen the particular make and model was because of its ample storage capacity. The problem was what to do with all of the other junk that would have to be moved for us to make a bed. In most places, we could set up the tent and use it to store our gear. Not in bear country. Almost everything has to stay in the car. "@#$% !" quoth Senator.

"I'm not doing this. Isn't there an inn or hotel?" he

---

campers deserve one.

asked.

"There is a lodge in the national park, but I don't know if they'll have availability on a summer weekend..." I ventured, trailing off as I tried to brainstorm other ideas. Senator was now alternating between swatting mosquitoes, which had found me as well, and blowing his nose. I could see his annoyance growing severely. It was going to be a long night, or three.

In fifteen minutes we were at the front desk of the lodge. As Senator would later describe it, throngs of happy people with their secured reservations for rooms that were not made of nylon and zippers were casually enjoying the lounge, taunting us. He mustered his best impression of a cheerful tourist and inquired about vacancy. We were told there was one available room for that night, but nothing for Friday or Saturday night, barring a cancellation. "We'll take it!" he announced. At least we were down to two nights of homelessness.

As long as we were already on the way, we continued along Going-to-the-Sun Road. The first thing we noticed was that it could just as aptly have been named Going-Over-the-Yellow Road, as an inordinate number of drivers crossed over the middle stripe into our lane haphazardly. The speed limits also seemed too fast for the steep and curvy conditions. It was also far busier than either of us had anticipated. The road had only been open for a week, and we later learned that park attendance had been hitting record highs for the previous few years, thanks to melting glaciers. Needless to say, Senator did not get to see much as he drove.

When we reached the highest point, at Logan Pass

Visitor Center (6600'), we knew it would be our last trip to Glacier. Whereas I had been picturing a more remote version of Rocky Mountain National Park, we were instead met with a packed parking lot full of the type of people who think flip-flops are appropriate footwear for hiking in snow... and wonder why their toes are cold when they do so. We walked up the snow field for a while, but it was hard to take in the alpine views with so many loud people around. Senator was feeling the altitude, and I was squinting against the glare, so we cut it short and drove back down the mountain, carefully navigating the sharp drop-offs.

It was late afternoon and we were getting hungry, so we drove back to the camp to at least enact one of the rituals of camping-- outdoor cooking. The mosquitoes were ready for their dinner too, unfortunately, but there were fewer of them than there had been. Between the two of us, we managed to concoct a delicious camp stove version of pizza. We downed it with leftovers to spare, and much evidence to erase. Being in bear country meant scrutinizing the area for any traces of food or crust that normally would have been tossed into the brush. Once everything was cooled, it all had to be packed back into the car, which meant it had to be completely clean before doing so. Otherwise we might be spending the next five days riding with nasty dirty dishes.

We still left our basic site intact, though. After all, we had no alternate lodging planned for Friday night or Saturday night, so there was no point in taking the tent down. There was also no point in packing up sleeping gear or the lantern. With full tummies, and feeling somewhat better, we headed to the lodge to take advantage of the evening program.

Despite the hefty price of the room, there was no television, radio, or internet connection, so we took our computer to the great room to see if we could link up to the outside world with our special, twenty-four-hour-only secret guest password. Along the way we stopped at the front desk, hoping to find a cancellation for the next two nights. Not surprisingly, we were out of luck. We had about forty-five minutes to kill until the ranger talk, so it was time to work on Plans C, D, and E if necessary.

Once connected to the internet, our first task was to check the weather. The night looked beautiful, but Friday's forecast still predicted rain for the afternoon and evening... and night... and possibly Saturday morning. *So much for that.* We shifted our focus to finding accommodations for one of the year's busiest weekends in northwest Montana. "Where is Columbia Falls?" Senator asked, half hopeful and half irritated.

I think it's quite a ways away. Maybe half an hour?" I ventured. In this case, the inconvenient distance could possibly work in our favor when it came to availability.

"Well it looks like there's a B&B with vacancy there." With the weather forecast, exhaustion, and Senator's growing anger-laced allergies, we agreed to book it. Phoning was not an option, so he began to enter his information online. When he finished, they sent him a reassuring confirmation notice. For the first time since we had arrived in the mountains that afternoon, I started to relax a little. Perhaps Senator's physical state and mood would improve after a good night's sleep.

205

As things were looking brighter, I felt we were regrouping to get the vacation back on track. Now that we knew we would not need our campsite, there was no point in leaving our gear there unattended. Though I was not afraid of theft, the tent and bedding would surely be soaked overnight, sitting on the bottom tier of a 90%-chance-of-overnight-rain campsite. The only common sense alternative was to skip the evening program and drive the fifteen or twenty minutes to the campground. Once we broke it down, everything would be back in the car with us in one place. I presented my idea to Senator, happy to have a positive solution. His reaction I could not and did not expect. Amid a mild explosion of very different vocabulary than he had been using the first few days of the trip, he let me know in no uncertain terms that, not only was he not going back to get the gear, but he would only be more upset if he even saw it again, because he would never camp another night in his life.

There are times when one should assert one's position, and there are times when one should back off. To date, no relationship in the history of humankind has quite nailed down exactly when each person should choose either of these options. Feeling very level-headed at the time, however, I chose the former. Senator might not have been willing to go back to get the gear, but I was not willing to throw it all away, not to mention leaving a mess for someone. It seemed like such a simple, reasonable suggestion, that I was sure it was only the frustration and allergies talking. Thus, I asserted my position once again, trying to provide the logic behind it.

Senator packed up the computer and started up the

stairs to our room. He announced simply that he was going to take a shower and get ready for bed. My strong gut feeling was still that we should get the gear, so I volunteered to go get it myself. It was an easy drive, I knew my way, and if I worked quickly, I could get back before dark. "I don't care what you do," was his curt reply. I knew he meant it, especially when he added, "But leave me my license and credit card, in case you don't come back."

These were not encouraging words, but I had to bank on the fact that he did not really mean it, and someday we would laugh about it. I was just about to leave, when I had one of those pesky responsible adult thoughts. It went something like this: *1.)Senator doesn't feel good, so he's in no shape to deal with a real problem, should one arise. 2.)I'm leaving in our only mode of transportation. 3.)We have no working phones. 4.)We have no way to email each other. 5.)With the way the day was going, this would be the one time someone would hit me or the car would stall or a bear would attack. 6.)It could go from an annoying and time-wasting night to a very, very bad night.* I decided I had nothing to lose, so I quickly rattled off a request that he come with me, promising that I would drive both ways, do all of the breakdown and packing, and have him in bed plenty early. To my amazement, he got dressed, pulled his shoes on, dropped the keys in my hand, and walked out with me. For both of our sake's, no words were exchanged.

In sixteen minutes we were at our campsite. Under different circumstances, we might have noticed the beautiful fuchsia sunset. Minutes seventeen through twenty-two were spent setting the land speed record for campsite breakdown. Despite my protests, Senator jumped out of the car at the same time as I did and immediately went to work alongside me. Even under duress, I had to admit we moved together like clockwork. Seven years of live recording set-up and tear down had welded us into an efficient machine.

Soon we were back at the lodge, and Senator commenced crashing into his pillow as I commenced reading a history book for the next two hours through intermittent tears. I knew nothing truly terrible had happened, but the mood was 180 degrees from what I had envisioned. For months I had fantasized about a snuggly slumber under the stars, enveloped in chilly, dry mountain air and the seclusion of the night. We had both been joyfully anticipating the break. Instead, we were fairly miserable and paying heftily for the privilege. At least we were not sleeping in a puddle.

*   *   *

They say everything looks brighter in the morning, and it did, but that was mainly due to the sunny sky. It had not rained overnight as predicted. Senator ensured that this fact did not escape my attention. It was true; nothing would have been soaked, but I was still glad to have the gear secured in the car. In fact, I was feeling brave enough to ask Senator if he had any interest in a ranger-led hike that morning, since we were up plenty early. He nodded in agreement, in an attempt to rescue the other two-thirds of our Glacier National Park experience.

With snacks, water, pepper spray, and other hiking essentials, we parked the car at the appropriate trail head. As we climbed out, a mosquito greeted Senator intimately, welcoming him to a new day. I hope that mosquito got allergies. Calmly, he took it in stride, dousing himself in a shower of deet. We then walked to the meeting point and waited. A few other people meandered around, but no ranger was in sight. At a quarter after nine we gave up and started up the trail ourselves.

Senator, pushing on despite feeling uncomfortable, had returned to complete silence, which made me really wish that the ranger was with us. The one way you are *not* supposed to hike in bear country is quietly. With this in mind, the next two miles were spent in awkward, mainly one-sided conversation. I think we scared the bears away for the wrong reasons.

We did get to take in some great scenery, since the trail followed a waterfall, but we could not see any mountain tops. The west side of the national park is enshrouded in forest, so while the trees are impressive, we could not really tell that we were in mountains. Still, we saw several birds and an array of forest-floor fauna. When we reached the bottom, we took a side trail along a boardwalk.

As long as I was pressing my luck and the rain was holding off, I decided to suggest another easy hike. For reasons only he knows, Senator again agreed. Up we walked along an easy, practically deserted path. It led to a lake, where we startled a wildlife photographer. Nodding as we passed, we continued down the gentle slope through the woods to the other side.

I will here note that, when we parked the car, we could actually see both sides of the trail loop. We chose one direction, assuming we would 'loop around' as the name

209

suggested, and return to the other side. This did not happen. We found ourselves at a completely different road, even though there had been no forks or turn offs. Having taken enough risks for the day, we turned around to return the familiar way we came. That is to say, we again passed the giant bear warning signs, the creaking birch trees that sounded like they wouldn't make it to the end of the day, and the interrupted photographer. Just as we were in the last quarter-mile stretch, a few drops of rain plopped down. I played dumb, opting for complete denial over looking back to see Senator's reaction. I kept my head down, momentarily focused on navigating a rocky section of the path. I soon looked up again when a deer and I surprised each other.

By the time we reached the car, the rain was streaming down. I was pleased that we had been able to hike for the morning, and I meant it sincerely when I thanked Senator for going with me. He nodded. When I suggested we go grab some hot coffee in the nearby café, I got an even bigger nod. Thankfully, it was starting to feel like us again.

Near the entrance of the park we found a bustling diner with friendly servers who kept the java flowing. It was only noon, so we had an entire afternoon to decompress. Sitting across from each other, we planned the rest of the day, glad to be on the same page. Things were looking up. When we finished our last drop, we sprinted out through the rain, not minding it as much now that we knew we had another dry bed waiting for us.

We had two hours until check-in at our bed and breakfast, so we left the national park for the town of

Columbia Falls. Armed with a satisfying lunch and coffee, it was a pleasant drive of less than half an hour. Enjoying the light rain, we took our time, playing it by ear in case we found anywhere that we wanted to stop. It was a good thing we were early, due to the adventure that ensued.

We set out armed with the name, address, and phone number of our reserved bed and breakfast. Somehow, during the chaos and angst of the previous evening, this seemed like enough information to get us to our destination. I had been too stressed to think of the potential complications with this plan. For the first time in many, many years of navigation duties, I did not get specific directions. I will not repeat this mistake anytime soon.

When we arrived in Columbia Falls, we cruised west on Route 2, (the main drag for the entire southern border of the mountain range,) assuming any lodging establishment would fall somewhere along it, as is the case in most small towns. There were two problems with this approach: 1.)the town was bigger than anticipated,* and 2.)the name of the street we were looking for was nowhere to be found. Complications increased when we realized that we had no way to access the internet and no phone service to call for directions.   Needless to say, it was getting mildly uncomfortable in the car. I could have kicked myself for not checking a map the previous day. I then had the dark thought that, even if we did somehow succeed, all of this was based off of the assumption that the place actually existed. I dared not explore other possibilities regarding that scenario just yet.

---

* stoplights and everything!

Still, we were keeping it all in perspective. After all, until virtually the most recent nanosecond of human existence, we would have had to rely on other tools of the tourist trade, so why not do the same now? Senator pulled into a gas station and I went in to ask to use the business' phone book. Apparently no one had made such an odd request in years, as they looked at me like I had asked for the nuclear code book. After a moment, they produced the dusty, clunky mass, and I began my search. Four yellow-page categories and two white-page listings later, I had nothing to go on. Naturally, the clerk had never heard of the place.

On to gas station #2 we drove. With no false hope, I asked that clerk if she had ever heard of the name of our bed and breakfast. It was another definitive, "Huh?" *I thought all you small-town people were supposed to know each other!*

I was striking out, and I was fairly sure my next question would yield just as much uselessness. "Do you know of anywhere in town that still has a pay phone?" She thought for a moment. I wasn't sure if she was trying to remember where she had seen one, or just trying to understand what in the world a pay phone was. Thankfully it was the former. She gave me directions to a place about a half mile away that still (reportedly) had one out back.

With renewed vigor I dashed back through the rain into the car. Senator just looked numb. I was truly sorry things were turning out so messy during our 'relaxing' getaway in the mountains. At least we were working together. "Hey-- there's a café!" yelled Senator, just as we were turning down the street that supposedly contained a pay phone.

"Wait! Where?" I was trying to look for the phone booth while navigating. Senator was trying to find a place to do a quick turn around. A pay phone was iffy, but a café might have internet access. With probably more immediacy than the situation called for, we turned around, pulled in the lot, parked, grabbed the computer, and bolted toward the door.

Inside, we ordered a simple black coffee. Then we asked for what we really wanted-- the internet access password. "There's no password. Just log on," answered the girl behind the counter. Then she added, "... but just so you know, we close at 3:00..." I thanked her and glanced at the clock. It was 2:15pm. All we needed was about three solid minutes to find out where in the world our bed and breakfast was. That is, we only needed three minutes given the place existed.

Happily, we easily found our route online. It turned out that it was just far enough outside of Columbia Falls to evade all sections of the local phone book. That was bad for our frustrating search, but good for a wonderfully remote location. In ten minutes we were pulling into the driveway of a few acres of private wooded property. In another ten minutes we were stepping into an immaculate, quiet, spacious room. Simple.

As tempting as it may have been to stay in the room the rest of the night, a shower and a nap revived us for another trek back to Glacier. Again we drove to the lodge, with far less stress than the previous night. Since we were early for the evening program, we improvised a car picnic

213

out of items originally planned for the camp stove. A few rounds of Farkel in view of Lake McDonald and a short wander through the gift store eroded the next hour, and soon it was time to go to the small, timbered auditorium.

During the ranger's talk we gleaned a brief education on the national park system and Glacier in particular. At last count, there are fifty-nine national parks in the United States, all of which joined together in celebrating the 100th anniversary of the first park's unique legal designation as a national park. Glacier National Park sported 150 glaciers in 1850, but they have gradually been melting, bringing the 2016 total to just twenty-five. While scientists have agreed that the Glacier glaciers would eventually be gone, they have moved up their predictions for when this would take place. I had heard anywhere from 50 to 100 years, but now some experts are estimating that it could happen as early as 2020. To be clear, this does not mean there will be no snowcaps in Glacier. As we learned, not all snow-covered peaks are created equal. In order to qualify as a glacier, as opposed to merely a snow field, the mass of white must meet three distinct criteria. It must span an area of at least twenty-five acres. It must also be at least 100 feet deep.* Finally, it must be moving. We learned that this is often tracked via recording the scraping sound.† The good news is that even if the glaciers all become lakes, there will still be snow on the mountains.

We walked arm-in-arm out of the auditorium. It was still raining steadily, but we would be high and dry for the night. Driving the lonely, dark road back to our room was

---

* Think of a ten-story snow drift!

† Do I detect a new branch of Senator's mobile recording studio?

enjoyable, but the clouds wasted an otherwise perfect backdrop for stargazing. In fact, we had not seen any good stars since leaving home, despite being in prime dark sky country. The next day was supposed to be clear, however, so we still had another chance. In the meantime, deer poked their heads around to see who the new kids driving through the meadow were. Poor Senator sneezed a greeting to them.

*   *   *

Saturday morning we were up early, and I was excited for the main highlight of the trip. A few months earlier I had booked a boat ride on St. Mary Lake, along with a hike in the surrounding region. It was still raining, but we had at least a two-hour drive until we reached the lake. I knew the park was big, but when I had originally planned to camp on the west side, I did not quite realize just how long it would take to get to our boat. You would think with all of my planning, I would have absorbed this fact, but I did not. When camping went out the window, had I been thinking clearly, I would have started looking for a room on the east side. Anyway, traffic was light, and the views were gorgeous.

It was not a bad commute, and we were making very good time, which allowed us to stop for homemade pastries and coffee. It was good to have fortifications before entering Route 49. Though it was a legitimate state highway, we concluded that the rules must be a little different on the reservation. Not only was the road bumpy and sharply curved, but there were no guardrails along the steep drop-offs. Occasionally on the straight sections we stopped for roaming cattle or horses. The grand payoff came when we rounded a corner to witness a full rainbow that curved down from the mountain top to the valley below. It was a promising clue to the differences between the east and west sides of Glacier National Park.

When we arrived at the boat launch, it was extremely windy, and considerably cooler. Thankfully, mosquitoes would not be a problem, but I hoped we would not be too chilly. I bundled up in an extra sweatshirt and went to the ticket booth. As I was waiting for someone to open the window, another woman who was waiting greeted me. "Where are you from?" she asked.

"Chicago," I answered generically.

"Oh, we're from Illinois, too," she continued.

My condolences was the automatic response in my head, but I resisted the urge to say it out loud.

Before I could craft a better reply, she jumped in with more detail. "We live in De Kalb."

When I told her the name of our small town, she was delighted to note that she had cousins who lived there. I was surprised. Imagine coming 1,500 miles to meet someone who knew people in your town of 5,000 people. I chose to take it as a good sign for the day ahead.

Right on schedule, we boarded our boat. The scenery was gorgeous as we rode along the turquoise lake, given its color by tiny suspended 'rock flour' particles. Unlike the west side of the park, the St. Mary Lake region is open to sweeping vistas of various colors. On one side, steep mountains and valleys roll into the distance, with visible waterfalls and snowy peaks. On the other side, a regenerating forest thrives after a 2015 fire.

It was only the day before our boat ride that I

216

learned that our hike would take place in a burned out forest. *Great*, I thought. The camping was a bust, Senator was fighting his worst allergy attack since I had known him, and now I was going to take him to an ugly, empty trail to see some dead wood. Fortunately, this was not the case. Because of the increase in sunlight after the tree canopy is destroyed, the forest floor teems with new growth, occasionally interrupted with small meadows. The flowers are especially lush and colorful due to the nutrients left behind from the ash in the soil. The unique setting is also home to black-backed woodpeckers, who can blend in with the charred bark. The ranger told us that it was rare to see one, but we saw three.

Our hike culminated at a bridge over the rushing St. Mary Falls. We stepped just far enough out to safely navigate the wet rock and snapped a picture. In the distance we could see Virginia Falls. Though we probably could have made it there and back, we did not want to miss our boat. Instead, we returned along the trail, enjoying lake and mountain views the entire way.

The only interruption to our serenity was a few moments while we passed a family of four. Though the young daughter was a trooper, encouraging the family to valiantly press on, the toddler son was in more of a screaming-and-crying-while-sightseeing mood. The dad apologized, but hey, at least the kid was keeping the bears away. If I have not said it before, I will say it here: I have no idea how my parents managed to competently drag four kids around the country to so many magnificent places. That had to require the type of patience of which I am not in possession.

On our return boat trip, our captain pointed out a few geologic highlights. Among them was the Continental Divide, which formed the backbone of North America, separating almost all of the fresh water into three routes. We could also see the Golden Staircase jutting out from the side of the mountain. He told us that it contained some of the oldest land on Earth. This caught our attention, because three years earlier when we were in Hawaii, we had walked on the newest land on Earth. I found it interesting that both are located in the United States.

The afternoon was ours to wander, so we continued up the east side of Going-to-the-Sun Road, encountering some mountain goats in one area. As we had found all morning, the views were superior to those on the west side. In addition, the drivers were decidedly more sane. Adding insult to injury was the fact that when we had first arrived at Glacier, we drove two hours further to get to the less interesting end of the park. *Well, live and learn.* Reader, I advise you to plan your Glacier trip accordingly.

On our way out of the park, we stopped at the St. Mary Visitor Center. The main exhibit presented the perspective of the Blackfeet and other tribes from the east side of the mountains. Essentially it was bittersweet. While the National Park Service has brought protected status to land the natives consider sacred, hunting and ceremonial rights on Glacier National Park property were lost, due to misinformation about what was in a treaty. As is the case with many First Nations, the relationship with the United States government is complex.

The relationship between our car and native-maintained Route 49 was also complicated. To put it into

218

perspective, motorcycles are actually prohibited on the uneven, daring road. The best way to come down from the adrenaline of navigating it, we decided, was to devour a fresh piece of huckleberry pie.* If you have not had Blackfeet huckleberry pie, you have not been to Glacier.

After the long drive back to the room, we relaxed for awhile and watched the hummingbirds at the home's feeder. Then we made one more foray to the park's west side to attend the evening ranger program. The topic was groups of inhabitants who had come and gone through the land that is now Glacier National Park. Early on, there were North American camels, which obviously are now extinct. Currently, the porcupines seem to be mysteriously disappearing from the region. Of course, the biggest group that is rapidly making its way out of the park are the glaciers themselves. (Given our relationship with the places we visit, we will most likely be blamed for this.)

After the program, we left the lodge and Glacier National Park permanently. Though it had not rained since early that morning, it was still cloudy enough to obscure any noteworthy amount of stars. Perhaps we would still have a chance to see a great sky during the next few nights. After all, how much light pollution could there be in Saskatchewan?

*   *   *

Sunday morning we shared a meal with the other lodgers at our bed and breakfast. All of them were hikers, mainly from the Southwest. Interestingly, none of them had been to the eastern national parks. During our travels,

---

* part pie, part cheesecake, with a berry that tastes like a cross between a blueberry and a raspberry

we have found that people really do tend to just hang out in their region of the country. No one is as bad as New Englanders, though. To this day, some of them still aren't aware that there are more than six states.

After breakfast it was time to leave the mountains. We drove back east along Highway 2 and turned north when we reached the Blackfeet Reservation. It was a clear morning, and we were on our way to Canada via a minor Montana highway. It was so minor that at one point the pavement randomly turned to gravel. *This doesn't seem right...* I would have been more concerned that we had taken a wrong road, except that there was no other road. Despite the lack of signage, we had to be on the right road. That was the day I learned that just because a road is an official state highway does not mean it has to be paved.

A few miles later, the gravel was replaced with pavement again, and we increased our speed as we headed to the Del Bonita border crossing. As Del Bonita is just a dot on the map, we knew we would not be waiting in any traffic jams, unless there were illegally crossing cattle. It was so remote, in fact, that it would have been believable if we were the only people who had crossed during the past week, or even month. Senator stopped the car as a border patrol agent emerged from the small building, probably glad to have something to break the monotony.

He asked for our passports and began the litany of usual questions. When he came to the part about our travel plans, I explained that we had come through South Dakota and Wyoming, up into the Glacier National Park region, and that we would be heading east through Canada before dropping back south into Minnesota. A northern loop

220

seemed to make perfect sense to me, but I think he was still suspicious of anyone who would cross the border at Del Bonita. "So you're going to travel through Saskatchewan and Manitoba until you see the mountains, right?" he asked.

"Noooo," I began, wondering if I had said something wrong. "No mountains, just prairie and some trees in Manitoba..."

"Just kidding!" he jumped in. To this day I do not think he was kidding. Nor do I think he was really bad at Canadian geography. I believe he was testing us to see if we really had a plan or reason behind our visit to his country.

Satisfied with my answer, he went on to inquiring about weapons. *What defines a weapon?* I thought of our little container of pepper spray. Normally I would not have thought to mention it, but here, where a border guard could lead a pretty boring existence, he might decide to search us, even if we did know there were no mountains in the middle of Canada. If he thought we were hiding something, it might not go over too well.

Whether he would have searched us or not, I will never know. It was probably a good thing that I mentioned the pepper spray though, since I learned that it is, in fact, an illegal defense weapon in Canada. I assured the man that we only had it for hiking protection. Nevertheless, we had two choices: either we could surrender the contraband item, or we could stay south of the border.

We opted to leave the item, following the guard inside to sign papers. As I filled out the necessary lines, a portrait of Queen Elizabeth II of England posing with the

Canadian flag smiled down approvingly at me. Her North American daughter-nation would not be imperiled by my mace. "By the way, this wouldn't do anything against a bear," the border agent commented. "Get some bear spray."

Senator rejoined me at the desk. "That was the absolute cleanest public bathroom I have ever seen-- anywhere!" he announced. Thoroughly impressed by the state of the border toilet and one can of pepper spray lighter, we nodded to our border guard and got into the car. Making our way northeastward through Alberta, we checked one more province off the list.

Alberta is known for the scenic Rockies, but this part of the province is like the American prairie. Among the ranches and grasses, we noticed very pretty, distinct wildflowers. They were almost a neon shade of yellow. When viewed at a distance on the flat landscape, it looked as though God had taken a giant highlighter and striped across certain bands of the horizon.

In addition to the unusual background, we also had entertainment in the foreground. Rodents we had never seen before ran into the road excitedly. They were something between a squirrel and a prairie dog, with the enthusiasm of both. As they reached the middle of the road, they would stop, and then bounce up and down. We concluded that they saw so little traffic that a car coming down the highway was cause for celebration.

The weather was beautiful as we continued to follow provincial highways. We were on our way to the main Trans-Canada Highway, enjoying the emptiness as we drove. Apparently Alberta had taken a cue from Montana, or vice-versa, because the pavement on the highway abruptly stopped, leaving us in a combination of chunky gravel and reddish dirt. We crawled on like this for fifteen miles, only seeing one semi-truck go past. I can only imagine what he thought when he saw our Illinois license plate. The crowning moment of the stretch was when we passed a sign that ominously read, "This road banned 75% of year". In other words, no one should even attempt this idiotic trek unless it is summer, and-- let's be honest-- no one in a Honda Fit with phones that had not worked in a week should do so even then.

"I gotta' get a picture of this," Senator announced. We pulled off to the side of the road, although we could just as easily have stopped in the middle of the road. Now we are in possession of a photograph that perfectly captures the overall experience of that week. Senator is standing with only fields in the background, expressionless, pointing to the sign above him. In the distance, you can see that the sky is quickly turning dark.

We drove on, smirking when a sign informed us that the road would be changing to pavement. *That* they did not need to tell us. It would have been useful, on the other hand, to know when the pavement was ending. Oh, Canada.

At last we reached civilization, in the form of a few houses, one intersection, and what may have been a community building. The town of Foremost, with perhaps 100 residents on a good day, lacked nothing in local pride. Their welcome sign billed them as a gateway to "Canada's Badlands". Senator and I looked at each other. Then we surveyed the landscape. Then we looked at each other again. That explained why neither of us had ever heard of

223

the Canadian Badlands, despite visiting the U.S. Badlands several times. The sparse mounds and mesas that occasionally poked up from the earth seemed tiny by comparison. They did not even vaguely resemble the sharp, color-catching spires that rose dramatically from South Dakota's soil, forcing pioneers to rethink their route. At best, the Canadian Badlands could be called the Canadian Mildly Inconvenientlands.

Leaving Foremost brought us to the strangest sign yet. On a board the size of an interstate sign was a giant warning to watch out for rattlesnakes. *Thank God we were not getting out of the car*, I thought. I was appreciative of their concern for our safety, until I saw the next sign. "Save our snakes!" explained why they wanted us to watch for the rattlers. Apparently the poisonous reptiles outranked the humans. So much for priorities.

We continued on into Saskatchewan, where I set a record for the longest stretch of uninterrupted cruise control usage. For three and a half hours I did not move my foot, thanks to a great deal of nothing along the Trans-Canada Highway. One thing we did have to get used to, however, was that even though it felt like an interstate, cars still crossed it and turned onto it from full stops. There was no entrance/exit ramp system. This was fine when no one was around, but as traffic built up near Regina, it was tricky to navigate around cars that entered at such slow speeds. At this point Senator was driving, and after dealing with it for the better part of an hour, he deemed it the Purgatory Highway, vowing never to drive it again.*

---

* I didn't have the heart to tell him that we would most likely be on the highway several more times in our lifetime, as it stretches all the

Finally we arrived at our hotel. We checked in and went out to park the car. I pointed to the box in front of the parking space. "Know what that is?" I asked Senator.

"For electric cars?" he guessed.

"Nope, they're engine heaters for winter. I learned about them when I was a kid. By the time January arrives, and 50-below-0 wind chills roar down from the Arctic, they just assume anyone staying somewhere overnight will have a dead battery by morning." He shook his head. We like the snow, but you can keep those kinds of temperatures.

With that, we checked in and scoped out dinner options. We were tired and glad to be on the way home, so comfort food was in order. We found it just a few blocks from our room, at an Indian restaurant. Garlic naan and veggies with sauces that I will never be able to duplicate went down easily. All that remained on the evening's agenda was relaxing to some quality Canadian television, which was abuzz with the news that the leader of Iceland had a Canadian wife.

*   *   *

Monday we slept in an hour later than usual. It also took us an hour to get out of Regina, due to construction. When we finally got on the road, Senator declared that he was sick of the Purgatory Highway, and he wanted to drop back into the States sooner than planned. *Hhmmm.* I thought this might add more time to our trip, but he was determined. It was time for a bargain. "Okay, but can we at least cross into Manitoba, just to cross it off the list?" I don't think he was aware of my imaginary list.

"Sure..." he agreed, "...and then we are taking the

_____

way across the country.

first highway south. Where does that put us?"

"In the middle of a field in North Dakota."

"Perfect."

Again we found ourselves crossing a tiny border stop. It was, indeed, in the middle of fields. I wondered how they could keep people from just randomly crossing through some guy's farm. There was no one for miles around the small booth, except the single border patrol agent. She was very friendly and looked more like a neighbor kid's mom than a defender of our country's border. In a round about way, she cheerfully tried to decipher what in the world we were doing crossing there, of all places. I gave a short explanation, consciously leaving out the part about Purgatory Road. She continued to smile sweetly, remarked that our trip sounded very nice, and then proceeded to search the car. We popped the hatchback obediently. When she moved a few things around and mentally pronounced us harmless, we were free to enter our homeland, and she was free to go back to doing whatever it is border patrol agents of obscure gateways normally do.

There was corn, a few lakes, and not a lot else in North Dakota. The biggest landmark we passed was the geographic center of North America. Maybe that was the place to live. Then we would be able to traverse the continent from a convenient central location. The only problem with that plan was that I did not care about too many places south of Chicago.

In the late afternoon we crossed into Minnesota. Traffic picked up, blocking much of the view of the road. By the time we saw the large board on the ground, it was

226

too late to avoid hitting it, hard. We both cringed, knowing we did not escape at least some damage, but the extent was unknown. No emergency maintenance lights came on in the car, so we found a gas station and checked the tires. Senator determined that we had a slow leak, so we scheduled stops every two hours or so until we reached our hotel. Between the allergies, the leaky tire, and a lot of driving, we were glad to be within a day's drive of home.

*   *   *

Tuesday morning we could see evidence of a night's worth of air leakage from our tire. This time the dashboard light came on as if to say, "All right you guys, get me some air and get me home-- pronto!" Now the car was upset, too. Senator was not enjoying himself. Neither was I, making it a unanimous trio. Sitting in the passenger seat flipping through the owner's manual was not how I had envisioned our romantic trip to the mountains. As the saying goes, "You win some. You lose some." I guess we were about due for a dud of a vacation. Still, I have some very fond memories of the museums we visited, the view of St. Mary Lake surrounded by snow-capped mountains, and driving parts of Canada that, until this trip, I was not entirely sure existed. At least I had figured out how to reset the car's air pressure monitor. As Senator topped off the tire, I wondered if he realized that we were leaving again in a week. "Aaaahhh-chooo!" came his answer to my thoughts.

Chapter 5
Albatross & Lavender:
Early July 2016

We had been home for a week to recover and reset from the last trip. Now it was time for our almost-annual excursion to Door County. It was always a short trip, with the benefit of many familiarities. We knew each part of the route, and none of it contained stretches of gravel. We knew where we would be staying, and it did not involve a tent. We knew who we would see, and they would not be wearing sandals while hiking in snow. It was time for some easy, mindless hanging-out, against the backdrop of the convergence of Lake Michigan and Green Bay.

Of course, when two individuals who are often overly ambitious get together, 'easy' does not usually top the list. For various health reasons, Senator had been toying with the idea of quitting caffeine. Though he had been through this a few times before, and it had involved a guaranteed degree of temporary misery for him, it became necessary. When he originally mentioned his plan, I assumed it would gradually go into effect around the time I went back to school in early August. Instead, I learned that he was quitting cold turkey, when he politely declined coffee with the breakfast I had made for him and my brother, who was in town for a day. We had only been home from Glacier for three days, and we had two more trips planned during the next month. It seemed extra challenging to attempt it mid-vacation season, but I was game if he was. In solidarity, I skipped the java as well.

The next few days of Senator's decaffeinated world went about as expected. The house was a quiet, calm place, and not a lot was going on, other than fending off migraines and fatigue. The night before we had planned to leave brought on a particularly strong headache. He decided to go to bed early. Since I had everything ready and was due for a good night's rest, I joined him. Lying there listening to an old radio show as Senator dozed, I had my doubts as to whether he would really be in a condition to travel in ten hours, but we would see.

*   *   *

With so much time spent asleep the night before, Senator, and consequently I, was up early. He claimed he felt well enough to go, so I started to load the car. Just in case, we packed plenty of ibuprofen. By 6:10am we were pulling out of the alley behind our home to head out on the road. The sky cooperated with the potential migraine state by keeping the sun mercifully behind the clouds without the hassle of rain. In fact, the six-hour drive seemed to go quickly, thanks in part to scheduling our trip a few days after a major holiday weekend.

After the last trip, I was determined to hit the 'reset' button and make the best of this one for both of us. Thus, I was happy that Senator was feeling better and looking forward to the traditional activities that lay ahead. When we passed a farmers' market, we decided to stop and have a look around. "I've always wanted to stop here," I mentioned, "but we never arrive before they close. This year we're early."

"Good, let's check it out," Senator replied. We parked the car and got out to stretch our legs. It was much hotter and more humid than a typical Door County summer. It had been an intense summer all the way around, and even the coast of Lake Michigan was warming up. Between the climate and the lack of any items that piqued our interest*, we were back in the car within five minutes.

Still, we were having fun. I glanced at my best friend and said, "I love you, Z."

He immediately returned the affection. "That's *your* problem!"

Sense of humor had fully returned, and the boy was on a roll. We had to make a quick stop at the post office to send out a business-related package. Noticing the older locals, I commented, "Looks like a lot of senior citizens around town today."

"That's just because you're with me!" he shot back. We were having fun, despite the less-than-ideal weather.

A short while later we were catching up with our friends, Bill and Marge, as we unpacked our gear. I then ran upstairs to make the old bed up with sheets and blankets from home. My ritual also included killing a few

---

* At what point did farmers' markets shift away from fresh produce to stale baked goods, overpriced handmade soap, and ugly jewelry?

random small bugs and spiders around the bathroom before bringing in our towels and other items. I can go a little rustic, but bugs are beyond my mercy. Once the mild transformation was complete, I went back downstairs to join the others.

For the past few years, podcasting had been a regular component of our Door County adventures. Bill liked to build up an archive of recorded memories and musings, so we produced several 30-minute episodes as we went along our activities. Our first one this time took place during an errand run to the local Shop-Ko. I can only imagine how suspicious it must have looked as three adults wandered around aimlessly, talking into a hand-held recorder while waiting for their fourth member. Marge was there on legitimate business; we were just confusing the locals.

Our next item on the agenda was slightly more serious. We returned to the house for a read-through of a radio drama Bill had written. The previous fall he had written the first play, and we had performed it at a Victorian mansion near our home. In reference to our time in Door County together, Marge named our group Pilot Island.* Assuming we could get our collective act together, we would again be performing the following October. It was casual, but there was still plenty of work to be done if we were to perfect several dozen voices and sound effects.

After rehearsal we took a drive down to one of the many scenic county harbors. This one had the added

---

* Plus, we were fairly certain that no other thespian society would be named after uninhabited, desolate, crap-covered islands, so there would probably not be any copyright infringement issues.

benefit of a lighthouse in the distance. Since we had last been there, the town had installed a walkway on the natural pier. It was a perfect spot to catch a breeze and some relief from the heavy air. Parasailors also took advantage of the wind, as did several terns. It was entertaining watching them hover and then dive straight down for food. A few times an ambitious sea gull or two tried to mimic their technique, but they always chickened out when it came to the 90° drop.

Two blocks away we claimed an outside table at a local grill. Every year I forget that in Wisconsin you can get bad-for-the-body-but-good-for-the-soul fried cheese curds. I don't mean the frozen junk that is rolled in cardboard and shipped around the country. These are the real deal, made with the squeaky part of the cheddar, true breading, and a whole lotta' northern love. With this delight as an appetizer, the rest of the meal is merely eaten to balance the onslaught of cholesterol.

Of course, satisfaction with dinner did not stop us from trekking to Wilson's for dessert. After all, you can't get a cherry malted just anywhere these days. As we enjoyed our various incarnations of ice cream, Senator and I told our tales of whoa from our previous trip. Needless to say, they were not all rosy memories, but the four of us were able to have a good laugh about most of it. Now the stories are probably captured on a podcast somewhere in Bill's vault.

After we finished as much as we could, we waddled our way toward the front door. As is usually the case on a July night, the place was very busy. It was truly an art form navigating and squeezing through the crowd to make an exit.* The real fun occurred when Marge accidentally encountered the take-a-penny-leave-a-penny jar that sat by the register. No real harm was done, but it turned into the spill-a-penny jar, adding to the chaos and craziness. Perhaps a little kid even pocketed a cent or two. As Bill, Senator, and I could not get near the register to assist, all I could do for my part was to laugh like an idiot.

Back at the house it was time for a movie. In honor of working on a radio show performance, we watched Abbott & Costello's *Who Done It?* As the comedic pair muddled their way around a radio station amid a murder mystery, I felt myself drifting off to sleep on the couch. I only woke for a moment when there was a scream or two (in the movie). The last thing I remembered was trudging up the steep stairs on our way to bed. I have seen the movie half a dozen times, but I have only made it to the end once or twice.

*　　　　*　　　　*

Wednesday morning I was up early enough to take a walk alone. It was an easy route along the paved country road. Only a few random cars passed to interrupt the view of the fields and the orange, blue, white, and purple flowers. The sun poked through the clouds, burning the overnight rain into a steamy haze for a few feet above the ground. There was no getting around the humidity. July was relentless throughout much of the country, but northeast Wisconsin still offered more relief than home.

As I walked and thought, I also prayed. While the details are personal, the sense of peace was amazing. A new approach to a consistent problem was laid before me,

---

* I can't imagine the fire chief would approve.

and I was injected with a renewed strength. There was no blast of sound or giant light in the middle of the road, but it was an altering experience. I was reminded that the birds and bugs and flowers do not strive so hard. Why should we?

By the time I reached the house, I was already sweaty and clammy. Senator was making a conscious effort toward coffee abstinence, but it was not even a temptation for me. Fresh fruit and funny conversation about spoiled children's birthday parties, on the other hand, drew me in. We sat with our friends at the kitchen table for a while as we planned our day.

Since a picnic was the main objective, we started with a run through Koepsel's. Koepsel's had become a tradition a few years earlier, when we realized that we could obtain (almost) all necessary elements from pickled garlic to dried cherries. This time, we also added the delight of a giant rope of smoked mozzarella string cheese. I had never seen cheese in that shape; it was as fun as it was tasty.

The only desired item that we could not get at Koepsel's was a loaf of sandwich bread to go with the homemade peanut butter. For this, Bill stopped at a gas station. The three of us waited in the car while Marge ran in. A few moments later she was back in the car, carrying her bread. "Find something, honey?" asked Bill.

"Yeah, it looks like we have a lovely loaf of 'Mrs. Freshley's' wheat," replied Marge, laughing at the name.

"Oh, well then, if it's *Mrs. Freshley's*...." joked Bill. Before heading to the park, we made one more stop at the Sister Bay Public Library. Bill and Marge checked email and did a little computer work. I helped Senator with a bit

235

of business correspondence, and then he continued to work for fifteen minutes or so on his own. Rather than start on a book I would soon have to surrender, I decided to work on the communal jigsaw puzzle. I love puzzles, and usually I find it relaxing to knock out the occasional piece or chunk or even frame. This time my brain was not functioning in that mode. I worked and reworked and moved around the rectangle, but I could not connect a single piece. Perhaps my jigsaw skills had diminished during the past year. Come to think of it, I probably had not worked on a puzzle since the last time I was in Door County.

I was rescued from further puzzle embarrassment and frustration when the others were done with their tasks. It was time to go to Newport State Park. Not surprisingly, Marge and I had both had the same idea when we were coming up with places for the four of us to explore this year. We have been on the same wavelength in this way so many times it is almost uncanny. With all our picnickery in tow, Bill drove us to the quiet state park.

Unlike the other parks in the region, Newport is more remote, and consequently less crowded. This makes it more conducive to talking with friends and slowing down the overall pace. One thing it does have in common with the other state parks, however, is a nominal fee for foreigners from 'south of the border'. I went inside to pay the Illinoisan fee and was ready to step back outside, when the ranger stopped me for a moment. She just wanted to point out that our pass was only good until 11:59pm on that day. "Okay," I acknowledged. *What happens at midnight?* I wondered. *Do we turn into wedges of cheese?*

Claiming a table with a waterfront view was easy.

We then proceeded to unload the spread of goodies, including a variety of taste sensations. Though we had not specifically packed napkins or plasticware, I had grabbed what Senator and I call our 'emergency picnic kit'. For years it has ridden in our car with us everywhere, alongside the first aid kit and spare tire, just for such a situation. We had everything we needed, until Marge went to make a sandwich. Sadly, not even the emergency picnic kit could rectify the mold on the bread. "So much for *Mrs. Freshley's!*" said Bill. I think they jinxed themselves with that name.

Nevertheless, no one starved. We then followed our outdoor meal with a walk into the woods. We had done this once before at Newport, but it had been drizzly then. This time it was nice to parallel the shoreline without as much dampness.

When we came to a group of suitable rocks, we each maneuvered into a comfortable position. Over the lake, more terns were expertly scanning the water for their lunch, probably laughing at our moldy bread. As we watched the show, the recording device came out, Senator situated it on a smaller rock, and the stories continued. I can't remember what we covered, but I think we may still have been purging the tales of our trip to Glacier National Park. I seem to recall various interpretations of what "banned 75% of year" meant.

Back at the house we tried our hands-- or voices, as is more accurately the case-- at another radio play. Bill had been on a writing frenzy, cranking out a third radio drama. Anxious to hear the characters come to life, he asked if we would read through *The Case of the Crooked Horseshoes*. It was fun, but my brain was starting to swim between the three plays. Thinking about the chaos that was sure to ensue as soon as the school semester started, I decided I could only focus on one at a time.

It was soon time to clean up and get ready for the highlight of the trip. Our friends had graciously invited us to attend a play by the Peninsula Players. The unique theatre setting was an indoor/outdoor hybrid, set among beautiful, lush gardens. There was a roof and walls, but the sides opened generously to let in the night air. It turned out to be the ideal setting in which to see an Agatha Christie murder mystery on a stormy night; the rain stayed out, but the thunder and lightning wove their way into the play.

I had not read an Agatha Christie story in years, but *The Hollows* was the perfect reintroduction. Senator and I also realized that we had never been to a play together. We may now be spoiled. The cast gave the gripping plot its due, and it truly was a mystery. Out of only eight or ten characters, our foursome guessed four different suspects. None of them turned out to be the murderer. Having logged hundreds of hours of mystery books and movies between us, fooling all of us was a feat to be commended.

It was still raining steadily when we got out of the play. Even so, the sky was dark enough that we could see the Milky Way and a few stars peeking out between the clouds. At home, the Milky Way is a rare treat to see on a clear night. We were also enjoying the mild drop in temperature.

It was too late to grab dinner, but that left more room for dessert. Back at the house we downed homemade berry

238

cheesecake in between playing rounds of Farkel. No one was surprised when Marge clinched the big win. I have no idea how she does it, but somehow she manages to win more than the rest of us combined. The fact that she traded in her normal mature composure for a childish "I won! I won! Na-na na-na na na!" sent us into hysterics all the way until bedtime.

*   *   *

Thursday morning Senator joined me for a walk to start our day. The no-caffeine thing was actually going rather well, especially since the temperature was quickly heating up. There was some reprieve in the fact that it was not as humid. I was enjoying chatting and holding hands as we discussed our day, our summer, and our upcoming busy autumn. As we walked and took in the country view, a truck with a senior citizen couple pulled up next to us to ask for directions. We gave them the information they needed, and they offered us a ride. We thanked them, politely declining, but it was nice to know that strangers could still be friendly and sincere.

After rejoining Bill and Marge, we drove to the northern tip of the peninsula to catch a ferry to Washington Island. In the past we had taken bikes across, but this time we had our friends' car. This was partly because the weather did not look like it would hold out too much longer before drizzling. Having wheels would also allow us to explore more of the island than the two main streets we normally rode along. With the car sandwiched in on the lower deck, we marched upstairs to claim seats with a view. I actually enjoyed the foggy atmosphere, which obscured much of the horizon. It was just thin enough to make out the silhouette of Pilot Island, for which we all hold a strange affection.

On the north shore of the island we pulled into the woods at Schoolhouse Beach. The campground there has a vague road that meanders irregularly between pine trees, creating odd turns and makeshift parking spaces. Bill adopted one, and we exited the car to claim a picnic table near the water's edge. As we walked, the sky grew darker.

Right on cue, as we unpacked a few items to get ready to podcast, a few drops fell. We had a little shelter from the pine tree we were under, but that would not hold out for long. None of us would melt, but we were concerned that the equipment might get damaged. The wind had also picked up, roaring over the lake from the north. In the end, our beach break lasted all of ten minutes. That was just about long enough to stare in amazement at people who were attempting to swim, march back to the car, and turn on the heat to dry out a bit.

Generally a summer excursion to Washington Island results in a trip to the Albatross at some point. I suppose the name may have something to do with mariner superstitions, but locals and tourists know it as the place to grab diner food, without the diner. They also know they can expect to wait-- for a long time. In fact, employees proudly flaunt their anti-fast food establishment with the simple slogan "We are not fast" on their shirts. When you go to the window to order, a handwritten card essentially instructs you to relax, because you are not going to eat anytime soon. If you want faster service, they suggest you go to Chicago, as you are now "north of the stress line". Perhaps latitude is attitude.

Bill ordered a burger, which I could only assume was made from 100% albatross. Senator and I went the grease route, nibbling fried cheese curds and French fries that tasted like they did when we were kids. I can't remember what Marge had. By the time she returned from waiting at the window for their order, I had almost forgotten who she was.

It was time to go exploring. With only a few miles of radius to the entire island, we knew it would not take long. We were interested in seeing what lay beyond the main few roads, though. Driving virtually every road on the island, we found our answer. After leaving the 'busy' district, signs of life fell off sharply. We first saw the remnants of an old 1940s motel, complete with antique gas pump. Further down the way, vibrant birches and maples thickly covered entrances to long driveways that led to properties where people clearly did not want to be disturbed. Someday I hoped to be one of those people-- not on Washington Island, but somewhere where there are more car accidents involving animals that oblivious texters.

Making our way back to civilization, we decided to stop at a lavender shop and farm. The purpose of this was threefold. First, it is not every day one can bask among rows of lavender, at least without the added expense of traveling to Provence. Second, we had time to kill until the next ferry. Finally, the curiosity surrounding the kinds of items that could be contained within a store whose entire stock featured lavenderia was too great to resist.

Our curiosity was soon satisfied. Of course there were soaps and sachets; that was a given. I did not expect the food items. For $12.00, a small bag of lavender popcorn

241

could be yours. For almost as much, you could be the only kid on your block to have sampled chocolate containing lavender.

Senator and I decided we could live without either, so we went outside to roam the fragrant field. Inside a small replica of a Scandinavian church, we could see bundles of lavender handing along vertical ropes to dry. It was interesting, but I still could not figure out how it could be a profitable industry. Maybe it was the next great trend. That would be okay; I could think of worse fads.

Having made no lavender purchases, the four of us got back into the car and headed for the ferry dock. We had entered the lavender shop from one direction, and now we were continuing in the other direction. Less than a mile away, I couldn't help bursting into laughter. Believe it or not, there was a competing lavender farm. At first I assumed they were related or jointly owned. After some informal research in the car, we confirmed that they were actually separate. Maybe lavender isn't the obscure niche market we thought it was.

We arrived at the dock just in time to catch the next ferry to the mainland. It was not as foggy as it had been in the morning, but it was still overcast, which always enhances the mood. As we floated along, we watched a large v-formation of cormorants flying just above the lake's surface. Their close proximity to the water gave the horizon a unique, shimmering effect.

Once on the peninsula, Senator needed to make a quick stop at the library. While he ran in to check his email, Bill, Marge, and I waited in the car, talking and watching the rain, which had now decided to spend the rest of the afternoon and evening with us. Despite sitting on my butt most of the day, I caught myself almost dozing off. When Senator came out, it was unanimously declared that hot comfort food was in order. When in Door County, that means Al Johnson's.*

It smelled like a grandma's kitchen as soon as we walked in. We relished the dry, cozy, warmly lit atmosphere as we took our seats in view of the bay. For a few moments we perused the giant menus. I almost didn't care what I ate, as long as it involved good melted European cheese†. I am a mutt of seven different nationalities. Based on my dietary preferences (addictions), surely there must have been cheesemakers somewhere in my ancestry.

We took the long way back to the house, because we needed a solid half-hour drive. Bill had a particular Jack Benny episode for us to listen to. In keeping with the old radio theme, we laughed hard at "Going to the Drive-In". I have officially decided that Benny is my favorite comic of all time. He also wins the Timeless Award. If you have not checked out his work, devote an evening or at least a few commutes to it.

There was enough time to transition into our own radio show, so we squeezed in one more read-through. When that was finished, we shook out the dice and played a few more rounds of cheesecake-infused Farkel. Through the large picture window in the kitchen we could see the

---

* or Al Jolson's, which, for some reason I always want to call it. It's definitely Johnson, though. Otherwise there would be a man kneeling and singing with his hands clasped over his heart (instead of goats) on the roof.

† I believe it is actually illegal in the state of Wisconsin to be vegan.

243

last fading attempt at daylight through the rain. Every aspect of the scene was screaming for coffee, but Senator and I held out. Anyway, the only other planned event was falling asleep on the couch to a British comedy about the French Resistance.

*   *   *

Another few days in Door County had sped by. Senator and I went through our normal routine of packing up after a vacation. Everything had its spot in a bag, and everything had its spot in the car. The only pain was the wet towels. There was just a free half-hour or so to join our friends over the breakfast table, and then we were off.

"Hey!" I interjected. "We never got around to buying maple syrup from the sugar bush down the street."

"That's okay. We can always get some elsewhere," answered Senator, backing out of the driveway until next year.

Chapter 6
Eagle & Pine:
Late July 2016

As I stated earlier, 2016 was our third attempt at planning a visit to see my parents at their part-time residence in Ontario, Canada. In line with the old adage, number three was a success. Though the original plan was to take one grand trip around the northwest, combining a camping trip in Glacier National Park with a few days at the cabin, we were both grateful that Senator's schedule made it necessary to break the trip into two. In all honesty, I probably could not have even packed for both of them. More importantly, divine Providence knew it would not be a good idea to stay with family at the tail end of a rather challenging trip.

Instead, we were refreshed, caught up on work and small projects, and mentally ready to take on a new adventure. Though it had been about three weeks without coffee, Senator was doing well. On my end, the very hot and humid summer was making it easy for me to support him. The thought of any steaming food or beverage was a complete turnoff.

Still, I was apprehensive about the trip. I was definitely excited to return to Birch Harbour, a place that held so many wonderful family memories, but I was also nervous.* The last time I had slept under my parents' roof was when I was eighteen years old. Adult life had only magnified my natural propensity toward independence. Then there was Senator. I so wanted him to enjoy himself, but that can be tricky when staying with your girlfriend's parents, particularly in a remote environment. He seemed to have absolutely no concerns, and he had heard many great stories about the place, but I started to wonder if maybe we were all biased because of our happy memories. I hoped we had not oversold the place. Maybe it would not be his cup of tea (or coffee). If that was the case, it might be the last time I ever visited, since I would not return without him.

With this in mind, I decided that communication and preparation were our best tools. For months before we left, my mom and I ironed out details to ensure that everyone would be relaxed and comfortable. She worried too much about what to feed us, because we were the only vegetarian guests she ever had. I solved that by suggesting that we bring some homemade, one-dish meals that we could all eat. In return, my parents made up a cozy room for us and

---

* From the time I was in junior high, the cabin has been in my family, originally owned by my grandparents, and now owned by my parents. Between junior high and high school, I went with my parents and siblings four times to see Papa and Grandma there. Each time we stayed for about a week, and we always crammed in a ton of fun. Now I am an aunt, which means the property has been enjoyed by four generations of us 'kids'.

reserved a prime spot for us on the porch couch.

*   *   *

It was Sunday, a week before we were about to leave, when Senator's back starting hurting. He said it was not major, and he figured that it would work its way out during the next few days. By Thursday he was feeling mostly normal, which was good timing since we had to work in Chicago that night. As we were driving on the Dan Ryan, Senator sneezed. At least once a week I am startled by his signature vehement sneezes, so I did not think much of this one.

Then I looked over at him. He was stunned by pain, and almost close to tearing up. When he could speak, he told me that he had just thrown out (or sneezed out, in this case) his back. I didn't even know that was possible. Not only did I assume this meant no Ontario, but I wondered how in the world he would manage two nights of recording with a day of studio work in between.

With much teamwork, we made it through the evening's gig. Senator insisted that there was still a chance that he could make it, so Friday morning I continued to pack and get things ready as originally planned. Doubtful, I drove to the grocery store to get necessary food items. He stayed behind and hosted a client in his studio, doing his best to hide the fact that just about any small movement sent him into the red zone.

I cranked the air conditioning in the car, cursing the miserable and relentless summer. As I parked and walked toward the store, I called my mom to break the news that we were probably in for strike three. I hated to disappoint any of us, but I really could not see Senator being able to travel in two days. A long car ride seemed like a very bad idea. "Oh, I feel so bad for him! We completely understand. Just tell him to take it easy, and we are certainly thinking of him and keeping him in our prayers." It was a perfect mom response, but 'taking it easy' wasn't on the agenda unfortunately.

Senator continued to work in the studio the rest of the day. Eventually he cut it off and took some time to watch a movie with me. It didn't take long for him to fall asleep. That was a good thing, since Saturday was the big recording event around which we had scheduled the rest of the month.

The next morning Senator woke up with the idea to purchase a waist brace. Driving extra carefully to minimize the bumps, we went to a local farm/labor supply store. Among the many manly aisles, he spotted a wide velcro belt that would help get him through the night's work. It wasn't cheap, but it turned out to be a great investment. With a heat index well over 100°F, a strong summer storm brewing while loading in, torrential rain while loading out, and severely restricted movement, any added support helped.

I did not bring up anything about vacation. I doubted that Senator had even thought about it; he had been so focused on getting through the night. Not wanting to add any pressure, but curious to know his thoughts, I played it casual as we crawled into bed. "Do I need to set the alarm clock?" I ventured, fully expecting him to say "No", or just to yelp in pain.

Instead, he surprised me. "Yeah, I'd like to try it. I think this support band helps." I was just about to voice my concerns when he added, "Besides, we can always turn around if it's too bad." *Okay, good-night.*

*   *   *

If Senator was willing to attempt the ride, I was willing to do all of the car packing and driving. The only dilemma was the cooler situation. There was so much food to bring that there was no way I could carry the big cooler out of the house to the garage. I solved it by placing the cooler in the car, with just a few items inside. I then ran back and forth with a small cooler, bringing cold items out to the big cooler in multiple trips. Frankly, I thought it a brilliant solution. Before Senator could attempt any ill-fated assistance, the deed was done.

Thus, we were off. I phoned in the update to Dad and Mom, who were delighted to hear that there was at least half a chance we would make it. Once Senator was situated with a tightened support belt and a few soft sweatshirts for added padding, we pulled out of the alley and began the ten-hour drive toward the Canadian border. I suggested we stop every hour for Senator to stretch, but he told me we could just play it by ear. I tried to fend off thoughts of him being stuck in the car, unable to move, and me not being able to get him out. *I guess if we are really desperate, there is always 9-1-1. Oh wait. No, that's for people with phones that work.*

We continued into Wisconsin, driving our familiar stretch of I-39. After about two and a half hours, we took a break. Things were going much better than anticipated, but in a few more hours we would be literally past the point of no return. I confirmed one more time that Senator actually wanted to attempt this for the next week. "Yes, definitely," was his reply. I sure hoped he was not just doing this for my sake.

Somewhere in northern Wisconsin we ended up behind a man with a boat on a trailer. This is a normal sight when in the Upper Midwest, but this guy could not keep his trailer from wavering back and forth. It was impossible to pass him for a long time, due to the risk of being side-swiped in the process. Finally we separated from him when we took another stretch break.

Getting back on the road, we crossed into Minnesota and left the interstate for a state highway. Traffic immediately dropped off, except for a few souls who preferred deeper wilderness. As we soon found out, Swerving Boat Guy was one of them. Even though we had changed roads, we met up with him again. Unfortunately, during our brief separation he had not mastered any further skills associated with towing a trailer. Another two hours passed before we were permanently rid of him.

We had arrived. I had proudly set a new personal record for my longest stretch of driving in a single day. Senator was hurting, but he was not regretful. Like me, he was anxious to see the lake, the cabin, and whatever else we would encounter in the Great North. As a bonus, our hotel was convenient and easy to find, if not anything special. Sure the towels were thin and cheap, and I could have easily gone through four of them for one shower, but the place was clean and we had entered a cooler, drier climate.

After a soothing pizza in an almost-empty restaurant, we returned to our room to relax a bit before bed. As soon as I turned on the television, we were hooked on what we saw. Once we discovered that there was a history travel program that followed Ozzy Osbourne around America, we never changed the channel. You really have not witnessed great programming until you have seen the former Black Sabbath front man tour Colonial Williamsburg.

*   *   *

Monday morning Senator woke up feeling a little better. He was also encouraged by the prospect of a much shorter drive than the day before. I woke up with the realization that, for the first time since high school, I was actually going to see Birch Harbour. A cool, dry, bright morning motivated us to get on the road a little earlier than planned.

Just a few blocks away, we stopped at the International Falls/Fort Frances border. It seemed like there was always a long line and a dependable wait any time we crossed when I was a kid. Now, it was nice to find that Senator and I were the only ones in line. That is, it was nice once we could find the line. The path had changed since I had last been there. What I remembered as a straight road was now a series of convoluted twists and turns around industrial rail spurs and closed metal gates. I later learned that some of this had changed because of the terrorist attacks in September 2001.

Entering the town of Fort Frances, Ontario, does not feel especially ceremonial. Leaving the town of Fort Frances, however, ushers the traveler into the next level of wilderness. Suddenly there are clear lakes everywhere. The highway winds in and out of northern birch, pine, and maple forests. The slight raise in the road at some points offers wide views of thinner forests and ponds that open up

251

to the sky. Above, eagles might swoop by your car. In the opposite lane, large logging trucks piled with timber may do the same. We soon learned that the posted 80km per hour speed limit meant nothing to anyone. Rather, driving at a steady 90km meant you were guaranteed to get passed. In an area like that, no one was going to be pulled over unless there was a deer, moose, or bear involved.

In less than three hours we were on the gravel road that led to my parents' cabin. It is not often that a special place from your childhood holds the same magic when you return as an adult. As we pulled onto the property at the Birch Harbour sign, created on a boat oar by my dad, the sight of it all literally made me gasp. In an instant it was even better than I had remembered. To the right we could see the small, neatly maintained cabin, nestled into the embankment. A little beyond it, tucked at the edge of the woods, was the outhouse, but I will come to that later. Directly before us lay the yard, dappled with wildflowers on its descent to the lake and the uninhabited islands beyond. From the back kitchen door, my mom called out to us as my dad started toward the car.

When words came back to me, I looked at Senator. "It's really all still here!" I said excitedly and stupidly, as though it would have vanished in my absence. "And we're here!" Of course, I instantly wondered what his reaction would be. Would he be as awestruck by the natural beauty of the inviting scene, or would he hear game-show-loser music playing in his head? Despite the extra effort it took him to get out of the car, and the mosquitoes that zoomed toward him in search of new meat, he was drawn in as well. I exercised self-control, choosing not to put him on the spot

252

by asking what he thought.

Senator insisted on carrying a couple of bags inside, while my dad and I relayed an army of food into the kitchen. My mom had left room in the fridge, but it would still take some expert efficiency strategy to cram in everything else. In five minutes I had invaded her kitchen, and we were already having a good time. "I hope everyone eats, because this stuff is not going to fit back in there once it comes out," she said. I was sure we all would, especially if the weather held out and we got our fill of fresh air.

Inside, the cabin was better than ever. My parents had kept many of the treasured features of the home, while adding their own touches of woodsy décor. Over a new heater hung the memorial photo of my smiling grandpa, superimposed over a lake scene. Birch Harbour, I believe, was his favorite (or favourite) spot on Earth. It was not hard to see why. It really was beautiful in every direction. Occasionally boaters would enter the harbour, or a friendly face would drive down the road, but for the most part, it was a very private retreat.

Naturally, the best place to watch the world go by was the enclosed porch, whose view of the lake and Moose Island was unmatched. Among the antique lanterns hanging overhead and various books and articles about travel and the outdoors, my parents had added comfy seating and throw blankets, and a digital gadget that was Command Central for all things meteorological. Senator and I gazed in bliss at the temperature and humidity, which combined to make it feel at least 25°F cooler than at home. If only we could bottle it and take it back.

That was my dad's toy, and my mom had hers as

well. As part of the orientation, she introduced us to her new-found love: mosquito rackets (or raquets). These little devices are amazing tools to combat the evil little vampires. Imagine a hand-held paddle strung horizontally with seemingly harmless wires. Then imagine a mosquito hovering and drifting in the air, too smart to land or stay still, waiting to strike her prey.* Thinking she is at the top of the food chain, she is dumbfounded to suddenly find herself sizzling between the electrified lines, which the would-be victim has effortlessly waved in her direction. Resistance is futile.

When at Birch Harbour, sooner or later you will be initiated. This happens the first time you need to perform the natural human necessities. Unless it is during the night, you will step out the front porch door and make the seven-second walk to the simple brown outhouse at the edge of the yard. Yet this is no ordinary outhouse.

"But Wendy V," you interject, "doesn't the cabin have indoor plumbing?" Indeed it does, but as the story goes, when my grandpa bought the place, my grandma started thinking about the limited septic system and the potential of stressing it when company visited. One day she suggested to Papa that they put in an outhouse. He thought she was crazy. Then he thought she was pretty smart. After all, just because it was an outdoor john didn't mean it had to be dirty or uncomfortable.

Once they had settled on the prime location on the

---

* Yep, it's the girls that feast on humans. Males do not bite. Given their role in the procreation of more mosquitoes, (some of which are presumably female,) however, they are at least indirectly responsible for bites. Therefore, they are still kill-worthy.

property-- one that is cleverly situated in such a way as to offer privacy even if the door is wide open to the lovely lake view-- they set about constructing and decorating it. Yes, decorating. Follow the outhouse sign along the edge of the pines and you will be led to a personal stall that contains lush toilet paper, carpeting, a toilet seat with a north woods picture on it, various outhouse cartoons and nature scenes on the walls, a music box (for longer trips), and, of course, an electric mosquito racket. By all means, settle in and enjoy yourself.

Senator returned from his first trip to the famous outhouse. He was laughing at finally having a visual image to go with our descriptions of the loo by the lake. It had even been expanded to include an outdoor faucet with soap and hand towel. Once he passed that test, I knew he was in.

We spent some time relaxing on the porch and showing my parents photos from our last few trips. It was strange to see us in warm clothes, hiking in snowy mountains. I couldn't believe it had only been a few months since we took them. It was as though it had been summer for two years. Looking over pictures and being among some of Canada's best scenery put me in the mood to peruse travel guides for the Maritime Provinces, which my mom just happened to have on hand. Before there was the internet, there was the Marynet.

There was almost an hour until I planned to make dinner, so we decided to take a walk. Going up the hill warmed us up quickly, but it was still relatively comfortable thanks to the dryness. We were not gone long, but it was enough to give us an appetite. That meant it was time to

255

return to prepare the deli spread.

Between my mom and me, we set just about every item that mankind had ever thought to place on a sandwich out on the table, buffet style. Then I made some cole slaw. "Do you want to put out some chips, too?" Mom asked.

"Yes, I was thinking that. We've got some in the grocery bag we brought," I answered, assuming we would share them.

"Okay, I'll put them with ours," she replied. I looked over to see four different varieties of potato added to the spread. I guess we had over-planned a bit. "Everybody eat up," she invited.

Summer in a northern latitude brings late sunsets that offer plenty of daylight after dinner. We took advantage of it when my dad offered to take us out on the little motorboat.* I was a little hesitant at first, wondering how Senator's back would react to balancing and maneuvering into a vibrating boat. He, on the other hand, was not about to miss out, so he at least wanted to try. "I'm getting on the lake!" he declared. So in he climbed.

As soon as we left the dock, we were transported to a world of tranquility. In the far distance there were a few fishermen, but the foreground was occupied by eagles divvying up a fish dinner on the shore of one of the islands. Here and there loons would dive and pop up elsewhere along the water's surface. The breeze calmed down, but

---

* My brother keeps his boat, which was given to him by our grandpa, at the cabin year round, since that is the only place he uses it. It used to be a rowboat, but my dad enhanced it. Whenever my brother points out that the boat is his, my dad grins and quips, "Yeah, but the motor's MINE!"

there was still a light, dry wind, and not a single mosquito hitched a ride. The real highlight was when my dad pulled around to one side of an island and pointed out an eagle's nest in a tall, scraggly pine tree. We had seen eagles' nests before, but never this close. Size-wise, it looked like a car had landed in a treetop.

After our ride, we took our stations on the porch to await the gradual sunset. At about 9:30pm the sun slipped beneath the line of view, and dusk emerged. We were in the mood for a comedy, so the four of us went into the main room to watch an old Bob Hope movie. I think I was the only one who stayed awake for it, but that did not stop my mom from dishing up ice cream when she awoke from a snooze. "Nightly dessert is a tradition up here," she explained matter-of-factly. *...And a worthy tradition indeed.*

*   *   *

Tuesday morning we took our time getting up. The first thing one does when awakening at Birch Harbour is to check the lake. It is not as though one expects it to have drained out overnight, but one is instead eager to see the changes in light and wildlife at different times of the day. It's a great way to collect thoughts and remember what really matters in life. Plus, you can see it on your way to go pee.

As Senator meandered around the path down to the dock, I watched some minnows feverishly swimming around the posts. We then roamed around the yard, taking in different views from different angles. The road had been slightly widened since the last time I had visited, and I was glad there were still enough trees to obscure the cabin from the back end. Thinking about trees made me aware of how

257

big the trees my grandma had planted were now. On the other side of the cabin sat Papa's chair, a solid, empty, Adirondack-style chair that faithfully kept watch out over the lake in his stead. Among the inevitable sadness, it is tinged with a distinctly humorous mood. The chair sits on the hill about halfway between the cabin and the outhouse. As my grandma has told me, sometimes Papa would go out to make a bathroom run and not return for half an hour or more, due to being drawn in by the irresistible allure of sitting and watching the lake.

I went back inside to catch up on a few notes while we waited to leave. Later in the morning we were going west to Kenora to take a boat trip in the Lake-O'-the-Woods region. My parents had been wanting to go, and Senator was feeling quite a bit better, so we made the reservation and set our time of departure. With great weather and an hour-long drive that was scenic from start to finish, we looked forward to the whole day. Not having to drive made it extra pleasant.

We reached town and found the dock for the M.S. Kenora. Though we were early, there seemed to be no available seats inside or on the deck above. Staff members were stationed at the stairways and around the boat, but they just sort of shrugged in weak apology. Then I noticed that the stairs went down from the main deck as well. It looked like somewhere that was closed to the public, but I figured it was worth a shot. "Can we go down there?" I asked as I pointed to the stairway.

"Yes," the woman answered simply. *Well why didn't you say so?* I wondered. We stepped down carefully to find our own private deck with seating for about thirty. We were shaded from the bright sun, and we were closer to the water level, giving us a better view overall. We had stumbled onto the best secret of the boat.

If you want islands, Lake-O'-the-Woods is chock full of 'em, to the tune of thousands. As such, the area boasts 45,000km (28,000 miles) of coastline. How anyone learns to navigate these waters is beyond me. Apparently it is beyond some people behind the helm, as well. As our captain maneuvered through a particularly tricky narrow passageway, a woman who was not paying attention brought her boat across our path. Fortunately she cut it hard and fast to avoid hitting us. That would not have been pretty for her.

During the ride there was narration, which provided a wealth of local lore surrounding the islands. We learned, for example, that Whiskey Island was *the* place to be during Canadian Prohibition. When the United States went teetotaler (at least on the surface), well-to-do Americans flocked there as well. Supposedly Al Capone spent time there, although, so many places around North America claim that he frequented them, I am starting to wonder if the guy ever spent any time in Chicago.

The last twenty minutes of our boat ride was spent looking at two different water levels. Oddly, the port side sat up higher than the stern side. Then Senator put it together. "Oh, I know what it is," he said as he grinned. "Everyone roasting in the sun is crowded in the only part of the top deck with shade." I looked at the angle of the sun as compared to the angle of the boat. He was right.

On the way back to the cabin we stopped for a while at Dixie Lake. There was just enough of a pull-off to enjoy

259

an open view of the water from a picnic table. We nibbled our grapes and sunflower seeds as we talked and looked around. There were granite boulders and trees almost everywhere. It was strange to think that the major artery road through the entire country was just behind us. I guess that's the difference between a country with 36,000,000, and a country with 319,000,000. Canada has space!

Both Senator and I were dozing off during the rest of the ride back to the cabin. When we turned into the driveway, I suddenly thought to ask him how his back was. "Actually, it's doing really good!" he answered. He attributed it to a combination of prayers and the ride on the boat the night before. I would have thought that the ride was rough, but he pointed out that the vibration of the motor seemed to have loosened up the muscles. Plus, there was so much to see that he was constantly twisting back and forth, gently stretching it out. I'm sure the lack of work stress didn't hurt either. If the whole package could be funneled down to a pill and sold, someone would make a fortune.

Continuing in the spirit of relaxation and healing, Senator took a nap. I decided to try another walk up the road, just to see what I could see. As it was between trees, that turned out to be not much. It was still a nice walk, and the mild leg exercise was invigorating, but I did not expect to get an upper body workout as well. All the way back, for about twenty minutes, I had to walk with my arms flapping over my head to keep a vicious fly away. It never did attempt to bite me, but it was extremely determined to land in my hair. I'm sure the two trucks that passed wondered what in the world my problem was, but then again, perhaps they knew from experience. I now understand the appeal of the large-brimmed, netted hats that are sold in outdoorsy catalogs. Maybe next time.

The rest of the evening consisted of home-baked pizza-- imagine being able to run the oven in July!-- seasoned with a group effort to beat the television contestants on Jeopardy and Wheel of Fortune. In the end, I think we lost, but we definitely put up a good fight. In our defense, it is not easy to concentrate on a t.v. show when the lake is right out the opposite window. With that in mind, we settled in for a long evening on the porch.

Reading gave way to watching the ducks gradually gain the courage to come up further into the yard. By the time they retreated, the first few stars were visible in the southeastern sky. As time passed, each shade of blue gave way to a darker hue until the blackness firmly took hold. It was quiet, yet there was plenty to hear. For the most part, we heard loon cries, but then a train in the distance echoed in such a way that it sounded like it was coming at us from across the lake. Come to think of it, that would be a great premise for a ghost story.

We continued to watch everything and nothing. I didn't realize how much our eyes had adjusted to the darkness until I came back to the porch from the bathroom (indoor). As I blindly and gingerly stepped my way back into the room, Senator reached out to guide me to my spot next to him on the couch. As he did so, he joked a panicked warning: "DON'T fall through the screen!" I would not have been injured by the trip, but no one would have been happy with the dozens of mosquitoes that would have instantly launched a blitzkrieg. It was now official; Senator

261

was irresistible to foreign mosquitoes as well.

We were just about to call it a night and go to bed, when we were reminded that the nightly ritual had not yet taken place. My mom neatly folded her blanket, made her way to the kitchen, and started to pull out plates and forks. *Well, sure, I suppose I could be talked into spice cake with white, creamy frosting at 12:45 in the morning.* As we indulged in the cake and the 55°F air, I think Senator's back even improved a little more.

*   *   *

Wednesday morning, as I was brushing my teeth, my parents called me to come to the porch windows. Holding my chin to prevent my foaming mouth from leaking along the floor, I went to see what was going on. When I looked out, I could see a line of at least thirty mallards trailing along the lake's surface. Some were adults, and most were babies. I was just debating whether to wake Senator when I turned to see him putting on his glasses to focus on the duck parade. Though they squiggled around like a long whip, they never broke formation. Despite the ordered structure, they seemed to be having a pretty good time. We decided that we wanted to get on the water as soon as possible, too.

For years we had heard stories of my siblings having fun while kayaking around the bay. Given the invitation to try our hands at it, we accepted. My dad led us down the path to the rack he had built to hold the fleet and started to get the kayaks situated for us. We did not realize that they were single-seaters; we had been picturing a two-person kayak. Not knowing how Senator's back would take to paddling, and wanting to spend time talking together, we

262

asked if we could try the canoe instead. Graciously, my dad obliged, and we switched out the boats. Once inside, we made sure we had all of the necessities, including the Canadian-approved life jackets and the boat safety kit, which would likely float away in an actual emergency. A mosquito tried to hitch a ride, figuring she would dine on Senator with a waterfront view, but she was disposed of quickly. We shoved off from the sandy beach and glided through the reeds, waving good-bye to my dad and thanking him for being our outfitter. "Where do you want to head?" asked Senator.

"I don't know. I guess toward Moose Island, out there," I replied, indicating the closest island in the distance. It sounded like a good plan, but in reality, I wasn't sure we would actually make it that far. At that point, it seemed best to pretend I knew exactly what I was doing. "Have you ever been canoeing?" I asked, not remembering any such stories from Senator.

"Nope," was his short reply. We had kayaked together in Missouri once with my sister, and I had only canoed once, when I was about thirteen. That adventure, however, resulted in a group of junior high girls and their less-than-competent leaders trudging along in shallow muddy water while towing canoes upstream for a mile or so. It was not a high point in my nautical experience. This time I was determined to have more success.

As we found our rhythm, Senator continued to move around comfortably. I told him that I could easily paddle the calm waters alone, but he said he was enjoying himself. It was hard to believe that he had been in quite a bit of pain just two days earlier. Now the only thing that made him cringe was when he occasionally missed a loon sighting. It was good to be doing something new together. In fact, canoeing was kind of addicting. The further we went, the further we wanted to go.

Rounding Moose Island, I figured we better head back toward the dock. Under the high sun, with no watch or phone, we had no idea how long we had been gone. I estimated it had probably been at least an hour, so we paddled back. As anyone who has ever been a distance from shore will tell you, it never looks the same from the water. Though we had not varied our course, it took a moment to get my bearings and make sure we were going toward the correct little colored square of a building.

As we expertly (in our minds) slid back onto the sandy beach, we carefully stepped out onto the grass. We had been gone about an hour and a half, and so far we did not have any aches or pains in our upper body. The next morning would tell for sure whether we had pushed different muscle groups. My dad was not at the boat house, so we expertly (in our minds) hung the canoe and put away the supplies. In the end, we deemed it a grand success on three counts: 1.)we did not get lost or require rescuing, 2.)we did not capsize, and 3.)we did not lose either oar. We also did not tell my dad that we had next to no experience in a canoe, but I don't think it would have changed anything.

We walked up the hill to the cabin, eager to tell my parents about our pleasant outing. My mom was tending to a few things around the home, and she listened to our details, asking if we saw any animals. We chatted for a few minutes, and then I went to find my dad. Though the

264

property is not huge, there are various nooks and turns that can easily hide a person who has become lost in a project. I wondered what he was up to, so I picked the garage as my starting point.

On the side of the garage, hidden behind a row of pines in the thick of Mosquito Central, I found my dad. He had a spray bottle of something in one hand, a cloth in the other, and a deer-in-the-headlights look on his face. On the ground sat a bucket of soapy water. He had taken advantage (depending on your perspective) of our absence to sneak up to our car, which now boasted a fresh washing and waxing. "What?! Are you kidding me? Dad, we didn't come to see you so you could do chores for us! You've already been our chauffeur and gear outfitter; please come and relax!"

He just smiled and finished polishing the final touches. I was grateful, but I felt bad. I wanted it to be a day off for him, too. When I protested to my mom, she just shook her head and said matter-of-factly that it was "his thing", and there was no arguing with him. *Sneaky indeed. Okay, Dad. Thank you!*

It was still a bright afternoon, so I asked Senator and my parents if I could get a few pictures of them around Birch Harbour. As meaningful as the place was to me, I possessed no photographs of it. I wanted to do a nice job, so I took my time focusing, trying to position the camera just right to capture the wooded, lakeside setting. Just as I snapped, the edge of the frame caught Senator coming out of the outhouse. *So much for that one.* I retook it, then gathered everyone for a posed shot in the foreground of the lake.

As long as I was on a roll, I went inside to get a few pictures of the cabin's interior. The porch, of course, was of premier importance. I picked just the right angle to include the unique features across the room. I was satisfied with my amateur work, but my mom was not. "Oh, you didn't take that with my pillows sitting over here, did you?" I was then instructed to delete the photo until the decorative throw pillows had been restored to their proper seats on the couch. "There, that's much better!" she said as she perched the last one in its rightful spot. "Now you can take it," she permitted.

The afternoon was lazy, which works well when you have glider swings that sit on a hill overlooking the water. The four of us each chose our spot to continue catching up. Despite living only forty miles apart for most of the year, we do not get together nearly as much as we should. This is mainly due to work and travel schedules, but I am determined to make it happen more often. Senator and I always offer the same deal to friends and family: if you will drive out to see us, we'll make sure you don't go away hungry. You will also be exposed to a variety of music, usually handpicked to your taste.

As we visited, the ducks who had been hanging around the shallow water began their ascent up the hill. They would debate for awhile, stepping up into the grass and then retreating when the momma duck decided it might be too risky. Eventually she deemed it safe, and the gang worked its way closer to the humans. (Having a supply of stale bread expedited this process, as apparently the crumbs are irresistible to mallards.) Within ten minutes, they were our best friends. When I stopped feeding them, the mother followed me as if to say, "Hey you-- make with the treats!"

Because the weather was too ideal to waste, my dad offered to take us out on the motorboat again. Of course we jumped at the chance. This time Senator brought the camera. In between filming eagles taking off from their branches in the pines and scanning the horizon's many rugged islands, we agreed that this was easily the most fun we had had all year. Later we would each declare it one of the best trips either of us had ever taken.

We transitioned inside to read, each grabbing a different book or magazine to peruse. Intermittently, we each took a turn stalking two mosquitoes with the Raquets of Death.* I was in the middle of updating some notes, and Senator was browsing a health book when my mom reminded us of our required assignment. According to the bylaws, all guests must not only sign the cabin's official guest book, but must write some thoughts or memories in it as well. This is non-negotiable. Senator nudged me and whispered, "Go ahead. You can do mine."

"Wrong. Do your own homework..."

"I don't know what to write. No one can read my handwriting anyway..."

My dad was smirking as my mom discerned our conversation and reaffirmed her stance. "Nope, everyone has to do their own," she instructed. The she went in for the kill. Softening in that way that only a mom can make her voice sound, she added, "It means so much to me to read these memories. I always wait until everyone's gone, and then I love to read and reread them while looking at

---

* probably a Canadian metal band

the lake." It was a sweet and touching image. How were we supposed to argue with that? "Oh, and it has to be at least a paragraph. None of this 'had a great time' and signature stuff."

I took up the plume and found myself easily spilling over two pages. "Overachiever," scoffed Senator, reading over my shoulder. I laughed and passed the book over to him. He began by reading what everyone else had written over the past few years. Once he had sufficient inspiration, or just wanted to get us off his back, he began. What he wrote meant a great deal to me. It was a sincere reflection of everything I had hoped he would experience while at Birch Harbour. Maybe he should be writing this book.

It was almost time to start cooking dinner, which I was looking forward to preparing. Before diving into the small kitchen, I decided to walk down to the dock and see if anything was going on at the water's edge. Coincidentally, a mother duck (perhaps the one who had followed me earlier) was swimming toward me with seven ducklings trailing behind. The babies approached me and scrambled up the granite boulder, putting all of their energy into the necessary hop over a large crack. Evidently word had gotten around about the bag of stale hot dog buns my parents kept in case of a duck-feeding emergency.

The family was soon joined by a few random adult ducks who were relegated to the edges of the feeding mob. I kept moving back to see how far up the hill they would come. Though they were tentative, and occasionally had to be reined in by the mom, it was clear that they were now comfortable with us. I have to admit, I did this on purpose. Being the fun aunt that I am, I was trying to train them to come to my parents so that they would make an appearance a few weeks later, when my one-and-a-half-year old nephew would be running around the yard. One has to plan these things.

After the ducks had been taken care of, I made dinner for the four of us. I truly savored the experience of cooking for my family while taking my time and enjoying great views in all directions. Due to the prep work at home, there were not too many dirty dishes, either. *This must be what it's like to host one of those cooking shows, where the chef has all of the fun without any of the unpleasant bits*, I thought.

When we had ingested as much salad and pasta as we could reasonably hold, we took to the chairs and couches for an hour. On television was a program that featured different parts of Canada and their unique aspects. Nova Scotia and Prince Edward Island were the topic of the evening, and the scenery was too good to pass up, even on a small screen. Watching footage of the Bay of Fundy solidified my decision to travel there soon. PEI was, likewise, an irresistible palette of colors (or colours). While watching, I believe I perfected the extraction of the best of both worlds. If I positioned myself just right on the couch on the porch, I could look through the opening in the wall to the dining area and watch the t.v., while still seeing the real scenery through the windows. *Now that's a real art form, eh?*

As dusk emerged, we took advantage of another night to watch the sky. I am endlessly fascinated by the night sky, which is why you have been subjected to some no-doubt painfully boring descriptions of our 'nightlife' on this trip. For that, I apologize, Reader. On the other hand, take a cue. You owe it to yourself to get far away from cities and even small towns so you can gain perspective, let your imagination create your own constellations, and simply renew. It's like nothing on Earth.

*   *   *

Thursday morning we woke up after our best night of sleep in a long time. Building on our newly discovered love of canoeing (at least on Eagle Lake), we set out for another paddle around the island. This time we went even further and stayed out about two hours. Senator's back still felt good, and neither of us had any muscle pain in our arms. Either we were not in quite as bad of shape as we thought, or it was what I had started dubbing 'the Birch Harbour Effect'. More likely it was the latter.

As we approached the shore, we could see that our family of ducks was back. They were hanging out casually around the boathouse, waiting to see if we were bringing them anything interesting. On the other side of the dock a blue heron stood in the shallow water among the reeds. Maybe he was hoping someone would toss him a fish.*

Senator and I scooted toward the bank and pulled our canoe out of the water. As much as I had enjoyed our rides, I could not see us canoeing at home. For starters, we have nowhere to house a canoe, and no way to transport one. Furthermore, renting would not change the fact that we have rivers, not big lakes.† Rivers are unpredictable in

---

* It is a commonly known fact among amateur birdwatchers that herons consider themselves above stale hot dog buns-- the snobs.

† Yes, yes, of course I haven't forgotten about Lake Michigan, but that is more like an inland sea. We don't want to be a speck that gets sucked out into the deep, cold water, and we also don't want to be the idiots on the Chicago news who had to be rescued from the cold,

their movement, yet very predictable in their pollution. No thanks, says I.

We went inside the cabin for a light snack. As we munched chips and nuts, we browsed more of the porch's supply of reading material. Senator and my dad chose their books, and my mom handed me a slightly worn bundle. "What's this?" I asked.

"Look at it. Is anything familiar?..." I unfolded old papers to find letters that I had written to my grandparents while they were in Canada. I was surprised to find they had saved several from the time I was about fifteen years old. Most were handwritten, but one or two were typed, reflecting the fact that I was experimenting with my friend's computer. My friend, of course, was Pam, with whom I have been close since I was three years old. There was a reference to her at some point in every letter, which both amused and staggered me. Being able to read those letters and process what saving them had meant was an unexpected gift I will always treasure.

There was time for one last ride on North Star, so we accepted my dad's offer for an extended ride on the lake. We settled into our spots and unleashed ourselves from the post. As we puttered away from the dock, we looked up to see a trail of ducks following us out into the water. They must have been the family we had been feeding for the past few days. Evidently we had spoiled them. They kept up for a while, but eventually we outran them. *Sorry guys.*

The extraordinarily calm and glass-like lake allowed us to go far out from the small bay. Along the way we watched more eagles and some kids from a local summer

---

deep water.

camp being towed on a rubber inner tube behind a boat. When their ride turned into the boat's wake, all three of them flew off, laughing the whole time. We also saw someone paddling a canoe. It was the same shade of red as my dad's canoe. Later we saw two kayakers in kayaks the same color as my dad's. *Hhmmm....* Buzzing along, it was just great to see people seizing the beautiful day without media, video games, or smart phones.

I made dinner for our last night together, and once more we feasted. Maybe it was my replacement for missing holiday dinners at my parents. Maybe it was just the joy of not being rushed like we were on work nights. Either way, no one was losing weight that week. We could go back to dietary temperance when we returned home. It would probably be too hot there to want to eat, anyway.

After dinner we went back outside for a better view of the changing light on the water. It was still a few hours until sunset, but the animals were already winding down for the evening. I was going to feed a gang of ducks near the shore, but they swam off before I could reach them. I couldn't tell if I had frightened them away, or they just weren't interested in the old buns. Perhaps they had been talking to the heron.

I stayed out until the first mosquito outsmarted me. I did not see or hear the beast, but she got me. I decided I had better make one more outhouse trip before moving indoors for the night. Fortunately, the electric zappers were as handy as the three-ply toilet paper, since another one was on the hunt. BZZT! *Let that be a lesson to you all!* I etched another imaginary notch on the wall and ventured out.

Before entering the cabin, I performed the ritual dance of She Who Evades Mosquitoes. My arms waved, my feet stamped, and my hair swayed in various directions until I was sure that no hitchhikers were coming in for a wicked party. The dance then concluded with the traditional split-second opening and slamming of the door. Success! I had entered the house alone. My comrades congratulated me and together we rooted on our dragonfly allies that had begun to circle in front of the screens. There were bats in the area as well, but it had been such a wet winter and spring that the vampire population was winning. Hopefully they would all be taken off-guard by an unexpected early autumn freeze.

It was 1:00am before anyone made a move to go to bed. Somewhere in the wee hours of the night we had also managed to eat dessert, despite being stuffed only hours earlier. I took a last look at the stars that only existed in such places and then walked to the bedroom. It would be the last night that sleeping with a window open required a heavy quilt, at least for several months. I was not ready to leave, but my mid-summer playtime was drawing to a quick close.

*   *   *

Friday morning we got up and went into pack mode. We were not in a hurry, but it was amazing how much junk we needed to shuffle out to the car. Since the mosquitoes had rallied for a final vicious assault, I had Senator work as the inside man, while I relayed stuff to the car. Because it was the first time we had gone there, I had over-packed. If we ever go back, it shouldn't be as complicated.*

---

* famous last words

After saying our good-byes and drinking in our last view of the lake, we started east. "Sorry to break it to you Baby, but we're going to be on the Trans-Canada Highway for a few hours," I told Senator.

"Ahhhh! The Purgatory Highway?"

"That's the one, but I promise it will be nothing like Saskatchewan."

"We'll see...." He was a skeptic, but he was soon convinced. The road to Thunder Bay continued to be wooded and surrounded with granite boulders. As we neared the city, the terrain rose and plunged into considerable valleys. I had not remembered how beautiful it was. Then again, it had been many years.

South of Thunder Bay we crossed into Minnesota. There was about a fifteen minute wait at the border, and I think we were the only ones in line who were not planning to fish, boat, or camp. Once we reentered the homeland, we just followed the 'arrow head' down the coast of magnificent Lake Superior. The weather was fine, but we could already tell a difference in the temperature and humidity. The other thing we noticed was that in just half a week we had become so used to a lack of civilization, that we felt crowded and uncomfortable around the traffic and the people-- even though we were not near any towns of size.

At Temperance River State Park, we stopped briefly for a snack, bravely exiting the car among other humans. There was easy beach access, so we selected a bench with a view. It is hard to imagine that people pay outrageous amounts for tables in high-end restaurants, when such a spot is available for free. Here, the geology changed distinctly. The ground was now composed of rusty red and black rock, due to the iron content. This feature, conveniently situated at the end of a major shipping lane, allowed the area to thrive in the iron trade.

There was plenty of iron, but there were not plenty of accommodations. I realized this early on in the planning phase of the trip, so I had booked ahead. The best option at the time was a mom-and-pop motel not far from the lake. As it turned out, however, mom-and-pop were more like biker-momma-and-bartender-pop.

As we pulled into the gravel parking lot, it was clear that the property's advertised 'restaurant' was actually a loud roadhouse. Doubtfully, I looked around for an office or somewhere we could go to check-in. Seeing nothing of the sort, we ventured into the noisy bar. There was nothing inside that would suggest they also ran the motel next door, so I was a little stumped. "Well, I don't know. Let's go back outside." I suggested. A few people looked at us curiously as we walked back out the door.

I was mentally working on a backup plan when I saw a woman taking garbage out back behind the building. She was very thin, very tan, and rather wrinkly. She might have been forty-five or sixty-five. Maybe she could point us in the right direction. She was also friendly, eager to help the couple who looked completely out of place, and certainly not like anyone off of whom she could bum a cigarette.

When I explained that we had a reservation and were trying to figure out where to check-in, she got excited and told us that she could take care of us. *Well, that's a start, anyway.* She led us back into the bar, and I looked again to see if we had missed a desk or door to an office. Nope. She parked us at a table, asked us to wait a moment while she served another table, and then returned with a piece of paper and a pen. Everything appeared to be in order, which we took to be a good sign. Then she noticed that we would be there the next night also (at least in theory) and got very enthusiastic. "You're in luck!" she announced. "Tomorrow is Customer Appreciation Day!" *Well, well, what could this mean? 5% off of our bill? Free passes to the nearby lighthouse?* I need wonder no longer. "We'll have tents out back behind the motel, with a barbecue and live music starting at 3:00 and going into the night," she proudly explained. Then, just in case the immensity of our great fortune had failed to fully grip us, she added, "We have good food and strong drinks!"

Senator and I looked at each other, smiled politely to our happy hostess, and wondered what in the world we had let ourselves in for. We walked across the parking lot and entered the room. It can best be described as a giant paradox. The room was spacious, but it was also connected to other rooms. There were deadbolts, but it still felt a little too close to others. There was a view of the lake in the distance, but the ugly parking lot with the extremely bright security light took precedence in the foreground. The dresser was an attractive reproduction of a Victorian piece, but the bed sheets were a miserably cheap 100% polyester.* Somehow, there was no good lighting in the room, despite three lamps. The bathroom was the ultimate contradiction. The shower was large, bright, and clean, yet the small, high window had a hole in the screen. To be fair, a fly swatter

---

* Seriously, they couldn't have at least popped for a *blend*?

was provided.

"Well, it's not awful..." Senator said, summing up the situation adequately.

"There really wasn't anything else available," I said, not sure why I was defending the choice.

"It's okay. It's only two nights, and we'll be gone most of the time anyway," he reasoned. I could already tell we were thinking the same thing. *Would the celebrated Customer Appreciation Day result in a.)no sleep, b.)loss of property, c.)a call to the local police, or d.)all of the above?*

There was no point in worrying about it. It was time to find some dinner and make our plans for the next day. Afterward, a sunset walk along the breakwater made everything look better. I was still having some difficulty making the adjustment from Birch Harbour, which now seemed like it was in another world. Perhaps I would dream about it.

*　　　*　　　*

Saturday morning we were up early for a number of reasons. It was chilly and sunny, which motivated us to start our day with the local circles of old men at a busy diner for breakfast. Since we had plenty of time to kill before Split Rock Lighthouse opened, we also took a walk at Gooseberry Falls State Park. Because word had gotten out about Senator being in town, the mosquito population had caught up with us, making it a relatively short walk. Senator's mood was quickly dropping, and we hadn't even dealt with Customer Appreciation Day yet.

We drove on to Split Rock Lighthouse State Park, the main reason for taking the long way home. The coastal drive offered plenty of panoramic vistas of Lake Superior

277

with the morning sun emerging through the light haze. Soon the view opened up to reveal the iconic octagonal lighthouse jutting out over the water on its high cliff. We must have been at precisely the point from which the majority of the postcards were photographed. I could see the great glass windows, and I could easily imagine the beacon warding off potential shipwrecks.

A little further up the road, we turned into the park and began driving around semi-aimlessly to waste time until the place opened. I was excited to be there. The last time I had visited, I was in junior high. Senator, on the other had, was not enthusiastic. He had passed the point where he could not overlook the growing humidity for the sake of some fun. Still, I was determined to end our summer vacations on a good note, especially after such a perfect time at the lake.

When the doors opened, we followed the line into the visitor center and paid our admission. There was just enough time to peruse the museum room before our tour, so we wandered around for a while. Typical exhibits showcased the principle behind the 6.5-ton Fresnel lens and told the story of the disasters that led to the construction of Split Rock in 1910. There were a combination of factors that contributed to the need for a light on that part of the shore. Deep waters and a narrow passage were tricky enough, but the valuable iron ore that made the region also messed with the magnetism of the ships' compasses. In particular, 1905 saw one terrible storm that claimed twenty ships.

Our tour guide met us and walked us to the cliff's beautiful, rugged edge. Surveying the water on a calm, sunny July day, it was hard to picture it in a wild, wintry

278

blizzard. We listened to his stories and wondered how much determination it took for the earliest keepers to hoist all of their supplies up the side of the 100'+ precipice. Eventually, a tram was installed to make life 'easier'.

We moved on to the oil house, which was cleverly designed to explode upward instead of outward in the event of a fuel accident. Then we stepped into the fog signal house, which once blared the recognizable maudlin blast that sets a mood only a lighthouse can. Our next stop was the row of keepers' quarters. Three identical houses stood neatly aligned, ensuring that there would be no competition among the staff. It was important that all members were viewed as equals. Inside each home soothing colors covered the walls, as though they had been decorated during a later period. The colors were original, though, because their tones were believed to help stave off madness. Perhaps schools should take this approach.

After the tour we walked along the cliff's top and then down to the water's edge via the old tramway path. There was no denying it was uncomfortably warm, and too hot if walking. At least the mosquitoes were leaving us alone. Of course, that could have been because there was so little untapped flesh left on Senator. It was time to cool down in the gift shop while plotting to move to a colder, drier climate.

It was only midday when we left Split Rock Lighthouse, so we took advantage of the time by making a stop on our way back to Two Harbors. Along the edge of the highway, we pulled over by Silver Creek Tunnel. To our back was a mound of red rock. Before us spread another wide view of Lake Superior. There was not any shade, but

279

the breeze coming off the water was free to sweep up the face of the cliff, relieving us somewhat. Out too far from the shore was a lone kayaker. *No thanks; I'll stick to the little bay near the cabin.*

It was only another fifteen minutes or so until we reached Two Harbors. As we were certainly in no hurry to get back to our motel, we went back to the waterfront to sit on the rocks and watch the tide come in. Senator was enjoying himself again, and we perked up as we watched a freight liner slowly make its way to the enormous dock. The gulls were roaming the area, in the sky and on the land. A few people were around, but it was still peaceful.

Then Senator laughed. "Wait, gimme the camera. I gotta' get a picture of this!" I looked around to see what I had missed, wondering if he spied some rare bird or ship. As he lined up his shot, I saw what had amused him. There, further down the rock beach, sitting together on the boulders quietly like we were, was another couple. Unlike us, they were not aware of their surroundings, or even each other for that matter. They were each glued to their phones, focused on tiny, virtual screens while the beautiful 360° natural palette of the real world went unnoticed. How funny... and sad.

At the other end of the inlet was a park with a small museum housed along a railroad. With nothing on the agenda, we walked in. An hour and a half later, we were experts on the iron mining history and the role of the Duluth, Missabe & Iron Range Railway in it. Okay, maybe "experts" is pushing it a bit, but we did learn a lot about the discovery of iron ore in the area, and how smart investors flocked to the opportunity to help build the emerging modern country and their own financial portfolios. We also learned just how tough a steam engine could be.* In one case, it took four diesel engines to replace one steam engine.

We left the museum and walked back to the car to decide what to do next. I looked at the clock. "I guess Customer Appreciation Day is in full swing now..." I said, unenthusiastically.

"Yeah, I image the band'll be ramping up into 'Sweet Home Alabama' anytime," Senator replied.

"Or maybe it'll be 'Sweet Home Minn-e-so-ta'," I added, grinning at the scene we were hoping to avoid for as long as possible.

"Just so there's no drunken partiers," pointed out Senator. "What else can we do in town before going back to the room?"

Thrift stores it was. We entered the first one, walked to the back toward the books, realized they were about to close, and walked back out, all without stopping. The second one proved more profitable, yielding a nice hardcover travel book that highlighted sites along all of the major interstates in the country. I plunked down my money on the counter as the cashier wished me a nice evening and invited me to come back soon. *That all depends on how desperate we are to avoid the barbecue,†* I thought.

We were getting hungry, so we decided to check out the family-run pizza restaurant just a block or two away. It was early for Saturday night dinner, so we were the only ones in the place. This gave us a prime seat by the window.

---

* Remember *The Little Engine That Could*?

† emphasis on the 'bar'

People watching wasn't the only form of entertainment. Each table had a stack of Trivial Pursuit cards to challenge or shame its guests. Senator and I did okay, but neither one of us was going on Jeopardy any time soon.

As I shook parmesan and crushed red pepper on my third slice, I again thought of Customer Appreciation Day. "So, I guess we have to go back after this," I started. Senator nodded in agreement. "I am definitely ready for a shower," I added.

"Yeah, I'm getting tired. We were up really early. I just want to clean up, sleep, and get going home tomorrow."

"Me too, but I had a really great day. Thank you. It's been a great trip all the way around," I mused. "Sweet home Minn-e-so-ta..." I sang.

"...Until now!" joked Senator. "The band's probably playing 'Born to Be Wild' as we speak."

We finished up and drove apprehensively to our room. As we rounded the corner and the motel came into view, I craned my neck to see what was going on in the tents. Nothing looked too wild at first glance, but the tents were right behind our room. Senator turned into the parking lot and searched for a spot that seemed like it would still be safe after dark. I scanned the crowd and was pleased to see an older group than I had anticipated. For the most part, it was composed of harmless, happy, plump Midwesterners. The customers didn't look too threatening, despite being appreciated with "strong drinks".

Once in our room, we could hear the music through the open window in the bathroom. "Sounds like it's just one guy instead of a band," Senator said as he shut it. The volume was now significantly lowered and could easily be drowned out by the t.v.. "It's not bad."

That was good. Things were turning out much milder than we had pictured. We had accurately predicted one thing though. "Hey! Come here a minute! I don't want you to miss this," I called, just as I was about to step in the shower. Senator poked his head in the bathroom just in time to hear the first chorus of "Sweet Home Alabama".

*   *   *

The triple-whammy of no air conditioning, a closed window to keep the flies out, and polyester sheets did not make for a good night of sleep. Ironically, the party outside our room had not been an issue. Eager to get going, we got ready and packed up quickly. I went to check out, but there was no one around to whom I could turn in our key. In fact, the entire establishment was quiet. Maybe they were all recovering from Customer Appreciation Day. *Oh well*, I thought, and left the key on the dresser in the room.

Driving south initiated one big metaphoric slide into decay. In Duluth, many expensive homes showed the signs of heavy storm damage. Chopped up tree branches and property debris were in the process of being dragged to the curb for removal. The damage was substantive, spreading for many blocks.

An hour or so later, while driving through northern Wisconsin, we encountered a dark blob on the side of the road. When we took a second look, we realized it was a dead black bear. Most likely it was a female, presumably hit while wondering why all these fast, shiny objects had invaded her forest. Maybe she had been hit, or maybe she was just sick of summer, which had definitively reared its ugly, hot, humid head much farther north than usual.

I am truly baffled as to how my parents adjust to 'normal' life after spending an extended period of time at the lake. I could barely do it after a week. As we did our best to acclimate, however, I had the thought that maybe I just needed an attitude or perspective adjustment. Yes, perhaps that's it. That, or my map book to start planning 2017.

Afterword

In some ways, our latest travel adventures were our most challenging. This shouldn't surprise me, but common sense would dictate just the opposite; the longer you are with someone, and the more experience you have in planning, the smoother it should all go. Repeatedly, however, humans disprove this theory. Sometimes physical ailments alter things. Sometimes destinations disappoint. Sometimes people who love each other misunderstand each other. Sometimes your route is interrupted by an unexploded bomb. Things happen, and often they discourage.

Then, in a quiet moment of clarity, when you reflect on the big picture, you see the beauty akin to Whoville on Christmas morning. Despite problems and mistakes, the journey continues. You find yourself among serene churches in small, centuries-old town squares. You gasp from laughing so hard with friends. You cherish the perfection of watching a lake do nothing under a revolving canopy of stars, seated with your parents, who knew all along that everything would work out. You watch your favorite person while he is asleep. It's a gift I do not wish to squander.

~Wendy V
Christmas 2016

Appendix:
Peterisms

The following statements are a sample of the wit and wisdom we had the fortune to gain by sitting next to Peter, an English (not British) man from our Germany tour.

On travel:

"My wife and I enjoy taking skiing vacations. That's S-K-I, which stands for 'Spending our Kids' Inheritance!'"

On relations across the pond:

"England and the United States are two countries divided by a common language ."

"Are you familiar with Colonial Williamsburg?... Yeah, now those chaps know their place!"

On Canadians:

"I've always just thought of Canadians as Americans with good manners."

On France:

[when describing a certain English port city] "...It's very lovely. There's a nice breeze... and on a clear day you can see France... Well, I mean, nowhere's perfect!"

www.ingramcontent.com/pod-product-compliance
Lightning Source LLC
Chambersburg PA
CBHW032036080426
42733CB00006B/104